Conflicts of Rights

Conflicts of Rights

Moral Theory and Social Policy Implications

John R. Rowan

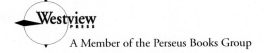

A Member of the Perseus Books Group

Copyright © 1999 by Westview Press, A Member of the Perseus Books Group

Published in 1999 in the United States of America by Westview Press, 5500 Central Avenue, Boulder, Colorado 80301-2877, and in the United Kingdom by Westview Press, 12 Hid's Copse Road, Cumnor Hill, Oxford OX2 9JJ

Library of Congress Cataloging-in-Publication Data
Rowan, John R.
  Conflicts of rights : moral theory and social policy implications / John R. Rowan.
     p.   cm.
  Includes bibliographical references and index.
  ISBN 0-8133-9122-9 (hc) —ISBN 0-8133-6564-3 (pb)
     1. Civil rights—Moral and ethical aspects.   2. Human rights—Moral and ethical aspects.   3. Social policy—Moral and ethical aspects.   I. Title.
JC571.R775   1999
323—dc21   99-21203
                                                                                          CIP

The paper used in this publication meets the requirements of the American National Standard for Permanence of Paper for Printed Library Materials Z39.48-1984.

PERSEUS
POD
ON DEMAND   10   9   8   7   6   5   4   3   2

For Leslie

Contents

Preface

It is sometimes thought that philosophy is in no way a practical discipline. While it is true that we philosophers often tend to value knowledge for its own sake, we also (most of us anyway) tend to believe that philosophy can have practical value, and that it can provide assistance in everyday life. This is demonstrated most easily in the field of ethics. In Western society (in which free speech is valued, thus allowing for open discussion of issues), ethical disagreements abound, some of more significance than others. Among the more important ethical debates are those that pertain to our social policies—the laws that delineate the operative frameworks within which we live our lives. To some, this may seem to violate the adage that "morality cannot be legislated," but this assertion is ambiguous. First, if that assertion amounts to the claim that morality is not a function simply of what the legislators decide, well and good; most of us these days are moral realists and would agree. The claim would thus amount to a rejection of relativist accounts of morality, and perhaps of old-fashioned positivist accounts of law. Second, if the adage amounts to the claim that legislators have no business formalizing moral principles into law, that claim should be rejected. There are good reasons for thinking that our laws should indeed reflect morality, and appeal to common sense will likely bear this out.

This book, then, is a philosopher's attempt to assess the ethical status of several candidate social policies that continue to be debated in the public and political arenas. It is, in other words, an attempt at practical philosophy, what Ronald Dworkin refers to as "philosophy from the inside out," as noted on the book's opening page. The central idea around which the book is written is the notion of a right. A reasonable hypothesis is that if ethics indeed ought to inform law, the relevant ethical principles can be captured in the language of rights. Because these are not legal rights, following from contingent decisions made by the government regarding our entitlements, they must have some other status and thus some other designation. Many of us may be familiar with so-called human rights, which are appealed to frequently in discussions of alleged government oppression. These refer to entitlements that claim to exist regardless of what government policy happens to be. The phrase human rights violations has in recent years been associated with activities of the state in China, Yugoslavia, and South Africa, to name a few. The term natural right often has the same meaning but tends to be used with less frequency, perhaps because of the negative connotations that sometimes accompany the notion. For purposes of this book, I will utilize the term moral right, since this is used in more academic contexts and does not suffer from the unfortunate baggage (much of it political) that tends to accompany the previous two labels.

The foregoing discussion suggests that ongoing debates over our social policies can be characterized in terms of conflicts of (moral) rights. An obvious example is the debate over the moral permissibility of abortion, in which the fetus's alleged right to life is pitted against the mother's alleged right to choose. Because the appeals to such rights are made regardless of what the current law happens to be, they are clearly moral rights, and the thinking is that moral rights ought to be relied on when assigning various legal rights. Here is where the philosopher can make a meaningful contribution, for what is now needed is a basis for ascertaining which alleged rights are morally justified—in other words which are valid—and which ought to be overridden in cases where valid (moral) rights conflict. This book examines two moral theories of rights-justification and applies them to four social issues: redistributive taxation, affirmative action, pornography, and abortion.

Of course, the working hypothesis noted above—that the language of rights is effective in capturing more complex ethical content—is itself not immune to criticism. Indeed, the proliferation of rights claims that has infiltrated political dialogue may cast serious doubt on the prospect of resolving ethical issues within this linguistic framework. Another objective here, then, is to assess the viability of the language of rights; should the attempt to apply rights theory to practical issues encounter significant obstacles, it may have to be admitted that such language is unhelpful and ought to be abandoned in public and political discourse. On the other hand, well-founded, consistent conclusions will lend credence to the contrary conclusion.

This book grew out of a doctoral dissertation written at the University of Virginia, whose faculty accepted it in the spring of 1997. A significant debt of gratitude, which I fear can never be repaid, is owed to A. John Simmons, under whose direction the dissertation was written. Over a period of several years, John read (literally) thousands of pages of philosophy (much of it not very good) that I presented to him. It is through his kindness, patience, and careful eye that this project eventually found its way into press. When mentioning John, I must also mention Nancy Schauber, without whose assistance I would not have progressed past my first philosophy course as an undergraduate.

The criticisms and suggestions of many others also helped shape the final product, and while I undoubtedly will fail to acknowledge certain individuals (here I appeal to the "absent-minded professor" defense), I wish to thank the following for their careful readings of earlier versions: Cora Diamond, John Marshall, Louis Pojman, James Sterba, George Thomas, and Patricia Werhane. I am grateful also to the students I have taught, as they have, though unknowingly, contributed to the content, structure, and presentation of this book.

The efforts of many individuals at Westview Press helped to bring about the final product, and I wish to thank project editor Lisa Wigutoff, copyeditor Jean Erler, Todd Tobias in marketing, assistant editor Liz Twitchell, and especially acquisitions editor Sarah Warner, who over the past several months has brought everything together beautifully. Thanks to Purdue University Calumet for providing the means necessary for completing this project. Finally, the support and encouragement of my family was unwavering, and the significance of their contribution to this book cannot be adequately stated. Thanks to my sister, Jen; my parents, Richard and Marilyn; and especially my wife, Leslie, whose friendship sustains me.

John R. Rowan
Hammond, Indiana

PART ONE

Moral Theory

1

Rights and Social Policy

1.1 The Problem

Natural rights is simple nonsense: natural and imprescriptible rights, rhetorical nonsense, nonsense upon stilts. But this rhetorical nonsense ends in the old strain of mischievous nonsense: for immediately a list of those pretended natural rights is given, and those are so expressed as to present to view legal rights.[1]

In a recent book, Ronald Dworkin claimed to be doing philosophy "from the inside out."[2] According to this process, the moral philosopher begins with issues that are of practical importance, and then relies on theoretical considerations insofar as they are germane to those issues. This approach is "from the inside out" in that the standard methodology has been the other way around. Traditionally, moral theories are worked out (sometimes in excruciating detail) first, with the architect perhaps choosing to shop it around afterward (if at all) only out of curiosity, to see if it might serve some function in the world. If, however, ethics is to retain the action-guiding characteristic often ascribed to it, Dworkin's approach has much to recommend it.

Bearing this in mind, I have undertaken this book from the inside out. The practical matters with which I am concerned are those social issues that tend to be dealt with in terms of rights; focusing on such issues will thus necessitate detailed discussion regarding theories of rights.

As the twentieth century draws to a close, it has become clear that the language of rights, often employed in political contexts and in debates over proposed social policies, has become detrimental to public deliberation about those policies. First, the sheer incidence of appeal to rights has skyrocketed. Rights talk rears its head in virtually every issue in which there is some degree of conflict. In decisions regarding allocation of government funding, for example, various advocacy groups appeal to rights to adequate education, rights to adequate health care, and rights to welfare assistance, among others. In the workplace, the notion of employee

3

rights has become common and has been used in defense of more specific rights to a minimum wage and, in the face of corporate polygraph tests and drug-testing policies, to privacy and due process. In the context of crime, several states have recently passed initiatives regarding victims' rights, and opponents of capital punishment frequently refer to the violations of criminals' rights inherent in that practice.

The massive expansion of rights claims in these and other contexts is undoubtedly a function of the success with which they have been deployed as political weapons in the past. What well-meaning voter would want to deny someone her basic rights? Presentations to the public have thus evolved into the following form: "Candidate A supports policy B which, if enacted, would violate the rights of certain individuals; therefore, do not vote for Candidate A." In short, the language of rights is intuitively compelling, especially in the United States where the Declaration of Independence and the Constitution (including the Bill of Rights) form the basis of citizens' freedoms. Politicians and interest groups have increasingly worked this observation to their advantage.[3] The result is that appeal to rights has ceased to yield a relative advantage in debates over social issues; but like nuclear weapons in an arms race, rights are not relinquished by either side, lest the opponent gain an advantage.[4]

A second difficulty that has evolved is the unfortunate absolutist connotation associated with appeals to rights. Where there is political disagreement, it is increasingly the case that one party to the debate points to the (alleged) existence of some right in support of his position and acts as if that "fact" settles the matter. In this respect, Bentham's quotation is apropos. Here, too, the intuitive force of rights claims is in play; if someone has a right to something, how could it ever permissibly be denied him? When the other side adopts the same strategy, pointing to some right that supports his position and ending his argument there as if that "fact" settled the matter, meaningful discussion is effectively halted. Rights, originally utilized in an effort to facilitate public deliberation, are currently having the opposite effect.

Regarding these policy debates, it must be emphasized that the rights appealed to by the various parties are moral rights; such rights are functions of morality rather than law or any other conventional system. This is evident from the observation that the rights claims are made in an effort to maintain or amend existing law. Prior to the 1973 Roe v. Wade decision, for example, there was no legally recognized right to obtain an abortion; yet the public argument for changing the law pointed to the existence of such a right, and suggested that the Texas statute banning abortion was morally impermissible in that it violated a woman's "right to choose." Of course, this description of the motivation behind the legal challenge is not quite correct if the rights in question are thought to be constitutional. Strictly speaking, the legal argument in favor of abortion rights suggested that such rights were already contained in the Constitution but had not yet been formally recognized by the courts. In this way, interpretation of constitutional law (rather than of moral law) was the operative task. Even so, that which is (or is not) contained in the Constitution is itself subject to moral assessment. Because we take ourselves to be living in an "enlightened" society, we tend to believe that the content of the Constitution is, for the most part at least, morally justified. But where there is tension, public sentiment tends to recommend constitutional changes in order to make it more morally acceptable. Adoption of the Fourteenth Amendment was seen as progress in just this way; the motivation behind its passage (even if not in just these terms) was largely the belief that certain moral rights were not adequately attended to by the Constitution as it existed prior to the 1860s.

In this way, the law is accountable to morality; that which is morally required (or prohibited or permissible) should inform that which is legally required (or prohibited or permissible).[5] The problem of the stalled and ineffective debates is thus even worse than it may have initially seemed, for there are no books or statutes against which the legitimacy of the alleged moral rights may be checked.

This is the nature of the problem I wish to address, and the primary tool for doing so will be, naturally enough, moral theory. Because the problem centers on assertions of moral rights with little (if any) accompanying moral theory, there is a real opportunity here for moral philosophy to make a positive contribution. The approach in this book will be to apply theories of rights-justification to certain ongoing political debates in contemporary society. Because the theories are theories of rights-justification, a concession is made from the outset that rights themselves are not the basic elements of morality but are derived from more fundamental moral principles. Dworkin elsewhere has remarked that morality at its foundational level must be right-based, duty-based, or goal-based,[6] and the above concession amounts to denying the possibility of the right-based hypothesis. The right-based approach (or one similar to it) has been a factor in the exponential escalation of rights rhetoric in recent decades; in justifying various moral positions, the retreat to the concept of a right has helped bring about the problem. Though some have defended a right-based morality,[7] others share this concern.[8]

If the objective is to address the problem described above, rights must be treated as nonfoundational. This realization will no doubt rattle the convictions of some (those committed to a right-based morality) while bolstering the beliefs of others (those skeptical of rights projects in general). But the force of the claim should be tempered with the statement that rights, pending the outcome of this book, may still be valuable moral entities. Moral discourse can be complex and tedious, and where possible, efficient notations should be employed. The concept of a nonfoundational right may well be such a notation. If this is the case, periodic review of its meaning and basis is still required, and the failure to engage in this review is a significant cause of our current predicament. This book is devoted to such a review.

1.2 Theories and Applications

In order to achieve this objective, moral theories of rights-justification will be applied to particular debates over social issues in which rights are frequently invoked. In all, two theories will be applied to each of four issues. The aim in doing so will be to attempt to understand which alleged rights follow from which theories of justification, and thus which policies follow from those theories. In short, the intention is to determine the implications of specific rights theories for specific policy issues.

No hypothesis regarding the outcome will be made, although an underlying assumption is that moral theory can be effective as an aid in sorting through intricate and sometimes thorny ethical matters of practical importance. The extent to which moral theory may be even more valuable can be assessed once the findings are considered, and those findings may point in one of the following directions. First, it may be the case that the attempt to apply rights theory to social issues utterly fails, in that the reconciliation of the theoretical notion of a right with "real-world" problems is found to be impossible. The analysis may simply break down, and no meaningful conclusions may be reached in individual cases (of applying a theory to a certain issue), in which case it should be resolved that the language of rights is genuinely unhelpful and should be abandoned. Second, it may be that application is possible and various meaningful conclusions are generated, but that those conclusions vary according to the theory that is utilized. For example, in the context of abortion one theory may recommend honoring the right to life (and thus a pro-life policy) while another theory may recommend honoring the right to choose (and thus a pro-choice policy). Here, too, the ineffectiveness of the language of rights would be demonstrated; should rights be appealed to in public debate, it would always be necessary to pursue the matter further and inquire as to the underlying justificatory theory. This second possible result, which would recommend abandoning rights talk in favor of the more foundational moral principles, would validate Bentham's warning about relying too heavily on the language of rights and too lightly on their meaning.[9] A third possibility is that meaningful individual conclusions are generated and, further, converge in each case. Because this result would allow for consistency in political discussions that appeal to rights, the functional value of rights would be salvaged.

The two theories were chosen for several reasons. They are not only popular among moral philosophers, but they also comprise much of what has historically been offered in defense of moral rights. Perhaps most important, however, is that given the aim of resolving the problem described in the previous section, they are the two best candidates for the task. Doing philosophy from the inside out requires keeping the practical goal at the forefront of considerations of this sort.

The first is the interest-based theory of rights, according to which certain people have certain rights because they possess interests whose moral strength (generally) renders their infringement impermissible. The second is the goal-based theory, according to which certain people have certain rights because the possession of those rights positively contributes to the achievement of some particular goal. This is not in keeping with Dworkin's tripartite classification scheme, but there are good reasons for deviating from it. The popular distinction in ethical theory is between backward-looking (or, broadly speaking, deontological) theories on one hand, and forward-looking (or consequentialist) theories on the other. In order to cover as much theoretical ground as possible (which is important if we are to account for a variety of motivations that may exist for the numerous appeals to rights), the two theories of rights-justification to be utilized in this book should be evenly divided between the deontological and consequentialist approaches. The goal-based theory satisfies the latter. The former may be satisfied by a right-based theory or a duty-based theory, as Dworkin goes on to indicate.[10] But an interest-based theory is also deontological and furthermore has the advantage of being broad enough to include various aspects of a duty-based theory. Because it is also more readily applicable to the problem of rights, an interest-based theory is the preferable deontological theory to employ.

The particular interest-based theory to be used is described by Joseph Raz, primarily in his book The Morality of Freedom. This may at first blush seem a strange choice for two reasons. First, Raz's primary concern in that work is not with rights specifically but with morality generally. However, the framework of rights he does provide is entirely appropriate for our project. Second, Raz to some extent renounces the straightforward liberal approach that in Western philosophy has gained widespread acceptance, and instead argues for the more controversial perfectionist approach to state policy.[11] Two defining aspects of traditional liberalism are neutrality and an atomistic conception of the self. Without delving into too many details at this point, the first of these is the thesis that the state must be neutral among the various competing conceptions of the good harbored by its citizens. Raz, in questioning both the meaning of and the possibility for such neutrality, argues for a more objective conception of value with which the state, in formulating policy, ought to be concerned. (He does not, however, deviate dramatically from the atomistic, unencumbered self.) Even so, his framework of rights can be applied to contemporary social issues in a neutral manner, thereby evading the perfectionist aspect of his otherwise liberal political theory.[12]

The particular goal-based theory of rights to be used is described by L. W. Sumner, whose book, The Moral Foundation of Rights, is an extended argument for the claim that only consequentialist moral principles can ground rights. While it continues to be somewhat popular, consequentialist theory also meets with much disapproval. Deontologists tend to have little patience for an approach that, they claim, fails to "respect persons," or that "does not take seriously the distinction between persons."[13] The attempt to incorporate rights into a purely forward-looking theory, in which the good is by definition prior to the right, generates even more hostility. On the face of it, Sumner's conclusion may therefore appear radical. However, to refrain from undertaking a goal-based analysis on this ground would be irresponsible, for consequentialism remains persuasive to a number of moral philosophers. Further (and again more importantly), to the extent that any justifications whatsoever for rights are given in debates over social issues, those justifications often pertain to forward-looking considerations generally (and occasionally even to social goals specifically). Philosophy from the inside out thus requires an investigation of the goal-based theory, and Sumner's model is the most coherent for this purpose.

The remaining chapters in Part 1 are devoted to delineating the finer details of these theoretical approaches. Chapter 2 offers a discussion of the general nature of rights and introduces some terminology that will be used throughout. In Chapter 3, the details of Raz's interest-based theory are explored. It must be remembered that the purpose there is not to critically assess the theory, but to illustrate it fully and clearly so that it can be applied to the various social issues discussed in Part 2. Sumner's goal-based theory receives a similar treatment in Chapter 4.

Then, the heart of the "experiment" occurs in Part 2, where the two theories are applied to each of four issues in order to assess which rights (if any) are valid on which theories, and subsequently to reach conclusions regarding various possible social policies. In Chapter 5, the long-standing debate over redistributive taxation is addressed. Unlike "service" taxes, which fund various government functions enjoyed by all citizens (such as defense), redistributive taxes are levied on those who are wealthier and then transferred to those who are needy. Welfare programs constitute the bulk of such redistribution of wealth in the United States. Some claim that redistributive taxation is morally impermissible, suggesting it simply amounts to theft; individuals ought to retain control over their money and should make their own decisions about contributing to the cause of the needy. Thus, property rights are appealed to in defense of this position, which will be referred to as the "libertarian" position. Others maintain that the beneficiaries of welfare programs are unable to help the fact that they are poor, and that because their need arises from factors beyond their control, they have rights to receive assistance.[14] "Welfare liberalism" will designate the position recommending limited redistribution. Taking this consideration to an extreme, it has also been claimed that all economic inequalities are to be avoided, and, therefore, there are rights to receive assistance to the point where individual levels of wealth are essentially equal across society. This will be referred to as the "socialist egalitarian" position. These three possibilities constitute the pool from which the most acceptable policy will be chosen on each theory of rights.

Chapter 6 takes up the debate over affirmative action, which continues to be a heated political topic.[15] Here, too, three potential policies are in play. First, affirmative action, understood as the preferential consideration of minority applicants for employment[16] simply because they are members of a minority, may be impermissible. Rights to equal treatment (or, as will be seen, "equal consideration") are appealed to in defending the "impermissible" position regarding affirmative action. Second, affirmative action may be required by law. Such a policy is defended in different ways, depending on the theory of rights that is invoked. A backward-looking theory, it is claimed, prescribes rights (held by minorities) to be preferentially considered because of past injustices that have been suffered, while a forward-looking theory is claimed to prescribe such rights in order to achieve a more just society. The third potential policy falls between the two extremes. According to the "permissible" position, affirmative action may be practiced by individual employers at their discretion, but doing so would be neither legally required nor legally prohibited. Hence, the rights of the employer may play a significant role in justifying this third possibility.

Although the debate over the permissibility of pornography may seem somewhat less significant than the others considered in Part 2, assorted controversies over the extent of First Amendment rights continue. Some issue involving the right to freedom of expression ought therefore to be discussed, and pornography seems an appropriate choice for several reasons. First, this topic will likely occupy increased political significance as Internet resources become more available in society. Second, the freedom to produce and distribute pornographic material, it will be seen, is somewhat different from freedoms regarding straightforward political expression (such as flag burning), and thus warrants different foundational considerations. Third, a variety of rights have been appealed to in this context by groups with diverse political agendas, and so the issue of pornography offers a relative wealth of theoretical material with which to work. Fourth, while discussions of pornography may be instructive for other controversial First Amendment issues (such as hate speech), the converse is less likely to be true. For these reasons, pornography recommends itself as the best First Amendment issue to consider. It will be assumed that certain restrictions on the pornography industry (such as the prohibition on the use of minors) are appropriate on both the interest-based and goal-based theories of rights. Thus, only two potential social policies will be considered. It may be that the production and distribution of pornography ought to be prohibited in the same way as the prostitution and illegal drug industries (though not necessarily for the same reasons). It may also be the case that such an extreme measure is unwarranted, and that the freedom to partake of the pornography industry ought to be upheld, subject only to the restrictions that are assumed to be appropriate. A variety of rights have been advanced in support of both of these positions.

What is perhaps the most intractable social issue of our time will be discussed in Chapter 8. Abortion continues to be at the forefront of public deliberation, and more than any other debate it exhibits the symptoms of the current problem of rights language. In arguing for their position, abortion opponents often allude to a "right to life" possessed by the fetus, and seem to think that this right settles the matter in their favor. In similar fashion, pro-choice responses often allude to a "right to choose" possessed by the mother, and seem to think that this right settles the matter in their favor. Three main policies will be considered in the context of abortion, understood as the intentional termination of a fetus and its removal from the womb. First, according to the conservative position, abortion is wrong and (in most cases at least[17]) ought not be allowed. An appeal to the fetus's "right to life" is the traditional defense of this policy. Second, according to the liberal position, abortion is perfectly permissible and ought not to be prohibited. An appeal to the mother's "right to choose" is the traditional defense of this policy. Third, according to the moderate position, abortion is permissible up to a certain point during pregnancy but (generally) impermissible thereafter.

These issues were chosen on the basis of their popularity in contemporary political discourse and the fact that each is a fairly unique sort of problem. Clearly, there are numerous other social issues that might be taken up. One of the more interesting conflicts pits the alleged rights of criminals against the alleged rights of law-abiding citizens in debates regarding, for instance, capital punishment, "chain gangs," and the informing of residents when convicted wrongdoers move into their neighborhoods.[18] Rights within the family pose interesting questions as well. Such issues are not necessarily less worthy of investigation, but in order to keep this book to a reasonable size, certain concessions must be made.

The same can be said of theories of rights-justification other than the two utilized in this work. Some of these are discussed below, along with a few other general moral strategies.

1.3 Alternative Theoretical Approaches

It was suggested above that because the aim is to attend to policies in a diverse society, adherence to the classical liberal tradition is advisable. Within this tradition, there are theories of rights other than the interest-based and goal-based theories that might be utilized in this project. This section attends (briefly) to two such theories (both of which are deonto-logical in nature), as well as to several moral approaches falling outside the scope of liberalism.

The most obvious alternative to the interest-based justification of rights is the duty-based justification, and the foremost version is described by Alan Gewirth. In his book Reason and Morality, Gewirth attempts a neo-Kantian construction of the foundations of morality generally and of rights in particular. The rights-justification begins with the claim that persons are "prospective purposive agents" (PPAs). Morality, he writes, pertains to the actions of rational agents who have (or, invoking the "prospective" qualification, can have) purposes and ends in life. In order to carry out actions aimed at achieving their purposes, PPAs must have freedom and well-being. This is initially nothing more than a descriptive observation, but in making the observation about herself, the individual agent endorses it, and adopts the attitude that she ought to have these goods. In other words, she comes to view herself as having prudential rights to freedom and well-being.[19] Gewirth then applies what he calls the "supreme principle of morality," which is the Principle of Generic Consistency (PGC). This principle is directed toward rational agents and takes the form of a categorical imperative, directing them to "Act in ac-cord with the generic rights of your recipients as well as of yourself."[20] The rational agent cannot, upon pain of contradiction, deny the validity of the PGC.[21] But this principle then allows the transition from the indi-vidual's recognition of her own (purely prudential) rights to freedom and well-being to her recognition that all agents possess these rights, and this transition justifies their being moral (rather than merely prudential) rights.[22]

This is a duty-based theory of rights because of the priority of the PGC, whose alignment with Kant should be evident. Gewirth begins with con-siderations regarding the self and concludes that, with respect to others, agents must act in accordance with normative rules. The PGC itself may be viewed as a (very general) duty, or it may ground the "Golden Rule" duty to accord others the same considerations as one recognizes for her-

self. This duty, together with the claim that one must recognize prudential rights for herself, force the conclusion that others must be recognized
as having rights. The key aspect of this framework is that the duty associated with the PGC is doing the morally significant work.

The task of determining exactly which duties (and thus which rights)
must be recognized would be attempted if this duty-based approach
were a focus of this book. (Gewirth has recently published his own views
regarding certain implications of his theory.[23]) The choice to proceed with
the interest-based theory as the deontological representative was based
on the comparative ease with which it can be applied to political debates
over social policy, as well as the fact that it contains significant aspects of
the duty-based theory, certainly more so than the duty-based approach
would contain of the interest-based theory. Nonetheless, Gewirth's duty-
based framework is a fitting theoretical tool for assessing practical issues,
and it would certainly be considered alongside the other two if practical
considerations did not necessitate restricting the scope of this project.

A second approach within the liberal tradition would be to focus on
agreement as the justification for the existence of certain rights. This
might seem a strange strategy since the problem at hand is a function of
there being no agreement regarding which rights exist or which take
precedence in conflict situations. But moral theories falling under the
rubric of "contractarianism" (or "contractualism") tend to focus on hypothetical rather than extant agreement. John Rawls's principles of justice are generated by this sort of hypothetical negotiating process, and his
framework represents perhaps the best-known example of this theory.[24]
Briefly, Rawls places each contractor in an "original position," behind a
"veil of ignorance" that prevents each contractor (who in the original position is self-interested yet remains perfectly rational) from knowing his
contingent attributes, such as race, wealth, and natural abilities, as well
as the sort of society in which he will find himself once the veil is lifted.
Thus, all individuals behind the veil, being ignorant of their contingent
attributes, are in an identical position. This guarantees Rawls's conception of justice as fairness and generates his two main principles of justice.
The content of the principles (and of the rights associated with those
principles) is irrelevant to the present discussion; it is the theoretical
framework that currently is of interest.

With this in mind, Rawls's approach may not be the best contractarian
representative. First, many idealizations are made in getting the contrac-
tors to the negotiating table, and consequently it has been claimed that
Rawls's conception of the self is metaphysically flawed.[25] Whether or not
this is a problem for liberalism generally, it may be a problem for Rawls's
particular scheme. Second, Rawls is concerned with justice specifically
rather than morality generally, and so his framework may not be wholly
appropriate for the project at hand.

In both of these respects, the contractualist theory offered by T. M. Scanlon appears to be less problematic. Not only is Scanlon explicitly concerned with general moral rules, but his only genuine idealization is that of perfect rationality on the part of the negotiators; there is no analogue to the veil of ignorance on this model, and thus individuals are aware of their contingent attributes and social positions during the negotiating process. Specifically, "An act is wrong if its performance under the circumstances would be disallowed by any system of rules for the general regulation of behaviour which no one could reasonably reject as a basis for informed, unforced general agreement."[26]

The "reasonable" aspect of this formulation is meant to indicate that moral rules are those that no one could reasonably reject, given the aim of finding informed, unforced general agreement. Scanlon's stress on rejection of potential moral rules rather than acceptance is based on his claim that the assessment of what is reasonable is clearer when the rules are proposed in this (negative) manner.

There are other versions of contractarianism as well,[27] though again, Scanlon's model would likely be the superior one for this book. However, there are good reasons for not pursuing this theory here. Primarily, it is redundant in that at its core it may amount to no more than the duty-based theory of rights. This is seen in contractarianism's focus on rationality and the idealization of perfect rationality that even Scanlon is committed to retaining. Indeed, Scanlon hints at Kantian reasons for constructing a "genuinely interpersonal form of justification." Rawls, meanwhile, is more explicit in acknowledging his theory's connections with Kantian methodology.[28] Thus, an agreement-based justification of rights will not be employed for the same reasons the duty-based theory is not being utilized. Furthermore, if this sort of framework were to be used, the agreement-based and duty-based approaches should work together in assessing practical issues rather than being applied separately.[29]

Because there exist very different sorts of moral approaches (other than the standard liberal ones) to addressing such issues, some brief remarks regarding a few of these approaches are in order. According to communitarianism, the liberal notion of the atomistic, unencumbered self is untenable. Michael Sandel's complaint against Rawls's conception of the original position is perhaps the best-known specific objection,[30] but the general idea is that the view of persons as wholly distinct from their political and social institutions is simply not realistic. Liberals are misguided in thinking that we are free to choose our individual values; rather, the ends we choose in life are largely a function of the communities into which we are born.[31] According to Sandel, it follows that individuals play certain roles in achieving the ends of the larger overall community. Sandel thus posits the existence of shared values from which we ought not to deviate, and these must be kept at the forefront in deliberations over social issues.

Other communitarian writers vary their attacks on classical liberalism. Charles Taylor is critical of the atomistic self for somewhat different reasons. He maintains the conditional claim that if the notion of rights is to be meaningful, the liberal self must be retained. However, the liberal self cannot be maintained; atomism turns out to be the thesis that individuals are self-sufficient and can develop their characteristics independent of societies, but this is implausible according to Taylor. It follows that the moral priority of rights cannot be maintained.[32] Amatai Etzioni goes so far as to suggest that continued emphasis on rights will undermine the role of individual responsibilities in a pluralistic society.[33] MacIntyre, meanwhile, suggests that attempts to resolve societal difficulties without abandoning the assumptions of liberalism cannot be fruitful. In illustrating this point, in fact, he utilizes the issue of taxation, which is the first of the problems to be discussed in Part 2. [34]

But if communitarianism is to offer itself as preferable, it must go further than merely to assert the existence of shared values that must be appealed to; namely, the nature of those values must be delineated if the framework is to be action-guiding. Yet Sandel and others fail to take this step, and the inference must be that such shared values are either nonexistent or unhelpful in attempts to maintain and justify our political institutions and the social policies therein. MacIntyre states that "our pluralist culture possesses no method of weighing, no rational criterion for deciding between claims based on legitimate entitlement against claims based on need."[35] Rather than inferring from the pluralistic character of society an inability to assess competing individual interests, an inference to the general implausibility of the communitarian approach seems more directly available.[36] The inability to furnish community-wide values is a problem for communitarianism generally, and another protest might be that its criticisms of liberalism are not wholly fair. In response to Sandel, for example, liberals can concede that the self is somewhat dependent on the particular society in which one finds oneself without abandoning the political (rather than metaphysical) self conceived by Rawls,[37] and certainly without having to adopt Sandel's position.

While there appear to be good reasons for defending liberalism against communitarian critics, the overall project does not necessitate spelling out a finely detailed argument. Philosophy from the inside out requires that we begin with the rights claims themselves, and as Taylor suggests, a communitarian approach seems unsuited to an analysis of those rights. Liberalism appears to be entailed by the rights claims and is thus preferable.

The notion of community plays a different role for pragmatism of the sort endorsed by Richard Rorty. Pragmatists would object to the methodology in this project, pointing to the existence of an underlying assumption that there is a "fact" of the matter about the morality of proposed social policies. Traditional normative ethical theories like those of Kant and Mill presuppose (or attempt to demonstrate) this reality, and Rorty's charge is that such theories are "outmoded."[38] In an attempt to resist being labeled a relativist, Rorty's specific complaint is against foundationalism (rather than moral realism per se), understood as the doctrine that there exist fundamental moral truths in which knowledge of all ethical truth is grounded. The notion of justification does not make sense apart from justification to a community, according to the pragmatist. Historical and cultural contexts must be taken into account in moral assessments and decision-making.[39]

Rorty would be correct that elements of foundationalism permeate this project, and so his protest must be addressed from this perspective. He could be challenged by distinguishing the metaphysical claims associated with foundationalism from the epistemological aspects. Thousands of years of failure to arrive at objective truths helps fuel the pragmatist's project. It could be maintained, however, that this ongoing struggle in no way implies the nonexistence of objective moral truths but instead an epistemological difficulty in coming to know exactly which truths there are. Of course, such a move insulates foundationalism and would likely be impatiently dismissed.

A second response would be to suggest that foundationalism does not deny historical and cultural contexts, but accounts for them in the form of normative principles that are hypothetical rather than categorical. Given the prevailing conditions, there exist certain ethical principles that, furthermore, are overridable (that is, not absolute). While these principles are indeed grounded in deeper truths about human nature, it is not the case that contexts are ignored in the way typically described by pragmatist opponents of moral objectivism and of classical liberalism.

The easiest route, however, would be similar to the one taken by Dworkin. Citing Rorty's acceptance of the existence of a "most reasonable" (rather than "true") answer in controversial moral cases, Dworkin suggests that we all take a pragmatic approach to this debate and recognize that it ultimately makes no difference which vocabulary we adopt.[40] This is because the ultimate aim, the resolution of social conflict, is practical in nature, and it can be achieved without having to come to a definitive conclusion on this matter. Further, regarding rights (which, again, are assumed not to constitute the basic principles of morality), Rorty in the end admits their usefulness, and in this way he would likely view the project in this book as worthwhile.

However, feminist approaches to political and social philosophy tend to be less charitable in this respect. Though the views constituting feminism are rather diverse, there is some convergence regarding the claim that the elements of traditional moral discourse, including the language of rights (as well as of duties and justice), are inappropriate and ought to be jettisoned. Emphasis on these so-called male notions has led to a misplaced emphasis on the value of equality (which will nonetheless play a significant role in upcoming chapters). Feminists like Susan Okin suggest that the pursuit of gender-blind equality in society is a disservice to women, since the removal of merely superficial inequalities would leave intact the basic social frameworks that are inherently damaging to women's interests.[41] Okin focuses on the family in particular, but maintains that this result would obtain for a variety of social institutions. A second predominant aspect of feminist moral philosophy is that justification of various actions toward others, rather than being a function of justice or rights, is instead a function of caring. Carol Gilligan is best known for this idea, which is as much psychological as it is philosophical.[42] The claim seems to be that as a psychological fact, people need other people, and in confronting difficult moral and social issues we would do well to recognize this fact, adopt a disposition of care, and utilize it in our decisionmaking.

The primary difficulty with feminism is that it is hard to see how such a general approach can be action-guiding. The idea seems to be that we will come to adopt the various feminist claims once the right kinds of experiences are had, but just which experiences those are (and why they should occur) is unclear. Feminists will likely maintain that such questions exhibit the male-oriented thinking they wish to dispose of, but that looks like classic question-begging. Regardless, this discussion is only of tangential importance since the task is to begin with the rights claims made in society and attempt to demonstrate what (if anything) follows from those claims. A feminist approach that rejects the notion of rights thus appears to be inappropriate from the outset.

Communitarianism, pragmatism, and feminism are just three alternatives to standard liberalism. There are others. One purpose in discussing these has been to point out explicitly that the methodology utilized in this book is certainly not universally accepted. Rather than attempting to begin with rights claims, others would suggest (for different reasons) that the ongoing difficulties associated with such claims are a function of the liberal framework within which they are made. Some of their conclusions may ultimately turn out to be warranted. Rather than jumping to that conclusion, however, a resolution of the current problem of the language of rights should be attempted from within the prevailing framework. Answering the question of whether an internal resolution of this sort is promising is the task of this project.[43]

Because the goal is to ascertain the moral implications of rights claims, some explanation of the nature of moral rights is a logical starting point. This will be the task in the next chapter.

Notes

1. Jeremy Bentham, "Anarchical Fallacies" in Works of Jeremy Bentham (volume II), ed. John Bowring (Edinburgh: William Tate, 1843), 501.

2. Dworkin, Life's Dominion (New York: Alfred A. Knopf, 1993), 28–29.

3. The importance of the seven-second sound bite in the expanding broadcast media should also be underscored. What better way to maximize the impact of one's (very brief) time than to employ the language of rights? Related problems are discussed in Mary Ann Glendon, Rights Talk: The Impoverishment of Political Discourse (New York: The Free Press, 1991), especially Chapter 1.

4. In Bentham's words, "What has been the object, the perpetual object, of this declaration of pretended rights? To add as much force as possible to these passions, already but too strong." (Works, 497.)

5. Further aspects of the importance of moral theory in assessing law and social policy are discussed in my exchange with David Messick. See Rowan, "Philosophy on Messick and Social Conflict," Social Justice Research 10 (1997); David Messick, "Philosophy and the Resoultion of Equality Conflicts," Social Justice Research 10 (1997).

6. Dworkin, Taking Rights Seriously (Cambridge, MA: Harvard University Press, 1977), 169–72. Dworkin's explicit remark is that these are classifications of political theories, but it is clear from subsequent remarks that they apply equally well to general moral theories.

7. J. L. Mackie, "Can There Be a Right-Based Moral Theory?" in Theories of Rights, ed. Jeremy Waldron (Oxford: Oxford University Press, 1984).

8. Joseph Raz, "Right-Based Moralities" in Utility and Rights, ed. R. G. Frey (Minneapolis: University of Minnesota Press, 1984).

9. The assumption is that the current general understanding of moral rights is roughly synonymous with Bentham's "natural" rights. See Works, 523.

10. Taking Rights Seriously, 172.

11. Raz, The Morality of Freedom (Oxford: Oxford University Press, 1986), Chapters 5 and 6.

12. Because this book is concerned with assessing social policies for a diverse and pluralistic society, it is assumed that the characteristic of neutrality is a desirable aspect of the rights theories to be employed.

13. This is the well-known charge leveled by John Rawls, A Theory of Justice (Cambridge, MA: Harvard University Press, 1971), 27.

14. In this description, government itself has no rights but plays an instrumental role. Thus, the discussion in Chapter 5 will focus on the competing rights of the citizens themselves, namely, the property rights of the well-off and the welfare rights of the poor. The government may be viewed as an agent of the poor, responsible for the collection and subsequent reallocation of this revenue.

15. One of the more publicized policy changes in recent times has been California Proposition 209, a measure intended to "prohibit gender or racial preferences in public employment, education or contracting," and which would effectively end the practice of affirmative action in the public sphere. The measure was temporarily blocked by a federal judge on the basis that it likely violated the equal protection clause of the Fourteenth Amendment to the Constitution. William Claiborne, "Judge Blocks Measure on Affirmative Action," Washington Post (November 27, 1996). It ultimately did pass, and subsequent petitions to the

Supreme Court to review the decision have been denied. A similar measure passed in the state of Washington in the November, 1998 election.

16. Other contexts in which affirmative action may be relevant, such as education, will receive very limited attention.

17. The qualification is introduced in order to accommodate conservatives who would allow abortion under certain circumstances, such as when the life or health of the mother is endangered.

18. "Megan's Law," which requires authorities to notify local residents when a convicted child molester moves into the area, is an example of this sort of measure. See Amitai Etzioni, The Limits of Privacy (New York: Basic Books, 1999), Chapter 2.

19. Gewirth, Reason and Morality (Chicago: University of Chicago Press, 1978), 63–67. The notion of a prudential right is rather unclear but appears to be analogous to a hypothetical imperative; the agent recognizes that if she is to achieve her ends (or at least be able to work toward them), she needs these goods.

20. Ibid., 135.

21. This claim is defended via reference to logical universalizability (105).

22. The transition is not, however, wholly unproblematic and is the focus of a strong objection by Alasdair MacIntyre, who questions what he sees as the sudden appearance of a moral right where previously there was only a (poorly defined) prudential right. See After Virtue (Notre Dame: University of Notre Dame Press, 1984), 66–68.

23. Gewirth, The Community of Rights (Chicago: University of Chicago Press, 1996).

24. A Theory of Justice.

25. This is a principal argument of Michael Sandel in his book, Liberalism and the Limits of Justice (Oxford: Blackwell, 1984).

26. "Contractualism and Utilitarianism" in Utilitarianism and Beyond, ed. Amartya Sen and Bernard Williams (Cambridge: Cambridge University Press, 1982), 117.

27. One of the best known is David Gauthier's Morals By Agreement (Oxford: Oxford University Press, 1986), in which there is a stronger emphasis on the egoistic motivations of the negotiators. Thomas Nagel, meanwhile, employs aspects of the approaches of both Rawls and Scanlon. See Equality and Partiality (Oxford: Oxford University Press, 1991).

28. A Theory of Justice, 584.

29. Some other initial suggestions regarding the connection between the two approaches are offered by Jan Narveson, "Contractarian Rights" in Utility and Rights.

30. Liberalism and the Limits of Justice, 45–46.

31. Sandel, "Morality and the Liberal Ideal" in Justice: Alternative Political Perspectives, ed. James P. Sterba (Belmont, CA: Wadsworth, 1992), 222–23.

32. Taylor, "Atomism," in Communitarianism and Individualism, ed. Schlomo Avineri and Avner de-Shalit (Oxford: Oxford University Press, 1992).

33. Etzioni, The New Golden Rule (New York: Basic Books, 1996), Chapter 2.

34. After Virtue, 244–46. MacIntyre's deeper criticisms of liberalism are delineated more fully in Whose Justice? Which Rationality? (Notre Dame: University of Notre Dame Press, 1988), especially Chapter 17.

35. After Virtue, 246.

36. Of course, since MacIntyre explicitly states his doubts regarding the prospect of a common good as a useful political mechanism, he is less subject than Sandel to criticism on this count.

37. Rawls highlights this distinction in "Justice as Fairness: Political Not Metaphysical" Philosophy and Public Affairs 14 (1985).

38. "Human Rights, Rationality, and Sentimentality," in On Human Rights, ed. Stephen Shute and Susan Hurley (New York: Basic Books, 1993), 117.

39. See also Rorty's "The Banality of Pragmatism and the Poetry of Justice" in Pragmatism in Law and Society, eds. Michael Brint and William Weaver (Boulder, CO: Westview Press, 1991). Claims that morality should be contextualized in this way seem to convict Rorty of the relativism he wishes to avoid. For further discussion on this point, see Hilary Putnam, Realism With a Human Face (Cambridge, MA: Harvard University Press, 1990), 22–23, 45.

40. Dworkin, "Pragmatism, Right Answers and True Banality" in Pragmatism in Law and Society, 367.

41. Okin, Justice, Gender and the Family (New York: Basic Books, 1989), Chapter 1.

42. Gilligan, In a Different Voice (Cambridge, MA: Harvard University Press, 1983), 124–26. The basic idea recurs throughout the book, however.

43. Another purpose of the preceding few pages has been to point out a number of potential problems associated with these alternative approaches. This is indirect and very superficial reason for thinking that liberalism may constitute the least problematic approach to resolving debates over social policy.

2

The Structure of Rights

2.1 The Hohfeldian Analysis

Much discussion regarding the structure of rights has at least begun with, and has often focused on, the work of Wesley Hohfeld.[1] It makes sense to do likewise in this project. It should be understood, though, that Hohfeld was a legal scholar and not a scholar of moral philosophy. The language he employed was specifically designed to describe the relations among the various fundamental conceptions of the law. Even so, many philosophers have felt quite comfortable borrowing the language and applying it beyond the law, to the realm of morality. Such a strategy is not only unproblematic but can be extremely helpful in understanding the different theories of rights that have been put forward.

While Hohfeld is thus a logical starting point, this chapter must proceed with the further understanding that not all questions will be answered herein. The goal for the present section (2.1) is introductory in scope, in that the discussion will focus on what Hohfeld's conceptions are and how they operate. It is likely, however, that further questions will arise. These additional inquiries will perhaps be addressed in section 2.2, in the examination of two possible conceptions of a right.

When discussing Hohfeld and rights, it makes sense to begin with what he called a "right in the strictest sense,"[2] which is a claim. Put simply, a person has a claim when he is in a position, morally, to claim some sort of performance from others.[3] Claims may be positive or negative. A claim that demands some actual performance on the part of others constitutes a positive claim. When I make a promise to meet my student at my office at noon to discuss utilitarianism, my student thereby comes to have a claim (or perhaps more than one, depending on the analysis) that I meet him at my office at noon and that I discuss utilitarianism with him. Many claims that moral thinkers assert are negative in nature. A claim that a certain type of act not be performed is negative. Many examples come to mind, such as the claim one has not to be assaulted, kidnapped, or in general harmed in any way.[4]

A closer look at claims reveals the existence of another Hohfeldian element—a duty. The simple definition of a claim may be restated more formally as follows: X has a claim against Y that Y perform (or refrain from performing) a certain act if and only if Y has a duty to X to perform that act. Indeed, Hohfeld appeared to believe that this definition is just what it means to have a claim.[5] Thus, the notion of a duty becomes crucially important in the Hohfeldian framework.

Understood in this way, claims are what many people mean when they speak of rights. But rights have other meanings as well; such meanings are commonly thought to be covered by the other Hohfeldian elements and will be addressed shortly, but first a couple of remarks regarding rights as claims are in order.[6]

An immediate observation here is that claims and duties are, for Hohfeld, strictly correlative. To have a claim means that there must be a duty on the part of the person toward whom the claim is held, and to have a duty means that there must be a claim held by the person to whom the duty is owed. The thesis that claims and duties entail each other is a popular one and has been formalized by Joel Feinberg as the "doctrine of the logical correlativity of rights and duties."[7]

Though popular, the doctrine is not universally accepted. First, some argue that there are claims that do not entail any duties. Feinberg himself points to this possibility, labeling such claims as "manifesto" rights. An example might be a right to an education—a legitimate claim that is held by a person, but against no particular individuals. (Defenders of the correlativity doctrine respond that the object of the claim to education—the party against whom the claim is held—might be the government or even society at large.)[8] Second, some argue that there are duties that entail no correlative claims. Mill, for instance, correlated what he called duties of perfect obligation (such as the duty not to harm others) with claims, but he did not think that duties of imperfect obligation (such as the duty to give to charity) entailed any claims. Thus, while I may have a moral duty to give to charity, the would-be beneficiaries of my donation hold no claims against me to make that donation. (Defenders of the correlativity doctrine respond that some "duties," such as "imperfect duties," are not really duties; they assert that only the stronger ones, the ones that do correlate with claims, are real, and thus the doctrine is intact.) No position regarding the doctrine need be taken at this point.

A second observation, which should be evident from the above discussion, is that claims and (if we maintain Hohfeld's picture) their correlative duties are relational. One does not simply have a claim, nor does one simply have a claim to something. There is an additional dimension—the claim is held against some determinate person or persons. My student holds a claim against me to meet him at my office and discuss utilitarianism; he does not hold the claim against anyone else, since I alone made the promise to meet him there. Because the source of this claim is a promise explains why the object of the claim is restricted to me. But it is widely held that many claims are not restricted in this way. My student also holds a claim not to be made to suffer unjust bodily harm, and he holds this claim against not only me but against everyone.[9] The source of this more extensive claim is the subject of much argument; the candidate sources, of course, are just the general theories of the justification of rights.

Conversely, I have a duty to meet my student at noon. I also have a duty to everyone not to cause them unjust bodily harm. The first duty is held by me alone and is owed to my student, but everyone possesses the second duty, and that duty is in turn owed to everyone.

The second of Hohfeld's fundamental conceptions may be called a privilege. Although not a right in the strictest sense, Hohfeld appears willing to count privileges as rights nonetheless. The simple definition of a privilege is clear enough. One is said to have a privilege to do something if doing that thing is morally permissible. An example might be a privilege to go to a baseball stadium, buy a ticket, and enjoy a game. There is nothing morally wrong with my engaging in this sort of behavior (assuming, of course, there is no overriding circumstance that demands my attention), and thus it is commonly said that I have a right to go watch the baseball game if I want to.

It should be emphasized that this sort of right differs from a claim; namely, no one has a correlative duty to ensure that I get to go to the game. It might be sold out, but that doesn't mean that someone already in the stadium has a duty to give up his seat to me. Even so, the element of duty is important in the more formal definition of a privilege. This time, however, it is the nonexistence, rather than the existence, of a duty that plays the crucial role. Specifically, X is said to have a privilege to perform a certain act if and only if X has no duty to refrain from performing that act. (Negatively, X has a privilege to refrain from performing a certain act if, and only if, X lacks a duty to perform it.) It makes sense, then, that since I have no duty not to go the ballgame (again, assuming there is no pressing duty otherwise demanding my attention), I have a right (a privilege) to go. Further, each fan who got to the stadium ahead of me, causing it to sell out before my arrival, has a right (a privilege) to refuse my request that he vacate his seat so that I may occupy it. (Each fan also has a privilege to agree to my request.)

Observations regarding the correlativity and relationality of privileges, then, are as follows. First, privileges, unlike claims, are not correlative with another's duty. My privilege of going to the ball game is merely my lack of a duty not to do so. Such a privilege itself says nothing about the moral permissibility of others' actions, say, to prevent my getting to watch the game. This observation should indicate just how weak privileges are. My evil neighbor may disable my car so that I have no means of transportation to the stadium; or, once at the stadium, I may be refused service at the ticket window (though plenty of tickets remain) because of the color of my skin; or, I may be tackled and beaten by a man trying to get to the ticket window before me in order to secure the last remaining seat. These actions cannot violate my privilege, because my privilege entails no duty on the part of others; they can be violations of my rights only if those rights are claims.

Thus, without any accompanying claims against others, such as the claims of noninterference necessary to secure my protection against any of the above actions, privileges do not seem to amount to much. Some preserve the moral importance of privileges by asserting that part of what it is for X to have a privilege to do something is not only for X to lack a duty, but for others to possess a duty toward X to allow X to do that thing. But if we are to be true to the Hohfeldian analysis, and if we are to maintain consistency in our descriptions of the structure of rights, this move cannot be allowed. Once the existence of a duty is in play, it must be accompanied by a claim, held by the person(s) toward whom the duty is owed; and once a claim is in play, there is something more going on than the mere existence of a privilege.

It seems, then, that for privileges to have much moral significance they must be accompanied by claims. The structure of such a privilege would then be that of a right with a "nucleus" (the main element of the right) together with a "periphery" (any elements that function to enhance or protect the nucleus). When people assert the existence of rights that are freedoms, such as the freedom to go to a baseball game, they typically (on the Hohfeldian analysis) mean a right with a privilege at its core, protected by a periphery of claims against interference.[10]

Privileges also differ from claims in that they are not relational in nature. My privilege to go to the baseball game is the lack of a duty, owed to anyone and anything, not to go to the game. Not only is it the lack of a duty owed to everyone else (in which case it would still be relational), but it is the lack of a duty owed to everything else in the universe.

Two remaining Hohfeldian elements have been used in the definitions of rights—powers and immunities. These elements might be labeled second-order elements, whereas claims, privileges, and duties might fall under the heading of first-order elements. Whereas the first-order relations (ways in which the elements are associated) describe what is (or is not) morally permissible or required, second-order relations describe the ways in which the first-order relations may be facilitated. In other words, they provide the rules for manipulating the first-order relations. First, an immunity may be defined, simply, as the moral ability to prevent one's (first-order) rights from being affected by the actions of others. It is commonly thought that individuals have immunities against their governments with respect to their claims to freedom of religious worship. Even if my government were to enact a law proscribing the practice of my religion (despite the fact that it harms no one, including myself), it would still be widely held that the act of legalization does not, indeed cannot, affect my moral right (claim) to freely practice the religion of my choosing. I thus hold an immunity against my government with respect to this claim, and my government can be said to hold a disability toward me with respect to this claim. Notice that the language utilized here is that of moral possibilities, while the discussion of first-order relations employed the language of moral permissibilities. This is just a function of what the two levels describe: first-order relations describe moral permissibilities, second-order relations describe moral possibilities.

Despite what Hohfeld himself wrote, it is clear that immunities are analogous to claims. He seemed to think that powers are the analogues of claims,[11] but in making this assertion, he must have been appealing to a semantic analogy,[12] for the logical analogue of the claim is certainly the immunity. Both are correlative with a certain sort of restriction on the part of their objects. Whereas the objects of claims are said to possess duties, we have noted that the objects of immunities are said to possess disabilities. Further, immunities are relational in just the way claims are. I may have an immunity against certain individuals (or institutions) and not others, or I may have an immunity against everyone else in the universe, such as my immunity against others with respect to my claim not to be tortured.

A power, meanwhile, appears to be the second-order (logical) analogue of a privilege. As a privilege signifies the absence of a duty, which is something that is impermissible for me to fail to do, a power signifies the absence of a liability, which may be defined as something impossible for me to do. A power, then, is the freedom to change the status of first-order rights, either one's own or those of others.

A common example of possessing a power pertains to property. I own my computer, for instance, and thus a certain state of affairs regarding first-order elements exists. Because I own it, I have a liberty to use it or keep it stored in the closet. If I decide to use it, I may use it for purposes for which it was designed, such as a means of writing, or I may use it for atypical purposes, such as for a target when I practice rifle shooting. I have a privilege to do all these things. Further, I have a claim against everyone else that they not use my computer without my consent, for any reason.[13] But my ownership also gives rise to a power I possess to change this state of affairs. I could, for instance, sell it, in which case I would lose the claims and privileges described above. Or the government might be able to appropriate it when it declares a national emergency (one might imagine some circumstance entailing a dire need for computers), in which case it too has a power. (Of course, if I cannot be made to lose my claims of ownership, through the government's declaration of emergency or through any other action, then I have an immunity against it with respect to my rights in my computer.)

2.2 Two Conceptions of Rights

On the table, then, are four Hohfeldian elements—claims, privileges, powers, and immunities—that have been used in various definitions of rights. Can any of these, individually, be a right? The answer to this question will be different for each of two conceptions of rights that will be examined. It has been noted that a privilege, without any accompanying claims to protection against noninterference, would constitute a right that is very weak, if a right at all. This same observation makes claims seem to be quite strong candidates. The ways in which powers and immunities might be rights have not been addressed, but as powers and immunities are second-order elements, they must be internally complex, containing any number of combinations of claims and privileges that can be altered (powers) or whose alteration can be resisted (immunities). Putting this discussion on hold momentarily, let us turn to the general characterizations of the two conceptions of rights.

First, there is the benefit conception of a right (sometimes referred to as the interest conception), for which Bentham is well known.[14] If we temporarily limit the possibilities to only claims, then according to the simplest version of this conception, a right (claim) is held if and only if the rightholder stands to benefit from the performance of the correlative duty. A right, then, is seen as a benefit, and a rightholder is seen as a beneficiary.[15]

In certain contexts, it may be doubted that one party's standing to benefit from the performance of a duty ought to entail a right for the beneficiary. Specifically, the case in which the beneficiary is not the party to whom the duty is owed seems to generate counterintuitive conclusions on the benefit conception. H.L.A. Hart has used this sort of criticism to reject Bentham's benefit account of rights.[16] I may, for instance, stand to benefit from your getting repaid by Joe (who owes you money), because you, in turn, owe me money, and the only way I will get repaid any time soon is for you to be repaid first. According to the benefit conception, it looks like Joe has a duty, owed to me, to repay you. But this is clearly incorrect as the objection goes; no acceptable account will ascribe actual rights to third- (or fourth- or fifth-) party members.

To maintain the integrity of the benefit conception, David Lyons has suggested that we accept a qualified version of it.[17] These sorts of problems can be avoided, he claims, by limiting the scope of beneficiaries to those who are directly intended to benefit from the performance of the correlative duty.[18] With this version, Joe does not have a duty toward me to repay you, and I thus do not have a claim against Joe that he repay you. More of our standard intuitions are captured in this way, and thus the benefit conception can be maintained.

According to the benefit conception, then, the general picture of the rightholder is one of a "passive beneficiary," as L. W. Sumner has aptly described it.[19] Duties are imposed on others, and claims are imposed on the rightholder (by whatever theory of justification is being employed); the rightholder plays no role in their generation or extinction.

Some would say that the rightholder is surely free to waive the performance of a correlative duty. It would seem odd to say that you have violated your moral duty to repay me the amount you borrowed if I explicitly informed you that you need not do this. Do I not have the option of acting altruistically and waiving my right to collect from you? If I indeed may do this (if I have no duty not to do this), then I have a power, and thus there is something here other than the existence of a mere claim. This discussion will be aided by briefly looking at the structural implications of the benefit account of rights.

It should first be observed that, while rights can be fairly complex (consisting of any number of combinations and orders of elements), a claim is a necessary component of a right. Mere privileges do not look like they qualify; it has been noted how very weak they are, and thus any privilege, in itself, will not be sufficient to provide a moral guarantee of a benefit. A right could perhaps be only a power or immunity, but again, since these are structurally complex, the statement that either of these in itself could be a right is misleading. Powers and immunities are complex, and on the benefit account of rights, must include claims—claims being the only element sufficient to guarantee a benefit to the rightholder. Second, it does appear to be the case on the benefit conception that claims alone can be rights. You owe me money, and I stand to benefit from your repayment. Thus I have a claim against you that you repay me. This does seem to be all we need for me to have the right.

But we can now address the puzzle of how I also seem to have a power, the power of altering the status of the first-order relation whereby I have a claim to repayment and you have a duty to repay. On the benefit account of rights, it may be the case, but it is not necessarily the case, that a claim is accompanied by other, separate elements, such as powers or privileges. In the above example, we commonly think that my claim against you is accompanied by the power that enables me to waive the claim, but there are other examples in which we tend to seriously question whether such a power tags along. In the United States, it is against the law for anyone to sell himself into slavery; the legal claim not to be enslaved is not accompanied by a legal power to waive this claim. If, as many believe, this law is based on some standard of morality, then we might come to see how the moral claim not to be enslaved may not be accompanied by a moral power to waive this claim. This account would also explain why some rights are seen as inalienable. Other examples might point to rights held by infants, animals, and other beings which stand to benefit from various actions of others but do not have the necessary abilities to waive their claims and thus cannot possibly have powers.

The overriding value inherent in the benefit conception, then, is welfare. In contrast, the choice conception of rights emphasizes the value of autonomy. It is explained nicely by Hart, who offers it as an alternative to the benefit account, which, again, he sees as problematic. According to this conception, a right is not merely a benefit, since there exists a choice on the part of the rightholder that the benefit be conferred. A right serves to protect this choice. In other words, because the rightholder stands to benefit from the performance of the correlative duty, he is in a special position to control which actions of the duty-bearer are permissible. The idea is that part of what it is to have a right is to be in a position to choose whether the duty-bearer should have to carry out his duty. The rightholder, then, is not a passive beneficiary, but an "active manager"[20] who has at his disposal some options regarding the status of others' duties, and thus also his claims. As with the benefit conception, the origin of the duty/claim depends on the chosen theory of justification of rights; the difference is that the choice conception necessarily ascribes to the rightholder the ability (the power) to extinguish the duty (and thus the claim), while the benefit conception does not. In other words, according to the choice conception, a power is necessarily part of a claim.

This difference between the two conceptions will be reflected in their structures. As was noted, the benefit conception allows that a right can be a simple claim. This claim may or may not be accompanied by a power to waive it. In contrast, the choice conception is unable to accommodate simple claims as rights. This is because any claim necessarily involves the power to alienate it.[21] So while a right may be a claim, the claim is internally complex, and so the choice conception admits of no rights that are mere claims.

While the possible variations of the structures of rights are numerous on each conception, given the various ways in which the Hohfeldian elements can be combined, we will focus on two main possible constructions of each. On the benefit account, a right can be a simple claim, as described above (with no accompanying privilege or other Hohfeldian element), but it can also be a protected privilege. The privilege to perform some particular act (the lack of a duty to refrain from doing that act) is based on an interest; but in order to make sure that the freedom to perform that act is effectively conferred, a perimeter of claims to noninterference, held against others, must accompany the privilege. The difference between these two structures will turn out to be of minimal importance, since most rights can be described in either way.

The choice conception can also accommodate a right whose structure is a protected privilege. Its second main structure is that of a claim, but not a simple claim, for the power to alienate or waive it is necessarily a part of the claim. Thus, on the choice conception, a claim can be a right, but the claim is necessarily internally complex and cannot be simple.

While the possible structures of a right constitute one difference between the two conceptions, a second difference pertains to what sorts of beings can have rights. The benefit conception will typically allow for a greater scope of rightholders. Part of this conception is that a necessary condition for being a rightholder is having interests, the protection of which would benefit the particular being. Certainly, adult human beings qualify on this model. But it is widely argued that other sorts of beings, such as fetuses, animals, and perhaps even plants, have interests that, if protected, would benefit those beings. Qualifying as a rightholder on the benefit conception is therefore not difficult.

It becomes more difficult, though, to qualify as a rightholder on the choice conception. According to this account, a necessary condition for having rights is the possession of the managerial abilities necessary to make choices as to whether the objects of one's claims must fulfill their correlative duties or may be relieved of them. Plants, certainly, cannot make such judgments; neither can animals or fetuses. Thus, none of these things can have rights on the choice conception.[22]

These two conceptions will be utilized in this book in the following ways. The interest-based justification of rights, when it is applied to the political debates in Part Two, will employ the benefit conception; the goal-based theory, meanwhile, will employ the choice conception. These connections are not necessary ones; others may mix and match the theories and conceptions as they see fit. For our purposes, and for the sake of efficiency, it is worthwhile to align just one conception with each theory rather than investigate all the possible combinations.

The attachment of the benefit conception to the interest-based theory seems plausible. Having one's interests satisfied and standing to benefit go hand in hand. The benefit conception also accords best with Joseph Raz's specific version of the theory, not just because he explicitly opts for it[23] but because he seems to allow room for inalienable rights.[24] In some ways this is not the most natural pairing, since Raz employs autonomy as a primary value, but all things considered, there seems to be nothing wrong with this alignment.[25]

Sumner opts instead for the choice conception on grounds that may be described as practical. In attempting to clearly mark the distinction between the values of autonomy and welfare, he claims that the choice conception, which centers on autonomy, does a better job. Only it can mark this distinction via the very use of rights language. Autonomy is a value that is sufficiently important to warrant a place of its own on the "theoretical terrain." Since the benefit conception, which centers on welfare, allows for autonomy to be a particular aspect of welfare, the language of rights would encompass both values, and thus not provide as sharp a demarcation between them.[26] Again, the pairing could be otherwise; it may be argued that Sumner, being a consequentialist, would be better equipped with the benefit conception. However, as will be seen in Chapter 4, he believes that possessing autonomy will turn out to be more worthwhile (from a consequentialist perspective) than denying individuals the opportunity to autonomously choose to waive their rights, even when doing so is to their detriment.[27] Therefore, aligning the choice conception with the goal-based theory, as Sumner does, is certainly permissible.

The definitions and concepts discussed in this chapter will be utilized throughout this project but will be of particular importance in the next two chapters, which delineate the details of the two theories of rights-justification to be employed. The interest-based theory will be examined first.

Notes

1. Hohfeld, Fundamental Legal Conceptions, ed. Walter Wheeler Cook (New Haven: Yale University Press, 1919).

2. Ibid., 36.

3. Again, Hohfeld himself did not define claims, or any of his fundamental conceptions, in terms of morality.

4. In his discussion of rights in Chapter 5 of Utilitarianism, for example, Mill seems to hold that most rights are negative claims.

5. Hohfeld, 38.

6. It should not be inferred that rights as claims are necessarily "claim-rights," a term that, along with its counterpart "liberty-rights," has become very popular in the literature. Instead, these terms should be ignored for now so as to avoid confusion.

7. Feinberg, "The Nature and Value of Rights" in The Philosophy of Human Rights, ed. Morton E. Winston (Belmont, CA: Wadsworth, 1989). Although Fein-

berg's title employs the language of "rights" and not "claims," his intention is to refer only to claims here.

8. Henceforth, the party against whom the claim is held will continue to be designated as the object of that claim; the holder of the claim will be referred to as its subject. The content of a claim will refer to that which is required by it.

9. The assumption at this point is that the class of possible objects of claims is limited to the class of rational human beings.

10. Those who assert the sorts of rights Hohfeld called privileges are typically, upon inspection, found to have this more complex nucleus-periphery picture (or something like it) in mind. A mere privilege, again, does not amount to much, and those who assert that they or others have these sorts of rights intend to indicate not just a freedom had by the rightholder, but a restraint on the part of others. The exception to this line might have been Hobbes, who described a state of nature in which all rights seem to be mere privileges, since "every man has a Right to every thing; even to one anothers body." See Leviathan, ed. C. B. MacPherson (London: Penguin Books, 1968), 190. For Hobbes, then, being at liberty is significant insofar as there are no restrictions on the permissibility of one's actions; but since everyone is at liberty in a Hobbesian state of nature, there exist no moral protections against any actions of others.

11. Hohfeld, 60.

12. This may be the case, in that a claim is understood as the absence of another's privilege, and a power is understood as the absence of another's immunity. But semantic parallelism does not necessarily correspond with a logical parallel structure, where our interest lies.

13. This example is intended for illustrative purposes. Certainly, property and ownership are complicated notions, and there is a fair amount of indeterminacy on rights stemming from ownership. This broader issue will be addressed in Chapter five. The present purpose is, again, solely to portray the notion of a power, and thus the first-order rights I have in my computer in the above example should just be assumed to exist.

14. The Works of Jeremy Bentham, ed. John Bowring (Edinburgh: William Tate, 1843), 159.

15. It might be noted here that Bentham's analysis is not strictly consistent with the Hohfeldian analysis discussed in the preceding section. While Bentham thought it was the case that the existence of a claim entailed a correlative duty, he did not necessarily think it was the case that the existence of a duty entailed a correlative claim. The failure to perform what might be called "barren" duties harms no one, and the failure to perform "self-regarding" duties harms only the holder of the duty; for these types of duties, there is no correlative claim held by the rightholder. (It is somewhat curious to argue that there even is a rightholder in these cases, since the bearer of the claim does not appear to benefit from the performance of the duty. If, however, Bentham is read as maintaining that the rightholder would benefit from the performance of, say, a barren duty, but would not be harmed from its nonperformance, then he would be more consistent on this point—albeit at the expense of being somewhat inconsistent with his utilitarian principles.)

It is also worth reminding ourselves at this point that Bentham rejected any notion of moral rights. His discussion was intended to cover primarily legal, and
perhaps more broadly conventional, rights, but as was the case with Hohfeld, the
conceptual apparatus lends itself to the moral analysis.

16. Hart, "Are There Any Natural Rights?" in Rights, ed. David Lyons (Belmont, CA: Wadsworth, 1979).

17. Lyons, "Rights, Claimants, and Beneficiaries" in Rights.

18. The qualification here, that the rightholder be "intended" to benefit, is also
of some importance. It is not necessary that the rightholder must actually benefit
on every occasion where the duty is carried out.

19. Sumner, The Moral Foundation of Rights (Oxford: Oxford University Press,
1987), 47.

20. Again, Sumner's characterization seems particularly apt. (The Moral Foundation of Rights, 47.)

21. This conclusion may be resisted, if it is believed that certain choices are by
nature incompetent, but without some argument for a necessary connection between such choices and incompetence, the suggestion begs the question. The observation that the choice conception apparently cannot accommodate any notion
of inalienable rights has led some to reject it as inferior to the benefit conception.
See, for example, Neil MacCormick, "Rights in Legislation" in Law, Morality and
Society, ed. P. M. S. Hacker and Joseph Raz (Oxford: Clarendon Press, 1971).

22. We have said that one of the political debates to be addressed is that of
abortion, in which each side typically centers its arguments on rights—either the
right to choice held by the mother, or the right to life held by the fetus. During the
discussion of this debate in Chapter 8, the choice conception will be discounted
in any assertion of fetal rights, since it must be the case that any argument for
such rights must not be employing it.

23. Raz, The Morality of Freedom (Oxford: Oxford University Press, 1986), 166.

24. Ibid., 170. Raz indicates that it is not necessarily the case that rights are conditional on the desire of the rightholder.

25. Further, Raz's emphasis on autonomy is a function of his commitment to
perfectionism rather than liberalism.

26. The Moral Foundation of Rights, 96–100.

27. Ibid., 97–98. This claim sounds similar to those found by Mill in the second
chapter of Utilitarianism. Mill claims that one who chooses to remain merely content with his simple life cannot, according to the principles of utilitarianism, be
forced to engage in activity which would in fact make him much happier.

3

The Interest-Based Theory of Rights

3.1 The Raz Version

Chapter 1 enumerated the reasons for including an interest-based justification of rights. Since there are different types of interest-based theories, we must detail the aspects of the one to be used in examining the social issues in Part 2. Before examining the preferred interest-based theory, the one offered by Joseph Raz, it would be helpful to frame it between two other, less appealing ones.

First, one version of an interest-based theory would spread rights too widely. Bernard Rollin has argued for the existence of moral rights possessed by animals. He appeals to Aristotelian teleology, stating that all beings, including animals, possess a telos, which is a "function, a set of activities intrinsic to it, evolutionarily determined and genetically imprinted" that constitute its nature. He then employs the notion of interests, defined as the "conditions without which the creature, first of all, cannot live or, second of all . . . cannot fulfill its telos."[1] As interests ground rights, Rollin soon derives not only a right to life for animals, but a right to the kind of life dictated by the animal's nature or telos. Some examples are a bird's right to fly and a gazelle's right to run.[2] From here, a right to virtually anything can be defended; a cockroach's right to darkness can be seen on the horizon.

Although there may be good reasons for thinking that animals do possess at least some moral rights, there are certainly good reasons for disliking the inordinate scope of the rights distribution implied by Rollin's argument. Given such a distribution, the number of situations in which there are conflicts of rights—not just concerning animals but between humans in any number of different cases—would be correspondingly inordinate. Rollin's method of adjudication in such situations is to assess which of the relevant parties has the stronger right, which in turn calls for an assessment of the strengths of the interests grounding the rights.

But now we are back to the problem alluded to in Chapter 1—that every situation of conflict seems to be a conflict of rights. And, as has been observed, when rights appear on both sides of almost every political dispute, their practical effectiveness disappears. Allowing just any interest to ground rights will therefore be ineffective.

A second version of an interest-based theory of rights can be envisioned, one that limits the interests that can ground rights by focusing on the concept of needs. This move requires addressing the ensuing question of what is to count as a need. This is a tricky job, given that one must assert not merely what counts as a need, but what counts as a need in order to do something. A thief can be said to need a jimmy in order to perform his task effectively, but this is not the sort of morally relevant conception of need we are looking for in a theory of rights. Which needs should count as needs worthy of grounding moral rights (or duties) is a matter of debate. Although some theories of need take into account interests that are both subjective and objective, and allow for a fairly wide list of needs,[3] many encompass a list that is purely objective and very narrow indeed. Some would limit what would count as a need to solely what is necessary for continued survival, claiming that such needs can be satisfied at a cost of about 75 cents per day.[4] Because the list would likely include only those items necessary for continued survival, many would argue that there would still be interests of moral relevance left unaccounted for, such as the interest in being free, which would ground such rights as freedom of action and freedom of speech.[5] This account, then, seems to capture too few rights.

Raz's version of the interest-based theory captures the appropriate scope of the distribution of rights. It is not the case that just any interest will do the job (as in Rollin's account), nor is it the case that a great many interests will get left out (as in the account just discussed). Much of what Raz says about rights is found in Chapter 7 of his book, The Morality of Freedom. (For the remainder of this chapter, the parenthetical page references are to this book.) The heart of his theory is found toward the very beginning of that chapter:

> Definition: 'X has a right' if and only if X can have rights, and, other things being equal, an aspect of X's well-being (his interest) is a sufficient reason for holding some other person(s) to be under a duty.[6]

This definition needs examination. The first condition, that the subject in question must have the ability to have rights, will be temporarily shelved while we look at the second and more complex condition—that "other things being equal, an aspect of X's well-being (his interest) is a sufficient reason for holding some other person(s) to be under a duty."

First, the concept of duty plays a key role in Raz's definition. A sound understanding might be achieved by again looking at Mill's discussion of duties. Recall (from Chapter 2, 2.1) that for Mill, being charitable and refraining from harming others (in a positive sense), to take two examples, are both moral duties.[7] The former is a weaker duty, what he called an "imperfect" duty (or duty of imperfect obligation), with which there is no correlative right. The latter is a stronger duty, what he called a "perfect" duty (or duty of perfect obligation), with which there does exist a correlative right—in this case a right not to be harmed.

Another view of this notion that will help to frame Raz's position is presented by R. M. Hare.[8] Hare distinguishes between that which one morally "ought" to do and that which one morally has an "obligation" to do. We ought to give to charity, and we also ought to refrain from harming others; the moral "ought" is widely applicable. But the notion of moral "obligation" is more constrained and applies (roughly) only to Mill's duties of perfect obligation. Hare's specific example is that of a stranded motorist on a bad night. While it is the case that I ought to give her a ride or otherwise come to her aid, it is not the case that I have an obligation to do so.[9] This example, then, looks like it falls into Mill's category of imperfect duties. Hare then goes on to tie rights to obligations. Thus, the stranded motorist holds no right against me that I assist her. The resulting ascriptions of rights are roughly the same for Hare as for Mill; the difference is that Hare refuses to label Mill's imperfect duties as duties (obligations) at all.

Raz appears to equate at least some aspects of the notion of duty in his definition with the notion of obligation offered by Hare.[10] Raz indicates that while some interests are sufficient for holding others to be under a duty, some are not sufficient. (Raz, 182) It appears that when someone has an interest that would be protected by some action of mine, then I have a reason—we can say a moral reason—for performing this action. We can also say, then, that when one has an interest that would be protected by some action of mine, then in some minimal sense at least, I ought to perform that action. But it does not necessarily follow that I have a duty to perform that action. For Raz, the reason for acting so as to protect the person's interest only becomes a duty if her interest is sufficient to warrant holding me under a duty. This may be the case in my having a reason to refrain from harming her, but it may not be the case in my having a reason to help her when she is stranded.

Duties are therefore special types of moral reasons for acting (or refraining from acting) in certain ways. They have what Raz calls "peremptory force." (Raz, 195) It is not the case that duties necessarily carry more moral weight than other types of moral reasons for action; it is the class of reason that sets them apart.[11] Raz compares the force of a duty to the force of a reason given by an authority. Because of the peremptory force that duties have, they are not very easily overridden, although they are not absolute either.[12] Here is another point of similarity between Raz's characterization of duty and Hare's characterization of obligation, namely the degree to which duties (obligations) are binding.

It would be misleading, though, to link Raz too closely with Hare when discussing the relationship between rights and duties (or obligations). For one thing, Hare appears to believe that obligations are prior to rights. His two-level utilitarian scheme implies rules of conduct that should be followed if overall utility is to be maximized, and the rules look to be in the form of obligations imposed by this utilitarian system, which in turn ground correlative rights.[13] Even if this reading is not exactly right, it is at best ambiguous whether obligations are prior to rights, or whether there is any priority at all for either, since Hare follows Hohfeld in asserting strict correlativity.

For Raz, however, it is quite clear, and quite important for a proper understanding of the interest-based theory, that rights are prior to duties.[14] This may seem a strange claim, given that his definition appears to call for things to be the other way round—that we first need to look at the prospect of holding others under a duty before we can ascribe a right. But this appearance is deceptive. In deliberations on rights, it is not the case that we first decide whether the potential duty-bearer does in fact have a duty, and then use our findings to make a judgment about whether someone else has a (correlative) right. Rather, we first decide whether the potential rightholder does in fact have a right, and we do this by assessing whether the interest on which the potential right would be based would itself be sufficient to warrant holding others under a (correlative) duty. If the interest is sufficient, then there is in fact a right. Thus, the right follows directly from the interest; the interest (if sufficient) grounds the right, and hence the "interest-based" label to this theory of rights. But once the right is established, it grounds the existence of the duty on the part of others. In this way, rights are "intermediate conclusions" in arguments that ultimately ground moral duties in interests. (Raz, 181)

A second way in which Raz departs from Hare's analysis is that Raz does not subscribe to the logical correlativity of rights and duties, and he thus also departs from Hohfeld on this matter. It is the case that rights entail duties, for rights invariably ground duties. But it is not necessarily the case that the existence of a duty entails the existence of a right on the part of the person to whom the duty is owed. (Raz, 170–171, 183–184)[15] Were this the case, then morality would be "right-based," since the only possible source of moral duties would be moral rights; but Raz rejects this.[16] Rights are one source of duties, but there may be other sources as well. One example is that the owner of a Van Gogh painting has a duty not to destroy it, despite the fact that it is her property. The basis of the duty is not a particular right; the painting itself has no right not to be destroyed (since it does not have interests and so cannot have rights), and no one else has a right that it not be destroyed (since it is no one else's property). The basis of this duty is respect, in particular respect for those things that give life meaning.[17] Thus, there is a duty on the part of the owner without any correlative right—indeed without any correlative party to whom the duty is owed.

To this point, we have been examining the aspects of "duty" and the role it plays in Raz's definition. Other aspects of the definition require attention as well. Before turning to those, however, it would be helpful to quickly review a distinction Raz makes that is not explicit in the definition itself. Some rights are grounded directly in interests, while others, though also ultimately grounded in interests, are directly justified by other rights. The former Raz labels as core rights, the latter derivative rights. (Raz, 168–169) He is hesitant to say which rights belong to which category; indeed, he makes it clear that he does not wish to suggest which rights might exist at all as a consequence of his theory. His aim is merely to explain what the justificatory framework of rights looks like.

An example he does use, albeit for explanatory purposes only, is the right to free speech. (Raz, 184) The right to free speech is fairly general and thus seems a good candidate for being classified as a core right in Raz's framework. This right does not seem to be grounded in any others but is directly justified in the interest one has in freely expressing oneself. More specific examples of claims to free speech rights, such as the right to protest against one's government or the right to produce and distribute pornography, would then be classified as derivative, being justified not by the interest directly but by the right to free speech generally (which in turn is grounded by the interest of free speech).

But this is not the only possible way to conceive of the right to free speech. For instance, it may turn out to be derivative, justified by the core right to freedom generally; or, it may be that there is no right to free speech, and that the illusion results because several individual core rights, such as the rights to protest and to produce pornography, have been generalized into something like the right to free speech.[18]

Again, Raz does not engage in discussion of what the hierarchical structures of specific rights might look like; he merely provides the underlying framework for such discussions. We will later be applying it to the contemporary debates in Part 2. We should not be at all surprised, though, if there is not one single way of understanding the structure of a particular right. As we discuss the debates, we will keep this in mind in the attempt to understand what this theory might say about the various rights to which appeal is made.

With the understanding of the distinction between core and derivative rights in hand, we should now examine the aspect of Raz's definition that stipulates that a necessary condition of X's having a right is the very ability on the part of X to have rights. The question of just who can have rights will directly affect only one of the political debates (the abortion debate, in Chapter 8), but addressing this aspect next makes good sense logically, since certain concepts employed here will facilitate later discussion in this chapter.

Raz follows up his primary definition with a statement of a general principle regarding who can have rights:

> An individual is capable of having rights if and only if either his well-being is of ultimate value or he is an "artificial person" (e.g., a corporation). (Raz, 166)

For our purposes, the notion of artificial persons is not particularly relevant. In this principle, Raz is attempting to capture the broad ways in which rights are used and in which things are said to possess rights, thus trying to capture not only moral rights but conventional ones as well. It may be that there is some moral basis for artificial persons to be the subjects of rights; but nothing Raz says leads us to believe that he thinks this. Since the political debates in Part 2 focus on the (alleged) rights of real persons, the second disjunct of the above will be ignored. Thus, future references to Raz's principle of capacity to have rights will pertain solely to the first disjunct, that a being can have rights if and only if his well-being is of ultimate value.[19]

The next question, then, is what is meant by "ultimate value." This notion plays a specific role for Raz, a role that will also bear on the question of what makes an interest sufficiently important to hold others to be under a duty, and it is therefore important that we approach its explanation in an organized manner. The best way to begin is by looking at the first main distinction he draws, which is between instrumental and intrinsic value. For something to have instrumental value it must be valuable as a result of its consequences, be they actual or intended. Conversely, to say that something has intrinsic value is to say that it has value even apart from any instrumental value it may have, that is, apart from any consideration of the consequences.[20]

Raz then describes three different types of intrinsic values, the first being "value in itself." Something possessing value in itself is valuable regardless of what else may exist. Second, there is "constituent value." A thing is said to have constituent value if it is an element of something that is valuable in itself, and in some way contributes to the value of it. Third, there is "ultimate value." A thing is said to be ultimately valuable if it is an aspect of something that is valuable in itself, and explains and justifies why that thing is judged to be valuable in itself. It is unnecessary, according to Raz, to explain or justify items of ultimate value by reference to any other values. (Raz, 177–179, 200)

The best way to illustrate these potentially confusing notions is probably with Raz's own example. Many people find pleasure in art. They find the activity of looking at art, studying it, and contemplating it to be a valuable one. This sort of activity is intrinsically valuable in that it is valuable in itself; its value does not derive from any consequences, actual or intended, and it would be valuable regardless of what else may exist. The specific works of art that are studied and contemplated are also intrinsically valuable in that they are constituently valuable; they are elements of the activity of enjoying art. Finally, the quality of a life in which art is enjoyed is the ultimate value here. A life with art is held to be of a higher quality than one without art, and it is thus ultimately valuable. It also explains and justifies the judgment that the activity of enjoying art is valuable in itself.

Here, Raz is expressing a commitment to humanism, according to which the moral goodness or badness something possesses is a function of how it contributes to human life and the quality thereof. As Raz notes, humanism is not itself a moral theory, but must be an aspect of any acceptable moral theory. (Raz, 194) The main focus for Raz is the relatively uncontroversial notion that quality of life is a source of value. A more detailed discussion of value requires an understanding of Raz's use of "well-being" in his definition. It is a particular conception of well-being, one he labels "personal well-being," and may be defined as the degree to which a person's life is successful from her point of view. Success, in turn, is a function of the degree to which a person achieves her goals. For now, the notion of a goal may be widely conceived, encompassing endeavors such as general projects, plans, and commitments. Goals may be short-term or long-term; they may be nested in various ways; and there may be orders of goals (such as goals about which goals one ought to have). Personal well-being is tied to goals because there seems to be little that can be done to improve one's well-being without in some way seeking to achieve the goals one has. (Raz, 288–294)

This conception of well-being, though synonymous with "interest," should be distinguished from what Raz calls "self-interest." Well-being and self-interest have often been used interchangeably, but Raz does not follow suit in doing this. When I pursue goals designed to improve only my well-being, then (assuming I am successful) I improve my self-interest as well. However, goals designed to improve both my well-being and the well-being of others (in addition to my own or as a means to achieving my own) do not pertain to self-interest. Well-being and self-interest could match up exactly for a person whose goals invariably focus only on herself; but it is unlikely that this will happen, and may not be a possibility at all.[21] (Raz, 295–299)

At this point, although well-being appears to be an entirely subjective notion, this will turn out not to be the case. Raz places a constraint on what sorts of aims can legitimately count as goals, and this is where he explicitly links well-being to the notion of value. A necessary condition for the legitimacy of a particular aim in life is that the aim be a valuable one. If the aim is not valuable, then what the agent takes to be her goal is only a false goal; its successful achievement will not have a beneficial impact on her well-being, and the failure to achieve it will not have a detrimental impact on her well-being (though she may feel frustration and disappointment).

The question of what makes a particular goal valuable, and thus legitimate, is answered via reference to the above discussion of types of value. A goal may be intrinsically valuable, or it may be instrumentally valuable if its successful achievement would have, or is intended to have, the consequence of advancing the cause of an intrinsically valuable goal. Thus, legitimate goals refer ultimately to intrinsic value. The intrinsic value of a goal, taking into account the above discussion of humanism and value, is seen in its positive contribution to the quality of human life. An extreme example of a valuable goal would be the purely altruistic ambition to do nothing in life but help others. Mother Theresa's overriding life goal was thus clearly valuable. Conversely, the goal of a person who spends his life attempting to become the best gambler he can be is not legitimate, since its accomplishment would not appear to contribute to the quality of human life.

It can now be seen how Raz combines elements of both subjective and objective interests into his notion of personal well-being. The more successful one's life is from her point of view (success being measured in terms of the achievement of goals), the better off one is in terms of her well-being. This subjective element is tempered by a requirement that negates the possibility that achieving just any goal improves one's well-being—the requirement being that the achievement of the goal positively influence the quality of human life. If a goal does not meet this requirement, then it is a false goal, and well-being will not be improved, regardless of whether the endeavor to achieve it is successful.

Thus far, we have reviewed the role of the notion of duty in Raz's definition. We have also spelled out what lies behind the notion of well-being, which has allowed for an answer to the question of who may have rights. According to Raz's humanistic principle, things whose well-being is of ultimate value can have rights, and since only the well-being of humans is of ultimate value (since ultimate value pertains to the quality of human life), only humans can have rights. Some humanistic principles

spread rights more widely by allowing for the quality of life of nonhuman entities to be morally relevant, thus paving the way for the well-
being of these entities to be of ultimate value as well.

Raz's understanding of well-being also allows us to address the issue
of what makes an interest (aspect of well-being) sufficient to hold others
to be under a duty, other things being equal. Consider two cases analogous to the ones above used to illustrate legitimate goals and false goals
(those without value). In the case of the altruist (call her Anne), an agent
possesses an overriding life goal to be the most altruistic person she can
be. In the case of the gambler (call him Gary), an agent possesses an overriding life goal to be the best gambler he can be. Does Anne possess a
right to a life of altruism? Does Gary have a right to a life of gambling,
understood in this same way? Can either justifiably claim a positive right
(to assistance) as well as a negative right (to noninterference), if this latter right can be justifiably claimed at all?

If an affirmative response is to be given to these questions, each case
must pass a couple of tests. The first is what might be called the "value
test,"[22] which assesses whether the interest on which the alleged right is
based is valuable—that is, whether it is a legitimate interest, one that will
positively affect well-being if the agent successfully achieves what she
takes to be her goal. Should this test be passed, we can say there is a
prima facie case for a right, or even that there is a prima facie (i.e., defeasible) right, since the interest's being valuable means that it is sufficient,
on initial inspection, to warrant holding others to be under a duty.[23] The
second test, the "other things equal test," then assesses whether this interest, though valuable, is sufficiently valuable to hold others to be under
a duty. It may be that the prima facie right is defeated by conflicting considerations, such as the unjust violation of others' rights, which may be
an unavoidable result of imposing duties on them. Whether the imposition of the duty violates another's rights at all, and if so whether it is a
justifiable violation ("justified" being evaluated in terms of the degree of
detrimental impact on the interest on which the violated right is based),
are questions to be addressed in this second test.

Anne's case can be examined in light of these tests. She is asserting her
right to a life of altruism. Consideration of the first test requires that the
interest on which Anne's alleged right exists be identified. If we take the
interest to be, simply, being altruistic, it appears as though the first test is
passed. The more altruistic she is, the more her goal will be achieved—
thus the more successful her life will be from her point of view, thus the
better the state of her well-being. What secures the passage of the value
test, though, is the value of the goal. Being altruistic and helping others
generally is indeed valuable, since such activity will positively impact
quality of life, Anne's life as well as the lives of those whom she is help-

ing. A life with some altruistic activity is of a higher quality than a life without any, and there does not seem to be a point of diminishing marginal returns in altruistic activity where quality of life (and thus well-being) starts to be negatively impacted. The more altruism, therefore, the better (assuming health and so on, will not seriously be adversely affected by one's giving).

Consideration of the second test requires that the nature of the duties to be imposed on others be specified. But this depends on the structure of the right under examination. Recall that the interest-based theory is employing the benefit conception of rights, according to which there are two main possible constructions of a right. First, a right might be a simple claim. If this is what Anne means when she asserts her right to a life of altruism, then there would exist correlative duties on the part of others to help her achieve her goal. It may be that this is too much, morally, to ask of others; such a demand might deprive them of their rights to privacy or liberty. But since the interest on which Anne's alleged right is based is of fairly significant value, in that it will benefit the quality of life not only of Anne but of others as well, it may be argued that others do have a duty to contribute something to Anne's effort, in much the way it is argued that people have a duty to do at least something for charity. Whether or not her claim would warrant holding others to be under a duty therefore requires further investigation of the relative interests on which the various rights are based.

The benefit conception also allows that a right may be a protected privilege. If this is what Anne means when she asserts her right to a life of altruism, she is speaking of the privilege to engage in altruistic activity. This privilege is based on the same interest specified above in considering the value test. (It should perhaps be noted that throughout this discussion we are therefore taking her right to be a core right, justified directly by the interest.) The privilege is the nucleus of the right, and is protected by a perimeter of claims to noninterference. Thus, the duties that others would have, given this picture of the right, would merely be negative duties—duties not to interfere in Anne's pursuit. Certainly this would involve no unjustifiable infringement of the rights of others. Such duties would amount to a mandate that they mind their own business, or at least not interfere in Anne's business. There would be no positive assistance entailed in the duty, as there would be if the right were seen as a simple claim. So Anne's assertion of a right, on the condition that the right is a protected privilege, passes the "other things equal" test as well, and thus may be asserted as a legitimate right.

The result, then, is that Anne does have a right, but she should be careful to avoid the ambiguity inherent in the assertion that she has a right to lead an altruistic life. More precisely, given that the right is a protected privilege, she has a right to attempt to lead an altruistic life, since no one would be under a duty to ensure that her goal is realized. Of course, if she means in her original assertion that her right is a claim, which would imply correlative duties on the part of others to assist her, then the original phrasing is more accurate. Again, whether or not Anne is correct about possessing this stronger right requires further analysis.

Turning now to Gary, who is asserting his right to a life of gambling, consideration of the value test requires that we identify the interest on which Gary's right is alleged to exist. If we take the interest to be, simply, gambling, it appears as though this first test will not be passed. The more Gary gambles and the better he gets (assuming he improves his gambling abilities), the more his goal will be achieved—thus the more successful his life will be from his point of view. But the state of his well-being will not be thus improved, because what Gary takes to be his goal is actually a false goal. It is not valuable since gambling, even successful gambling, does not contribute positively to the quality of human life—his or anyone else's. The assumption is that the activity of gambling, considered apart from potential income (which does tend to improve quality of life) and other considerations, fails to positively contribute in this way. The first test is failed, and the right to a life of gambling is not substantiated.

But it may be that Gary does not intend his right to be a core right, justified directly by an interest. It may be derivative. Indeed, the general core right to freedom appears to pass the value test easily.[24] The right to be free to spend one's life gambling is then seen as derivative, grounded in this more general core right. If this is what Gary means, then we must move on to the "other things equal" test.[25]

Again, consideration of this test requires that the nature of the duties to be imposed on others be specified, and which duties these are depends on the structure of the right in question. If Gary intends his right as a simple claim, then others would possess duties to positively aid him in achieving his goal of leading a life of gambling (whatever the specific duties may turn out to be). Again, such duties would likely infringe on the privacy and liberty rights of the prospective duty-bearers. Further, whereas in Anne's case it is more plausible to suggest that there are duties to positively assist her (and thus that some infringement on the liberty of others may be justifiable), in Gary's case the imposition of any such duties does not seem defensible. Thus, on the condition that the right is a simple claim, there are conflicting considerations that negate the possibility of Gary's right turning out to be legitimate.

The picture of the right as a protected privilege yields a different conclusion, however. As before, the duties imposed on others would be merely negative, requiring that Gary's pursuit of a life of gambling not be interfered with. This is not much to ask of others, and so, using the above approach, Gary's right to a life of gambling looks to be legitimate, although again it is more accurately described as a right to attempt to lead a life of gambling, or as a right to pursue a life of gambling.[26]

The cases of Anne and Gary are designed to illustrate the ways in which the various notions found in Raz's definition operate and interact with each other, and thus also to clarify their meanings. Understanding an interest to which appeal is widely made would simplify the project of applying the interest-based theory to specific cases. The following brief section is devoted to attaining such an understanding.

3.2 Personal Autonomy

Raz focuses on the particular interest of personal autonomy. We, too, will focus on this interest, as it will get much attention in upcoming chapters. Raz even treats it at times as if it has pride of place, rather than being one interest among several. (Raz, 394) One occasionally gets the feeling that personal autonomy is for Raz what happiness was for Aristotle. But this isn't quite correct, since Raz is also careful to indicate that personal autonomy is a "particular conception" of individual well-being.[27] (Raz, 369) For our purposes, it will play the more humble role of being one possible interest on which rights may be based, though it will be an unproblematic one.

The basic definition of personal autonomy is provided by Raz in several places in The Morality of Freedom. The central idea is that of being the author of one's own life:

> A person is autonomous only if he has a variety of acceptable options available to him to choose from, and his life became as it is through the choice of some of these options. (Raz, 204)

So there appear to be two necessary conditions for personal autonomy, the first being the existence of an acceptable range of options in deciding the course of one's life, and the second being that one's current life status results from the selection of some of these options. Raz asserts that this is an interest that passes what we are calling the value test, and thus grounds a prima facie core right.

Before examining further just what personal autonomy consists of, it would be wise to supplement this initial characterization with a statement of what it is not. First, Raz's personal autonomy is not to be confused with the Kantian notion of autonomy, a notion with which the term autonomy in its free-standing state tends to be immediately associated. Kantian autonomy pertains to positive freedom, the ability of rational agents first to regard themselves as makers of universal law, and second to follow that law; a person acts autonomously if the maxim on which she is acting can (through reason) simultaneously be willed as universal moral law. The autonomous person, for Kant, creates her own moral law via the categorical imperative, and is self-governing in accordance with it.[28] Personal autonomy is not so grandiose. For Raz, it pertains to a particular aspect of morality and is not a foundational element of morality itself. (Raz, 370) Personal autonomy, put simply, is about the freedom of individuals to pursue their own life plans.

Second, personal autonomy is not to be confused with self-realization, which is essentially the maximization of the development of one's valuable capabilities. The person who chooses (freely) to discard most or all of her available options is nonetheless acting autonomously in doing so. But if she autonomously chooses to act this way, she will not be achieving self-realization, since the possibilities for developing and ultimately maximizing her valuable capacities are correspondingly discarded. The two notions are thus distinct.

Returning now to the positive characterization of personal autonomy, three conditions for autonomy are individually necessary and jointly sufficient. First, an individual must possess the mental capabilities necessary for forming and executing a life plan. These can be fairly basic, such as the rationality necessary for reasoning about the available options, and the ability to foresee the likely consequences of one's actions. Second, the agent must have before her an adequate range of acceptable options from which to choose the goals she will pursue in life (i.e., from which to choose her life plan); otherwise, the possession of the requisite mental abilities would be of little significance. This second condition is treated as the primary element of personal autonomy. The third condition is that of independence, the freedom from coercion or manipulation. Though Raz lists this as a separate condition, it could arguably be assimilated into the second, since one who is coerced or manipulated into a particular choice (or a particular range of choices) can be said to lack the requisite number of acceptable options. But pending what is to count as "acceptable," it is conceivable that a person could be manipulated into choosing from among a range of options that is nonetheless acceptable. Thus, the third condition is appropriately added to the other two.

It should be obvious from these three conditions that autonomy is largely a matter of degree. The mental capabilities entailed by the first condition are assessed in terms of degrees; there is no magical point on the scale of rationality (assuming rationality is quantifiable or has a "scale" at all) at which the minimum capabilities necessary for autonomy are reached. This is no less true for the condition stipulating that the agent have an "adequate range of acceptable options." Though no specifications of precise, quantifiable minimums necessary for autonomy can

be or should be attempted, some idea of when one is or is not autonomous should be provided.

Raz suggests certain considerations that are relevant to the assessment
of whether the range of options open to an agent is adequate and
whether the options are themselves acceptable. First, he stipulates that it
is not necessarily the number of options, but the variety, that is relevant.
Having numerous options from which to choose is no better than having
only one if they all amount to virtually the same thing. Of course, what
makes for an acceptable variety is not specified by Raz, and probably
does not admit of specification; variety is offered as one component of
what constitutes an adequate range of acceptable options.

Second, the available options must pertain to goals of varying scopes,
longer-term as well as shorter-term. It may seem that, since the notion of
personal autonomy entails being the author of one's life, only long-term
projects are encompassed by autonomy. But short-term endeavors,
whether or not they are means to achieving long-term ones, are also to be
included. The control inherent in autonomy, then, should "extend to all
aspects of our lives." (Raz, 374)

Two other factors affect the assessment of whether one is autonomous.
One who is constantly performing particular actions because her very
survival depends on it is not autonomous; such a person does not have
an adequate range of acceptable options. In addition, if I have what appear to be acceptable options from which to choose but some of those options entail performing immoral acts as a means to achieving the goals
inherent in those options, then I may be more restricted than originally
would seem to be the case, perhaps to the point where I am no longer autonomous.[29] (Raz, 379)

For Raz, and for us, whenever autonomy is specified as the interest on
which the particular alleged right is said to be based, the value test is unproblematically passed. Others have pointed to some notion of freedom
as a fundamental element of morality, and thus of moral rights.[30] Personal autonomy can be seen as the concrete form of freedom (Raz, 394),
and thus an interest without which other interests are necessarily endangered, if not fully debilitated. This characterization makes autonomy out
to be fundamental, or existing at the top of an Aristotelian hierarchy of
interests (hence the similarity to Aristotle noted above). We have said
that this stronger position need not be defended; but, autonomy is certainly an interest that, when satisfied, contributes positively to the quality of human life. Its value as a legitimate interest is thus secure.

The observation that it is an interest widely appealed to in moral discourse will help us to tackle more efficiently the project in Part 2. It seems
safe to say that, in many cases, personal autonomy (or something very
close to it) is the interest that is serving to ground the rights people claim

to have in those debates. Both sides in the debate over redistributive taxation, assuming they subscribe to the interest-based theory of rights, are likely appealing in large part to this interest. Those who assert a right to receive benefits from others[31] can be seen as asserting that such benefits are necessary conditions for being autonomous. Conversely, those from whom the benefits would be appropriated can be seen as arguing that such appropriation unjustly violates their property rights precisely because it would intrude on their autonomy. The interest of personal autonomy is playing a similarly important role in both sides of the debate over affirmative action. Minorities can be seen as basing their rights to preferential treatment on the claim that the policy is a necessary condition for autonomy. Conversely, those who would be negatively affected by this policy can be seen as arguing that their autonomy would be unacceptably violated, and thus that they have a right not to be subjected to affirmative action. Autonomy can be similarly framed in the pornography and abortion debates.

But it is not just that autonomy will be "framed" (in Part 2) to fit the debates. Rather, the assertion is that autonomy is in fact playing a key role in the reasoning of those who employ interest-based arguments for their rights. This observation will serve to facilitate the discussions of the particular social issues. By having established autonomy as an interest of value (indeed of great value), the value test can be bypassed when assessing those arguments. Also, when applying the "other things equal" test, it will not be necessary to examine a veritable plethora of interests that might be grounding the alleged rights; employing the interest of autonomy will yield significant results. Focusing solely on personal autonomy, however, will not be possible, since other interests can be inserted into this interest-based model.

As a final note, it is not the case that the interest of autonomy should necessarily be thought to ground the (prima facie) right to autonomy. Autonomy requires the existence of a number of available options, which in turn generally requires that certain social conditions obtain. But it may not be feasible to hold others under a duty to ensure that such conditions do obtain. Autonomy will likely ground other rights, though, depending on the existing circumstances. It may, for instance, ground a right to education, not merely as a protected privilege but as a claim. It may also ground rights to abortion, preferential treatment, and other rights to be discussed in Part 2.

Notes

1. Bernard Rollin, Animal Rights and Human Morality (Buffalo: Prometheus Books, 1992), 75.

2. Ibid., 90, 98.

3. See, for example, David Braybrooke, who discusses "course-of-life" needs within a fairly complex framework in Meeting Needs (Princeton: Princeton University Press, 1992).

4. C. E. Lindblom, Politics and Markets (New York: Basic Books, 1977), 9. Although today's priceline might allow for a somewhat higher daily allowance, the force of the point is not diminished.

5. On this point, see Henry Shue, "Security and Subsistence" in The Philosophy of Human Rights, ed. Morton E. Winston (Belmont, CA: Wadsworth, 1989), 159. Shue allows for such things as "unpolluted air, unpolluted water, adequate food, adequate clothing, adequate shelter, and minimal preventive health care" to count as needs, and thus as items to which individuals have a right.

6. Raz, The Morality of Freedom (Oxford: Oxford University Press, 1986), 166.

7. Utilitarianism, ed. George Sher (Indianapolis: Hackett, 1979), Chapter 5.

8. Moral Thinking (Oxford: Oxford University Press, 1981), especially Chapter 9.

9. Ibid., 149.

10. Indeed, neither writer believes that there is any interesting difference between the notion of a duty and the notion of an obligation, and each indicates (Hare more implicitly than explicitly) that his choice of which term to employ ("obligation" for Hare and "duty" for Raz) is merely a matter of preference. (See Hare, 149; Raz 167.)

11. Though Raz explicitly makes this claim, it is unclear just how his characterization of what sets duties apart from other moral reasons is significantly different from explanations employing the "weight" analogy. See, e.g., Judith Jarvis Thomson, The Realm of Rights (Cambridge, MA: Harvard University Press, 1990), 61–65; and Hare, 148–149. Just how is being a separate class of moral reason different from being a weightier reason, in the sense provided by these and other writers?

12. Further detail is provided in Raz's "Promises and Obligations" in Law, Morality and Society, ed. P. M. S. Hacker and Joseph Raz (Oxford: Clarendon Press, 1971).

13. Hare, 149–150.

14. See 171, 180, 183 for some examples of Raz's commitment to this thesis.

15. Further, there may even be duties that are non-relational, owed to no specifiable class of beings.

16. It is actually unclear whether Raz thinks the claims that morality is right-based, and that all duties derive from rights, amount to the same thing. If he does think this, he should not. First, a morality is right-based if rights are morally fundamental, and do not derive from any other consideration. Raz argues that this is false, and that rights are based on interests. Second, even a morality that is not right-based might allow for duties to follow only from rights. Raz argues against this in the example that follows. The point, again, is that the two claims are not extensionally equivalent.

17. See Raz, "Right-Based Moralities" in Utility and Rights, ed. R. G. Frey (Minneapolis: University of Minnesota Press, 1984). Objections to this point will undoubtedly arise. They will not be considered, however, as the goal here is merely

to point out Raz's reasons for denying that all duties ultimately derive from rights.

18. Raz's analogy is that if one comes to own a street by purchasing, in separate transactions, each individual home on that street, then any notion of owning "the street" would just be a generalization from owning each individual home. In such a case, there is no "core ownership" of the street, as would be the case if the entire street were purchased all at once, which in turn would entail ownership of the various parts of it, i.e., the individual homes. (169)

19. A few pages later, Raz adds another method of assessing whether something can have rights. According to this second principle, the "reciprocity thesis," only members of the same moral community can have rights. (176) Raz believes that the two principles generate consistent ascriptions of rights subjects, and he thus confines discussion of the reciprocity thesis to just a couple of paragraphs.

20. This general description of the distinction between intrinsic and instrumental follows the demarcation of most commentators. See, e.g., Louis P. Pojman, Ethics: Discovering Right and Wrong (Belmont, CA: Wadsworth, 1990), 57–58.

21. Because one's goals, according to Raz, are a function of social forms (widely practiced behaviors in one's society) and because much of morality is also a function of social forms, the achievement of goals looks like it must pass through at least some moral activities and pertain to the well-being of others as well as oneself, in which case well-being cannot be limited to self-interest.

22. The new terminology introduced here and in the rest of this section is not Raz's own. It is being offered as a vehicle for simplifying what Raz is doing.

23. We should be hesitant to recognize a "prima facie duty" as a correlate of the prima facie right just recognized, as this might lead to confusion with W. D. Ross's notion of a prima facie duty described in the first chapter of The Right and The Good (Oxford: Clarendon Press, 1930). An argument could perhaps be provided that the two amount to the same thing, but this would be well off the current subject, and in any case their moral foundations would be quite different.

24. An interest as broad as freedom may seem to render the value test pointless, since it looks like it could generate derivative rights to do anything. Perhaps the "first-level" derivative rights (those immediately following from the right to freedom) are thus better seen as core rights. On this analysis, Gary's core right might be to freely pursue an income in a nonharmful manner, from which the derivative right to gamble would follow. Either reading is acceptable at this point, since the example is for explanatory purposes.

25. Raz and I part company here, as he seems to think that a life of gambling, even successfully, is not a very successful life, since it does not positively contribute to the quality of human life. However, as freedom itself (or, more specifically, the freedom to pursue an income in a nonharmful manner) does positively contribute in this way, I am taking the derivative right to gamble as passing the value test.

Further, allowing for this more general freedom to pass the value test unproblematically is necessary to retain a classical liberal approach, one which is neutral among competing conceptions of the good. Following Raz's framework too closely would necessitate adoption of a perfectionist political philosophy, which, as was suggested in Chapter 1, should be avoided in discussions of policies for pluralistic societies.

26. In asserting Gary's right here, I am leaving aside the possibility that some may challenge the acceptability of duties of noninterference. Some may see the activity of gambling as dangerous to oneself, or just inherently evil, such that interfering in another's pursuit of a life of gambling is at least morally permissible, and may even be morally required. If such a challenge is made, an investigation into the interest on which the alleged right to interfere is based (or, in this example, into the plausibility of paternalism or moralism as justifications for restriction of individual liberty) would be necessary in order to adjudicate between the competing rights.

27. He does seem to think that, in contemporary political societies that are democratic in nature, personal autonomy is a necessary condition for (his conception of) success.

28. Kant, Grounding for the Metaphysics of Morals, trans. James W. Ellington (Indianapolis: Hackett, 1963), section 440.

29. Raz refers us to Bernard Williams's well-known argument that integrity causes great problems for utilitarian moral theory. Raz extends this (perhaps to a questionable degree) to include the idea that one whose options entail actions contrary to one's commitments is not autonomous in the sense he describes. (284, 315, 379) See J. J. C. Smart and Bernard Williams, Utilitarianism: For and Against (Cambridge: Cambridge University Press, 1963), 108–18.

30. See, e.g., H. L. A. Hart, "Are There Any Natural Rights?" in Rights, ed. David Lyons (Belmont, CA: Wadsworth, 1979), 14. While not committing to the existence of moral rights, Hart allows that "if there are any moral rights at all, it follows that there is at least one natural right, the equal right of all men to be free." See also Thomson, The Realm of Rights, 272–88, who goes on to use her defense of a (Raz-like) core right to liberty to establish a derivative right to abortion.

31. In our discussion, the right to receive such benefits from others via the intermediate actions of the government is being considered. Another question, of course, is whether individuals lacking autonomy would have the right to directly receive (or take) benefits from others. This latter right (and some would say the former as well) looks very much like a right, within certain limits and in certain circumstances, to steal the property of others.

4

The Goal-Based Theory of Rights

4.1 A Consequentialist Framework

This chapter is devoted to examining a goal-based (consequentialist) justification for rights. According to consequentialism, an act's rightness or
wrongness is a function solely of its consequences. The reasons for incorporating a goal-based theory of rights into this project were provided in
Chapter 1, where it was also indicated that the existence of a strong commitment to consequentialism is accompanied by an equally strong hostility toward it. The hostility is compounded when rights, traditionally
thought to be deontological in nature, are incorporated into the theory
and attempts are made to make them compatible with, and more
strongly grounded by, the theory. Vehement anticonsequentialists see no
hope of any such reconciliation.

The aim here, recall, is not to persuade such individuals that consequentialism is a superior moral theory. The aim, more modestly, is to
make a consequentialist theory of rights understandable, even to those
who will not subscribe to it, in order to see what such a theory implies
about specific contemporary issues. The first part of the chapter will be
devoted to analyzing consequentialist theory specifically, and the second
part will discuss the incorporation of rights into the theory.

Contemporary analyses of consequentialist theories have focused on
the notions of the right and the good, which together are taken to define
the theory.[1] The good is the goal, that which is to be promoted, and the
right stipulates the way in which the good is to be promoted. Standard
formulations of classical utilitarianism identify happiness as the good
and its maximization as the right. A variety of protests have been leveled
against utilitarianism, including the claim that it prescribes never-ending
moral action and behavior that intuition informs us is clearly unjust. A
well-known example is that of a sheriff who must choose between framing and convicting an innocent hermit for a murder, or allowing his town
to be destroyed by riots incited by the failure of his department to cap-

ture the real murderer. Utilitarianism appears to prescribe the former act, since injury, property damage, and lost lives would occur in the riots.[2]

It is reasonable to think that the rejection of consequentialism in general stems from the fallacious assumption that the good and the right postulated by classical utilitarianism (or at least by contemporary formulations of it) must obtain, even in versions of consequentialism that are not strictly utilitarian. This failure is understandable insofar as we typically are taught that the utilitarianism of Bentham and Mill constitutes the standard competition to Kant and deontological approaches to morality. But happiness is certainly not the only good, and maximization is not the only means of promotion. As other possibilities are considered, the force of many initial objections may be eased if not altogether extinguished. It may still be the case that in the final analysis, some will deem consequentialism unacceptable; but if this is so, it will not be for simple reasons.

Various conceptions of the good have been offered over the past few centuries. According to Bentham, we as human beings are creatures of nature, and our primary aim is thus the attainment of pleasure, or, conversely, the avoidance of pain.[3] Everything we do is ultimately an attempt to achieve this goal of pleasure satisfaction/pain avoidance. Bentham undertook a development of a "hedonic calculus" which could serve as a reference when determining right and wrong actions. Leaving aside some of the obvious practical problems inherent in such a system, a major problem for Bentham was the idea that the good for human beings was something completely independent of the rational capacity typically seen as the characteristic trait of humankind. Indeed, Bentham's account at times implied a moral priority of animals over humans in a variety of situations.

This observation led Mill to develop a more general conception of the good, one that did incorporate the ability to reason. His notion of happiness included "higher" pleasures and satisfactions such that, in his utilitarian analysis, "It is better to be a human being dissatisfied than a pig satisfied."[4] "Lower" pleasures are not entirely irrelevant in Mill's view, but they are discounted in such a way that humans inevitably possess the capacity to be happier than animals and are thus morally prior to animals. In addition, he was able to avoid the messy quantitative approach required by Bentham's version. He therefore manages to avoid some of the unpalatable aspects of Bentham's utilitarianism.

But the high level of generality inherent in Mill's account of happiness, while necessary in order to improve on Bentham, breeds new problems, the most significant of which is perhaps the difficulty of comparing different instances or types of happiness. Alasdair MacIntyre makes this point in explaining the failure of utilitarianism as an instance of the general failure of the Enlightenment project. The happiness, or pleasure, derived from enjoying a drink, he says, is wholly distinct from the happiness derived from enjoying a swim. The two activities are not at all related; they are not different means of achieving the same end-state of happiness, for there is no such unified state of mind.[5] MacIntyre and others who make these sorts of observations state their cases persuasively. Unless some method of combining distinct types of happiness is possible, theoretical problems persist, and substantive practical applications of the theory may not be possible.

Between them, Bentham and Mill leave us with a dilemma: either we adopt a method of comparing various instances of happiness (for example, a hedonic calculus), which would entail some disturbingly counterintuitive conclusions; or we leave happiness in general terms, in which case adjudication seems an impossibility.

Moore's attempt at the beginning of the twentieth century to resolve this problem is also unsatisfactory, though for other reasons. Moore saw Bentham and Mill as guilty of conflating two distinct issues: that which is the case, and that which ought to be the case.[6] In other words, it is a mistake to attempt to define the good in terms of some natural property, q; any such attempt leaves open the question of whether q is good. The good, therefore, is a primitive and unanalyzable notion according to Moore, and it can only be known through intuition.[7] The problem with this approach, however, is that intuitionist theories are not only theoretically suspect but are typically quite unhelpful in resolving practical matters. If Moore's brand of intuitionist consequentialism is to serve as a model in such resolutions, the disputants will have to first agree (at least in general) on what "the good" is, and this looks rather unlikely given the broad range of intuitive moral beliefs that seems to exist. It is much more likely that agreement can be found regarding the good in specific cases, and I will return to (and use) this claim at various points later in this book. But the prospect of general agreement regarding the much more grandiose, universal good Moore had in mind is dim.

So among the various and sundry problems that have been associated with consequentialism generally are several that pertain to the good specifically. While it would not be fair to say that L. W. Sumner is successful in solving all of the difficulties, he does manage to put forth a fairly coherent and initially plausible picture; it at least provides a good starting point for constructing a reasonable consequentialist theory, and where it does encounter problems it lends itself to certain adaptations that might enhance its plausibility.

Sumner addresses the question of the good in two parts, the first of which he calls "a basic theory of the good." Here the aim is to pick out all those states of affairs that are seen as good or that are in fact good.[8] (Throughout the remainder of this chapter, the parenthetical page references are to Sumner's book, The Moral Foundation of Rights.) Now this way of speaking glosses over the question of whether the good is an objective or subjective notion. If it were objective, an underlying assumption would be that there are states of affairs that are in fact good, and this is why we have reason to promote them. If it were subjective, the order would be reversed: the assessment that some x ought to be pursued would be prior to, and be the source of, x's value.[9]

Neither of these works perfectly well. The objective account faces difficulties associated with intuitionism, and the subjective account encounters the problem of it being unclear why preferences, even if universal, should provide the moral force[10] that any acceptable moral theory must have. The latter problem leads Sumner to adopt the objective view (Sumner, 178–180), and we should not feel uncomfortable in doing the same. A good's being objective entails that it is valuable for everyone (Sumner, 179), regardless of individual preferences. In cases where preferences unanimously converge, the objective conception can be preserved if we take the view that the general agreement licenses an inference to the best explanation of why there is such agreement. It may not even be necessary (or, for the consequentialist, even possible) to choose between the subjective and objective conceptions; perhaps it is enough to say that whenever there is general agreement, x ought to be seen as good (for whatever reason). The quality of agent-neutrality is preserved on either account, and this should be sufficient to preserve the impartiality that is characteristic of an acceptable moral theory.

Sumner suggests that the second step, after identifying the various instances of the good, is to invoke a theory of rationality. He asserts that there must be some way of combining these instances into one global value that will then be the goal to be pursued. (Sumner, 170–171) If, to again use MacIntyre's example, swimming and drinking are both good, there must be some way of combining these (and any other) instances into the single, global value. The theory of rationality will be the means for accomplishing this rather daunting task. Consequentialist theories typically employ aggregation at this stage, although that need not be the case; distributive methods, for example, may also be utilized.

Regardless, concerns arise here about the feasibility of such a move. Specifically, MacIntyre's remarks, noted earlier, are apropos; the likelihood of combining such states of affairs seems poor indeed. If the method is too specific, there arise problems similar to those encountered by Bentham; if it is too general, such as the claim that the various instances of the good appear to fall under a common genus (such as happiness), there arise problems similar to those encountered by Mill. Even if a pluralistic theory were considered, that is, one that recognized several distinct values, there would have to be some additional means of collating them, a task that appears at least as unlikely as that of combining the specific instances of the good. If these doubts are legitimate, then the second step, that of combination, cannot be accomplished under any theory of rationality.[11]

I therefore propose that the following approach be taken in Part 2 of this book. Each of the Part 2 chapters covers a specific issue. The resolution of specific issues, contrary to what Sumner seems to think, does not necessarily require the assimilation (by whatever method of rationality) of all independently recognized goods into a single, global good. So I will propose, for each issue to be examined, a good to which all parties with a relevant interest should agree. Specifying such a good should not be as difficult as one might initially think. In Chapter 5, for instance, it will be seen that libertarians, welfare liberals, and socialist egalitarians all point to freedom as the good in which they all are ultimately interested. Although the good of freedom is still not precise, it is far less general than Mill's "happiness," and thus avoids the sorts of problems noted above. While the parties to the debate hold different views on the details of what freedom is, consolidation will be feasible (unlike the case of swimming and drinking) and thus the necessary comparisons can be made. In Chapter 6, the good of racial equality (or the existence of a "colorblind" society) is one that all should agree is worthy of pursuit. The particular goods in each chapter will then be seen as the goals to be pursued.

One drawback to this approach is that goods other than the primary one may consequently be ignored in the analysis. Despite its problems, classical utilitarianism, employing happiness as a global good, at least has the virtue of being all-encompassing. But this is also its defect. In order to render a consequentialist theory of rights practicable, the good must be somewhat restricted.[12] Within the context of each individual political debate, this should not be too problematic, since tangential goods tend to be seen by the debate participants to be comparatively much less relevant. If, however, more than one good might legitimately play a major role in any of the upcoming issues, then additional discussion will be provided to account for each good (or perhaps some pluralistic combination). Both liberty and equality might be relevant in this way to the pornography debate.

If this, then, is to be the treatment of the good, the next determination must be how to approach the right. A common assumption is that consequentialist theories must (following Moore) maximize the good. If it were the case that maximization were required, consequentialism would indeed be mired in a number of problematic objections. One common objection is the observation that the right, if conceived as a maximizing function, would appear to require constant moral activity, since any time spent not pursuing the good lessens the degree to which the good can be achieved.[13] This sort of normative implication is pointed to by opponents of consequentialism as evidence that the theory is self-defeating.[14] Rule-consequentialists have responded by maintaining that the right act is the one that conforms to the set of rules which, when followed, produces at least as much good as following any alternative set of rules. While initially more promising than simple act-consequentialism, it too runs into a variety of problems.[15]

Instead of trying to shoehorn a two-level version of consequentialism into a framework that employs maximization, a better response might be to deny that the good must be maximized. Again, maximization is not part of the basic definition of consequentialism, stated at the outset of this chapter as being that an act's rightness or wrongness is a function solely of its consequences. But other than a maximizing function, what else could the right be?

One possibility is that it could be what has been called a satisficing function.[16] This approach distinguishes itself by asserting that moral rightness is not dictated by whether or not the optimific outcome is produced, but by whether a satisfactory outcome is produced—that is, whether the good is achieved to a satisfactory degree, regardless of whether it could have been achieved even more. In everyday practice, we don't typically aim for the very best outcome, but for a satisfactory one. Further, being content with a satisfactory outcome, even in situations where a higher degree of satisfaction could have been achieved, is rarely seen as a moral transgression. The inability of the maximizing variety of consequentialism to cope with such cases has greatly contributed to the hostility toward the theory; but the satisficing version may be able to account for intuitions without giving up the essential nature of consequentialism.

Consider the following example, a version of one found in Commonsense Morality and Consequentialism, by Michael Slote.[17] A resort manager is confronted one cold night by a poor family whose car has broken down. Because the telephones are out, the only real options available to the manager are either to offer the family one of the cabins for free (which we might assume she ought to do) or to close the door on them, leaving them to spend a miserable and perhaps dangerous night out in the car. She in fact offers to house them and gives them the key to a very nice, yet modest cabin, even though she could have assigned them to a luxury cabin without incurring any additional cost.

What should we say about her choice to house them in a cabin that is merely "very nice"? The maximizing consequentialist would, apparently, be forced to conclude that it was wrong of her to offer the family a very nice cabin for free on a cold night—yet this conclusion grates harshly against our common-sense moral intuitions. When asked to assess the manager's actions, many people would say that she did what she ought to have done, and some might even characterize her offer as laudatory. Regardless, while most everyone would say that her actions were right, or at least permissible, almost no one would want to claim that she acted wrongly. Satisficing consequentialism can accommodate these intuitive concerns in a way that maximizing consequentialism cannot, by describing the manager's actions as "satisfactory" or "good enough" (despite their failure to produce an optimific result) and thus not wrong.

So the satisficing version is able to overcome a number of objections typically associated with the maximizing version. One such objection is the apparent clash with intuition (and thus, perhaps, the inability to be accommodated under reflective equilibrium). Second, moral agents need not be required to constantly engage in moral activity, since a satisfactory level of performing moral acts can be achieved. Third, this version allows for the possibility of supererogation. Fourth, the potential problem of utilitarianism's inability to accommodate any notion of integrity is eased as well, since the standard of achieving a satisfactory outcome, rather than an optimific one, is much more likely to allow an agent to act from his attitudes and commitments.[18]

A nonmaximizing approach can also meet the common objections that consequentialist moral theory is insensitive to distributive concerns. T. M. Scanlon appears to endorse such an approach when he advocates the fulfillment of needs before maximizing preferences, even at the expense of failing to maximize overall benefits.[19] The optimific outcome not only may be foregone but should be foregone on this view, yet he maintains (in that article at least) that he is nonetheless employing consequentialist reasoning.

The intention here is not necessarily to suggest that satisficing consequentialism is the cure for the ills that have plagued more traditional versions, especially since it raises new questions that would be at least very difficult, and maybe impossible, to answer. For example, what is to count as sufficient or good enough, and how is a formal elaboration of "enoughness" to be generated? What about slippery slope problems? And won't the responses to these sorts of questions be rather subjective, thus making the approach impractical in particular situations?

Attempts to provide specific answers to these questions will not be provided here, but concerns should be eased by the fact that the use of the satisficing variety, while present, will be minimal in this project. As indicated above, a certain good will be postulated in each chapter (for each social issue). It is important to remember that these are issues about general policies, and the aim will be to ascertain which of the competing policies would best achieve the stated goal. This approach will not consider dramatically unfamiliar policies or previously unconsidered ways of achieving the goal; the range of available options is thus restricted in this way. Such restriction is allowed for by implicitly assuming that at least one of those policies in the availability pool is "good enough" in that it provides a means of achieving the goal to a satisfactory degree. In other words, a satisficing approach will be (implicitly) employed at this stage. Then, from among those policies under consideration, the question of which policy best achieves the specified goal will be addressed. Thus, satisficing is being employed here only to the extent that there may be other candidate social policies (perhaps ones which combine details of familiar candidates in some way, or even ones that are radically different from any previously considered) which achieve the goal more effectively.

What remains before proceeding to these issues, then, is to develop a general understanding of how rights are supposed to operate in this theory.

4.2 Rights in the Goal-Based Framework

There is an almost immediate problem with attempting to incorporate rights into a goal-based moral framework. Within such a framework, attaining the goal is the only thing that matters, which means that all decision-making is conducted with respect to the goal. Thus the right decision (assuming the maximizing method of promotion) is the one that best promotes the goal, and all other considerations are irrelevant. A consequence is that, as Sumner says, "local losses may be tolerated for the sake of overall gains." (176) The earlier example in this chapter in which a police chief must choose between framing and convicting an innocent hermit of murder, or allowing his town to be destroyed by riots incited by the failure of his department to capture the real murderer serves as an applicable example. The hermit's loss of freedom is seen as a local loss which is justified in that it provides for the overall gain of the town, in that the town avoids the negative results of a riot. (Another example, from Judith Jarvis Thomson, is that of a doctor confronted with the decision of whether to remove five organs from a healthy patient in order to transplant one each into five other patients who desperately need them in order to survive.[20])

Rights, in contrast, may well constrain the pursuit of goals. In other words, the attainment of the goal ceases to be the sole consideration, and thus at least some local losses may not be tolerated simply on the grounds that greater overall gains would be achieved as a result. This is why, in the example, many people would share the intuition that the rights of the hermit would serve as a protection against this sort of "sacrifice" for a net overall gain. In Dworkin's terminology, the right not to be framed and convicted "trumps" the overall societal gain. This is what it means to take rights seriously. "The prospect of utilitarian gains cannot justify preventing a man from doing what he has a right to do."[21] For Robert Nozick, a right can only be understood as a moral "side constraint" on the pursuit of a goal (such as the maximization of happiness), but cannot be built into the goal itself.[22] So if taking rights seriously entails allowing rights to trump societal gains (which would constrain the pursuit of the societal goal), and if taking rights seriously is a requirement of an acceptable theory of rights, then the prospects for reconciliation do not look good. For rights to be generated by this framework, the goal would have to prescribe constraints against its own attainment, which seems self-defeating.

Another way to see this conflict is to understand that rights are synonymous with "agent-centered prerogatives," which may be defined as moral freedoms held by the agent to depart from the course of action that would best contribute to the achievement of the goal. Correlatively, "agent-centered restrictions," defined as moral prohibitions against engaging in the course of action that would best promote the goal, are synonymous with moral duties.[23] The alleged conflict between rights and goals can thus be seen as a function of rights being agent-relative in nature and goals being agent-neutral in nature.

A slightly less uncharitable way to describe this tension is to maintain that rights, as constraints, are irrelevant to the attainment of the goal. The approach apparently prescribed by a goal-based theory is a "linear" one: Given a goal, the morally incumbent option on each occasion of choice is the one that best promotes the goal. If this option happens to be required by the "constraint," then there is really no constraint at all. If, on the other hand, the required option is not prescribed by the "constraint," then adherence to the constraint will (impermissibly) frustrate the achievement of the goal. Either way, rights do not appear to be relevant to the decision-making process in this view.

These seem to be major difficulties indeed, and in the minds of many they constitute the primary reasons for rejecting a goal-based account of rights.[24] In summary, the problem is the linear approach to decision-making, described above, as an indispensable component of the goal-based theory. Thus, removing this linearity problem is a necessary and important step in attempting to demonstrate the initial plausibility (or at least a lack of initial implausibility) of a goal-based theory of rights.

The explanation of why the linear approach is not always the most efficient one in pursuing a given goal begins with the recognition of a distinction between a theory of justification and a theory of decision-making. (Sumner, 179) A theory of justification specifies the basic principle (or set of principles) that serves to indicate when an act is or is not justified.

In the goal-based theory, the theory of justification informs us that an act is right just in case it best promotes the goal (again assuming maximizing consequentialism). But this characterization of the theory of justification makes it out to be objective, in that it defines the right act as the one that actually does best promote the goal (or, conditionally, as the act that, if chosen, would in fact best promote the goal), regardless of whether the decision-maker(s) recognizes it as such. From the standpoint of the decision-maker, a particular option may appear best when in fact—or from the standpoint of an "infallible observer"—it is not.[25]

A theory of decision-making is therefore needed to discover just what the justified option (the one that best promotes the goal) is. In other words, a theory of decision-making, as separate from a theory of justification, acknowledges the fact that we are not infallible observers, and thus that the option that appears to be best may not actually be best. The function of the theory of decision-making is therefore to provide practical policies and other information to aid fallible agents in achieving their goals most effectively. The recognition of the distinction between these two types of theories, which some (wrongly, according to Sumner) see as one and the same thing, opens the door to solving the linearity problem but does not necessarily guarantee overcoming it.

There are various possibilities regarding the form that a theory of decision-making in a goal-based rights framework might take. Most obviously, it might prescribe a "direct strategy," according to which the agent, on each occasion of choice, should select the option that appears to best promote the goal. (Sumner, 180) Because such a strategy is used by fallible agents to achieve their goals, this direct strategy, when offered as a theory of decision-making, adds nothing new (or at least nothing very interesting) to the theory of justification. Adopting this approach will not enable us to escape from the linearity problem.

But the direct strategy is not the only candidate. An indirect strategy of decision-making will at times prescribe constraining the pursuit of the goal in an effort to better achieve it. The availability of the maximizing options can be limited by placing constraints on which options are permitted. An indirect approach, if a case can be made for it, would succeed in overcoming the linearity problem, and thus keep alive the possibility for incorporating rights into the goal-based theory.

The question then is, which of these two strategies we should opt for. Which, in other words, is superior? And for that matter how is superiority to be assessed? For the latter question, the standard for assessing superiority is the theory of justification. In this case, the method that provides for the better overall attainment of the goal is superior. The question of whether we should opt for the direct or indirect strategy is thus an empirical one.[26]

In arguing for the indirect approach, Sumner points to several problems associated with its competitor. The first is that inaccuracy in the initial cost/benefit analysis (i.e., the deliberative process by which one arrives at the option, from among the competing social policies, that appears to best achieve the goal) is likely to arise from time to time due to the fact that we are not perfect information-gatherers. (Sumner, 189–90) Because one strategy's superiority will be based on empirical considerations, we may not be able to acquire all pertinent information on which results are likely to follow from which policies. In addition, the relevant information is likely to come from individuals already committed to a particular view of what they think is best. The presentation of such information, even if not intentionally misleading, is for this reason at least likely to be affected by pre-existing perceptions of what is right, and thus is likely to bias, at the outset, the computation of the various costs and benefits. So the available information is not only likely to be incomplete but partial.

Another main problem is that the task of processing all relevant data may be sufficiently difficult that inaccurate conclusions will be reached from time to time. (Sumner, 189) Not only must initial bias (on the part of the information-processor now, rather than the information-gatherer) be absent, but the sheer computational challenges involved in collating the information may at times require almost superhuman abilities.

In sum, mistakes in the cost/benefit analysis are likely to occur from time to time, unless the individuals collecting and processing the information are "extremely powerful, highly knowledgeable, exceptionally bright, and rigorously impartial." (Sumner, 187) Most human beings obviously fall outside this description. Thus, even though an indirect strategy will frustrate the pursuit of the goal on various occasions, it is, according to Sumner, likely to lead to a better attainment of the goal in the long run than a direct strategy.

Of course, the constraint must ultimately be justified by the goal. In the instances in which rights frustrate the pursuit of the goal, it is acknowledged that, even though the initial cost/benefit analysis points to inflicting local loss (on the individual) for the sake of overall gains, the conclusion may be mistaken (due to errors in collecting and processing information). If, however, the conclusion was not in error, then an opportunity cost with respect to achieving the goal will be incurred. The frequency and seriousness of this cost must be compared to that of the frequency and seriousness of the costs of wrongly concluding that the cost/benefit analysis prescribes violating an alleged right for overall gains. In Sumner's view, the latter would more seriously frustrate the long-term attainment of the goal, since violations of (alleged) rights for no good reason (as it would turn out) tend to have dramatically serious consequences. Therefore, assigning the rights and thus allowing for the moral protections of individuals is justified with respect to the goal.[27]

Therefore, the conception of rights on the goal-based theory is likely to be very close to the one offered by Dworkin, including the moral ability of rights to "trump" overall societal gains. The goal-based theory can then explain why the hermit has a right not to be framed and convicted, and why Thomson's healthy patient has a right not to be killed in order to save the lives of five others. It may be that the right in question is already implied by the initial cost/benefit analysis of how the good is to be best promoted, but even when the right is not a function of that analysis, it should be respected, thus constraining the pursuit of the goal. Rights, then, are to be understood as protections, held by individuals against society, that their basic interests be protected regardless of whether the violation of them is (on the best information available) likely to generate an overall gain for society.

While some details of the goal-based theory of rights are perhaps more clear, others may, understandably, remain murky. In addition to merely describing it, comparison to another account can be useful for illustrative purposes. Sumner's theory might even become more understandable when contrasted with Hare's approach, for example, which initially looks quite similar.

A brief outline of Hare's theory, which has two levels of moral thinking, is as follows.[28] On the intuitive level we find the everyday, prima facie (nonabsolute) moral rules we appeal to in our normal deliberations (the rule requiring persons to keep their promises being a typical example). Among the prima facie moral rules are prima facie moral rights. The critical level is where we find the source and justification of these rules. For Hare, the principles employed in critical thinking must be utilitarian principles.[29]

The distinction between the two levels of thinking is important for the following reason. If we were to appeal to the critical level each time we engaged in the decision-making process, the deliberations would necessarily consume considerable time and effort, be based on imperfect knowledge, and be subject to bias. Therefore, it is much more efficient to appeal to the intuitive level and simply apply the rules, including the rights, we find there. Appeal to the critical level is required only when intuitive-level rules come into question (in which case a justification is sought), or when they come into conflict (in which case a resolution is sought), the justification or resolution being a function of utilitarian thinking.

Since Hare appeals to the same sorts of problems as Sumner, such as those related to information-gathering and processing, the two initially appear to hold almost identical positions. The difference between them becomes clearer, however, when we see that Hare, in the end, is an act-consequentialist (and an act-utilitarian specifically). His prima facie moral rules (or "rules of thumb") are a function of a direct cost/benefit analysis, and thus depend for their normative force on a utilitarian justification. An example (albeit in the realm of prudence rather than morality) that demonstrates this point is his claim that seat belts ought to be worn, even when it seems clear that no harm will occur, such as on very short drives. The reason is that "the rarity of the occurrence (of crashing) is compensated for by the gravity of the consequences" (such as serious injury or death).[30] This is straightforward cost/benefit reasoning.

Applying it to the example of the sheriff and the hermit given earlier, Hare would likely say that the hermit's right not to be framed, convicted, and punished is justified by the utilitarian reasoning that the severe consequences of such a cover-up in the sheriff's office becoming public[31] would overcome the small chance that the cover-up would somehow be exposed. In other words, when confronted with the options of framing or not framing the hermit, the sheriff ought not to frame on this occasion. Hence, Hare is properly classified as an act-utilitarian. The fact that a rule is being adhered to does not make him a rule-utilitarian, although some have read him as such.[32] If we accept the typical definition of rule-utilitarianism as prescribing action in accordance with a set of rules, the adherence to which produces at least as much utility as any other set of rules, then the difference is plain: Hare prescribes general adherence to rules, but, as the rules are defeasible, he departs from the standard definition.[33]

Sumner, in contrast, is not an act-consequentialist. Even in cases in which Hare's critical-level thinking would prescribe overriding an individual's right,[34] Sumner suggests that the constraint, that is, the right, ought to be upheld. This is because, for Hare, any "constraints" are themselves a function of the cost/benefit analysis and so are merely apparent. For Sumner, the constraints are outside the scope of the cost/benefit analysis; even when, on the best information available, the right ought to be overridden (in an effort to achieve the goal), Sumner claims that the best way to achieve the desired goal, in the long run, would be to honor the right.[35] His constraints are therefore (he claims) genuine. (Sumner, 184–87; 191–92) If this is correct, then Sumner is not, like Hare, an act-consequentialist, since he does not think the option prescribed by the cost/benefit analysis should (in every instance) be chosen.

Neither is he a rule-consequentialist, since these constraints, or rights, are not absolute. Because they are defeasible, Sumner fails to qualify as a rule-consequentialist for the same reason Hare does. This might sound like a retreat for Sumner; after stipulating that rights should be recognized (and thus "taken seriously" in Dworkin's sense) even when societal gains look to be greater, he then says that these rights may at times be defeated by what look like cost/benefit considerations. (He implies that rights may be overridden when there are "sizeable" benefits and "negligible" costs.) (Sumner, 193) Rather, this seems to be a statement about the degree to which such an analysis must prescribe overriding the right. Whereas Hare's consequentialist theory (along with others) appears to allow for overriding rights whenever benefits outweigh costs (rare though this may be), Sumner is mandating that benefits must "significantly" outweigh costs—and even more than significantly. (184–85) The situation, in other words, must be extreme.[36]

We are now in a position to apply this theory to contemporary social issues. Each upcoming chapter (except the concluding chapter) will consist of three parts. The first will be a general discussion of the problem. The second will apply the interest-based theory of rights to this problem, the aim being to ascertain which policy is morally superior on this view. The third part will apply the goal-based theory of rights to the problem, with the aim there being to ascertain which policy is morally superior on that view. Finally, in Chapter 9, we will take stock of the findings and will perhaps be able to say something interesting about the relationship between theories of rights and their normative implications. Depending on what sort of conclusion can be reached, perhaps some positive prognosis can be made regarding the status of "rights talk" in American political culture.

Notes

1. See, for example, G. E. Moore, Principia Ethica (London: Cambridge University Press, 1966), introduction and Chapter 1.

2. See Louis P. Pojman, Ethics: Discovering Right and Wrong (Belmont, CA: Wadsworth, 1990), 84.

3. Jeremy Bentham, "Introduction to the Principles of Morals and Legislation" in Ethical Theory, ed. Louis P. Pojman (Belmont, CA: Wadsworth, 1989), 111–14.

4. Mill, Utilitarianism, ed. George Sher (Indianapolis: Hackett, 1979), 10.

5. MacIntyre, After Virtue (Notre Dame: University of Notre Dame Press, 1984) 63–65.

6. Principia Ethica, 1–36.

7. Ibid., 15–16. Moore then goes on to say that the right is that which maximizes the good.

8. Sumner, The Moral Foundation of Rights (Oxford: Oxford University Press, 1987), 167–70.

9. For further discussion on the objective/subjective distinction, see Sumner, Welfare, Happiness and Ethics (Oxford: Oxford University Press, 1996), 27–34.

10. This term should be taken at face value. According to Sumner, a theory with moral force is simply one that provides "moral reasons" for its acceptance.

See David Lyons, Rights, Welfare, and Mill's Moral Theory (Oxford: Oxford University Press, 1994), 155–59.

11. See, for example, John Finnis, Natural Law and Natural Rights (Oxford: Clarendon Press, 1990), 111; and Fundamentals of Ethics (Oxford: Clarendon Press, 1983), 86. Finnis sees the combinatory step as not only irrational but perhaps also immoral, since acting on it may violate certain natural rights.

12. In applied ethics, it is the theory that must be somewhat malleable. When the issue at hand presents itself in a form difficult for moral philosophy to address, it is unrealistic (and wrongheaded) to expect the situation to change in order to accommodate the theory.

13. See, for example, Samuel Scheffler's introduction to his anthology, Consequentialism and Its Critics (Oxford: Oxford University Press, 1988).

14. Derek Parfit, for example, makes this sort of claim in "Is Common-sense Morality Self-defeating?" in Consequentialism and Its Critics.

15. See J. J. C. Smart and Bernard Williams, Utilitarianism: For and Against (Cambridge: Cambridge University Press, 1963). Williams argues that following rules regardless of whether they produce the optimific result in a particular case amounts to irrational rule-worship.

16. One of the more complete examinations of satisficing consequentialism is provided by Michael Slote, Common-sense Morality and Consequentialism (London: Routledge and Kegan Paul, 1985), Chapter 3.

17. Ibid., 45.

18. This is one of Williams's primary objections in Utilitarianism: For and Against, 108–18.

19. Scanlon, "Rights, Goals, and Fairness" in Consequentialism and Its Critics.

20. See The Realm of Rights (Cambridge, MA: Harvard University Press, 1990), 135–36.

21. Ronald Dworkin, Taking Rights Seriously (Cambridge, MA: Harvard University Press, 1977), 193.

22. Nozick, Anarchy, State, and Utopia (New York: Basic Books, 1974), 28–29.

23. A more detailed account of agent-centered prerogatives and restrictions (as well as the concept of "agent-neutrality" alluded to in section 4.1) can be found in Thomas Nagel, The View From Nowhere (Oxford: Oxford University Press, 1986), Chapter 9.

24. There are a number of such examples in the literature. See, for example, H.J. McCloskey, "Respect for Human Moral Rights versus Maximizing Good" in Utility and Rights, ed. R.G. Frey (Minneapolis: University of Minnesota Press, 1984); J.L. Mackie, "Can There Be a Right-Based Moral Theory?" in Theories of Rights, ed. Jeremy Waldron (Oxford: Oxford University Press, 1984); David Lyons, "Utility and Rights" in Theories of Rights. This skepticism on the part of Lyons is a change in direction from earlier writings in which he defended the compatibility of rights and utilitarianism. See, for example, "Human Rights and the General Welfare," Philosophy and Public Affairs 6 (1977) and "Mill's Theory of Justice" in Values and Morals, ed. Alvin I Goaldman and Jaegwon Kim (Boston: D. Riedel, 1978).

25. This is another aspect of consequentialist rights theories that seems to invite criticism. Mackie, for instance, focusing specifically on R.M. Hare's account, questions how we as fallible, biased and imperfectly rational beings are supposed

to reason from what essentially amounts to the standpoint of God. See "Rights, Utility and Universalization" in Utility and Rights, 101.

26. It is somewhat misleading to refer to the latter of these as "the" indirect approach. It would be more accurate to say "an" indirect approach, since there can be several, depending on what sorts of constraints are employed.

27. Recall that this sort of analysis is in order, given the approach of determining the "best" (maximizing) policy from a set of options.

28. The following summary is taken from various places in Hare's book Moral Thinking (Oxford: Oxford University Press, 1981). His discussion regarding rights specifically is found in chapter nine.

29. Utilitarianism at the critical level necessarily follows, he believes, from his meta-ethical universal prescriptivism, the details of which are not particularly relevant to the current discussion. Also, Hare seems to equivocate on whether the (utilitarian) principle at the critical level, in addition to justifying intuitive-level rules, actually generates those rules. At times he implies that this is the case: "For the selection of prima facie principles, and for the resolution of conflicts between them, critical thinking is necessary." (Moral Thinking, 45.) He also (on page 45) talks as if the rules are generated from culture, suggesting that "if a person is to have the prima facie principles he needs, (he) will have to get them from other people by education or imitation."

30. Moral Thinking, 47.

31. The riots might be much more severe (and even more widespread) if it were learned that the police were framing innocent citizens.

32. Scanlon, for instance, appears to view Hare's theory as a "version" of rule-utilitarianism in "Rights, Goals, and Fairness" in Consequentialism and Its Critics, 87.

33. Another way to make this point is to indicate that even though his system consists of rules, it collapses into act-utilitarianism. A rule is in effect for the very reason that adherence to it generally produces the best results on each occasion. In those instances where it doesn't, there appears to be a conflicting rule which has priority, the priority being a function of the general rule prescribing utility maximization.

34. This would come about when the results of the cost/benefit analysis would indicate that the societal gain is worth the "sacrifice" of the individual's right. Hare indicates that this result is unlikely to occur very often, but when it does we must act accordingly. (Moral Thinking, 150–53)

35. This almost makes Sumner sound as if he thinks rights are absolute, which isn't the case. See below.

36. This aspect of Sumner's theory is not necessarily inconsistent with certain deontological theories of rights which also deny the absolute nature of rights. See, e.g., Ronald Dworkin, Taking Rights Seriously, 193–94.

PART TWO

Social Policy Implications

5

Redistributive Taxation

5.1 Property

Any discussion regarding rights in the area of redistributive taxation must include a discussion of property, since the debate is typically between those emphasizing a strong right to property and those emphasizing a right to receive welfare (i.e., property in the form of money) from those of sufficient means. For our purposes we need only select one theory of property with which both sides of the debate will agree. Since both libertarians and welfare liberals claim John Locke as a predecessor of their respective views, the Lockean conception of property is a prudent starting point. (For the remainder of section 5.1 the parenthetical page references are to Locke's The Second Treatise of Government.)

First, though, a review of the competing policies to be considered in this chapter is in order. The libertarian position is that no taxes for the purpose of redistribution are justified, since it amounts to theft of personal property; only taxes that go toward the services provided by the state (such as internal and external security) are permissible. The welfare liberal position, by contrast, calls for the state to implement certain welfare programs so that all citizens are guaranteed a minimum standard of living. When this position is delineated in the context of a right to this minimum standard, the right is sometimes said to be held (by the poor) against the state, and sometimes directly against those who can afford to be taxed for welfare purposes (either individually or collectively).[1] For our purposes, we will incorporate only the latter of these into the upcoming discussion. This picture best captures the nature of the rights debate, since the conflict is between the alleged right to an adequate standard of living (or to the means for such a standard) and the alleged strong right to private property emphasized by libertarians. In welfare liberalism, the state can be seen as an efficient intermediary between the rich and the poor, or as the agency responsible for the collection of redistributive taxes from the rich and their subsequent allocation to the poor. (Direct collection by the poor from the rich is assumed to be problematic.)

A third position, that of socialist egalitarianism, will also be considered. Egalitarian theories of distributive justice call for holdings to be equally distributed in a society, which, given an initial unequal distribution, is likely to entail very heavy redistributive taxation. Socialist theories approach strict egalitarianism but stop short of mandating that wealth must be exactly equal across society. The two are lumped together under the heading "socialist egalitarianism."

Again, it will be suggested that one of these three policies—libertarianism, welfare liberalism, or social egalitarianism—will be recommended by the interest-based theory of rights (in 5.2) and by the goal-based theory of rights (in 5.3). First, however, the notion of property must be reviewed.

While Locke often intends "property" to be a widely inclusive notion in The Second Treatise, consisting of "lives, liberties and estates,"[2] his primary use in Chapter 5 of that work (the chapter in which the bulk of his theory of property is found) pertains to the third of these, external goods, or "possessions." (Locke, 36) It is Locke's view that the earth was given to mankind in common, for its use and preservation, in accordance with the law of nature. (26) The question, then, is how individual ownership, a right to private property (which for Locke is a claim against others, entailing correlative duties not to steal or otherwise use that which belongs to the rightholder), can come about from a context of joint ownership.[3]

There is little disagreement about the general answer to this question, which is that labor grounds property rights. Locke maintains that by laboring on external objects, the common is individuated, and persons come to own the products of their labor. (Locke, 27) There is more disagreement about just what this means. Alan Ryan suggests that those who labor deserve some reward or compensation for their efforts, and the product of their labor is natural and fitting.[4] In addition to questionable textual support for this interpretation of Locke, an immediate problem is that the fruits of one's labor may not fit one's efforts at all; luck is a powerful variable, frequently helping to produce returns out of line with what the laborer truly deserves, and compensating for the effects of luck is virtually impossible.[5]

Another interpretation of the claim that labor grounds property rights points to the alleged value that a person creates when he labors on the common. Locke indicates that most of the value of any good is a result of human labor. (Locke, 40) This is similar to the previous interpretation, in that the laborer is claimed to deserve the object, since he is the one who gave it value. Accordingly, though, there are similar problems; as Robert Nozick points out, it is not necessarily the case that laboring on something necessarily increases its value, or even if it did, that the laborer should come to own the entire object as a result.[6] Even if Locke intended this understanding, the argument is not very good.

The interpretation that best accords with the text while at the same time producing a defensible argument pertains to Locke's claims regarding mixing one's labor with external objects. (Locke, 27–30) We own our labor, and when we work on something our labor becomes part of that thing. By adding something that belongs to us (our labor) to something that does not belong to us (the object), the object becomes ours.

Nozick finds this interpretation problematic as well. "Why," he asks, "isn't mixing what I own with what I don't a way of losing what I own instead of gaining what I don't?"[7] But this question seems to misunderstand the notion of labor. It is not, as Nozick seems to think, a physical mass that actually mixes with external objects in some material way. Rather, when understood as an activity, as A. John Simmons has suggested,[8] the argument is perfectly plausible. In accord with Locke's doctrine of natural liberty, which allows for individuals to freely pursue a life plan, we need certain things in this pursuit, including external goods. Laboring, conceived as a purposive activity, is a way of bringing these goods within the scope of one's life plan. In this way, the right to acquire property is a natural extension of the right to self-governance, emphasized by Locke throughout The Second Treatise. (4, 54, 87, 128) This understanding of the labor-mixing interpretation of the claim that labor grounds property rights meets not only Nozick's objection, but others as well, including Hume's protest that the very idea of mixing labor with physical objects is incoherent,[9] and Waldron's complaint that labor-mixing results, at best, only in a very limited property right.[10]

This reading also appeals to contemporary libertarians and welfare liberals both. Each camp claims to be concerned with freedom and self-governance. The difference is whether property rights are fairly conditional, allowing for those who are needy to appropriate a portion of what belongs to others in an effort to meet their own needs (and, more strongly, to allow them to pursue meaningful life plans), or fairly strict, in which case such appropriation is impermissible. The former takes seriously the notion of positive freedom, understood as being able to formulate and execute a life plan.[11] Those who are needy are not free in this way, and thus require assistance. The latter takes seriously the notion of negative freedom, the idea that persons have the right to be left alone and not be forced into involuntary behavior, such as contributing to charity (which, according to libertarians, is what welfare programs amount to). More will be said later about these two notions of freedom; for now, the observation is merely that neither side should object to Simmons's reading of Locke's theory of property acquisition.

Disagreement does exist, though, regarding the interpretation of the limits Locke places on property acquisition. Two such limitations, often referred to as "provisos" in the literature, have received significant attention. The "spoilage" or "no waste" proviso is a limit on use, and stipulates that what is labored on (and thus acquired) must be used. (31) Although Locke at times writes as if spoiling is the actual perishing of the item (so that the limit on acquiring apples is set by their propensity to rot), when spoiling is taken in conjunction with the reading of labor as purposive activity, it is better understood as not being used for the purpose of advancing one's life plan. Failing to use one's acquisitions violates the rights of others to make use of the common, and this violates Locke's law of nature. The second limitation, the "fair share" proviso, is a limit on the amount that may be acquired, and stipulates that appropriation must be such that "enough and as good" is left in common for others. (27)

It may seem as if the fair share proviso in particular gives the advantage to the welfare liberal interpretation of Locke.[12] Unlimited capitalist acquisition is not permitted when others are not left with enough and as good, whether this is understood merely as meeting subsistence needs, or, more strongly, as meeting "meaningful life" needs; when a distribution exists that violates either interpretation of the fair share proviso, redistributive measures might appear to be in order. But this is not necessarily the case, according to libertarians who claim Locke as their predecessor. Nozick is a leading example, and he discusses this proviso as an aspect of his general defense of the libertarian interpretation of Locke.

According to Nozick, the proviso prohibits appropriation only when the condition of others will worsen as a result.[13] Depriving others of the opportunity to make any particular appropriation does not count as worsening in the relevant sense, since there will often remain in common other items that can be appropriated by other individuals. Thus, my appropriation of X is permissible, since items Y and Z are still available to you and will enable you to be as well off as you would have been with X. As Waldron notes, no net loss must be suffered by others according to Nozick's interpretation of Locke's limitation.[14]

Other aspects of Nozick's entitlement theory of distributive justice are, he claims, consistent with Lockean property principles. For Nozick, a distribution (of basic social and economic goods) is just if it accords with the principles of justice in acquisition, transfer and rectification.[15] While he fails to delineate exactly what these principles consist in, it is clear that they must be Lockean in nature. Despite his criticisms of Locke's labor-based theory of acquisition, his own view must be something similar, and includes as well the proviso limitation just discussed.[16] Nozick's principles of justice in transfer must also be similar to those of Locke, since he allows for the free alienation of property, made clear by his well-known example of individuals freely giving Wilt Chamberlain 25 cents in exchange for the opportunity to see him play basketball.[17] Nozick's principles of justice in rectification, the function of which is to allow for the reallocation of property where it has been illegitimately acquired (i.e., where the violation of natural rights has occurred), appear Lockean as well.

One additional similarity should be noted. Nozick makes much of the fact that liberty upsets patterns, where patterned theories of distributive justice are defined as capable of fitting into the phrase, "To each according to his _____."[18] Demonstrating how liberty is incompatible with any such theory is the primary purpose of the Wilt Chamberlain example. (Then, together with the claim that liberty is the priority, Nozick derives his entitlement theory.) Locke, too, may be read as denying the need for a distribution to meet any pattern,[19] in which case Nozick's libertarian interpretation of Locke becomes even more plausible.

Although a primary example, Nozick is not the only one to read Locke in this way. Tibor Machan, emphasizing the Lockean natural right of "self-development," argues for the existence of strong property rights in Locke,[20] and C. B. MacPherson reads The Second Treatise as allowing for unlimited appropriation.[21] The point is that one can, without unreasonable maneuvering, derive a libertarian understanding of property from Locke's work.

Conclusions more in line with the welfare liberal perspective also can unproblematically be found in Locke. According to James Tully, individuals must surrender all their rights to the government upon joining political society, including all personal property. The government, then, in accordance with the law of nature, must distribute property in a manner that provides all citizens with a comfortable existence.[22] Limits to individual accumulations (or, more accurately, individual allocations of government distributions) are inherent in such a scenario; the strong natural property rights argued for by libertarians would, according to Tully, upset Locke's view of God's plan. Thus, the right to property is only conventional (and no longer natural, as in the state of nature), and is therefore highly conditional at best. The upshot would be the need for a radical redistribution of holdings.

A number of other commentators interpret Locke's claims as calling for a milder degree of redistribution. Sreenivasan sees in Locke an emphasis on the right to property in common, and takes Locke to equate it with the right to the means of preservation. As this is based on the law of nature, which commands the preservation of (self and) others, those who are needy, according to Sreenivasan, hold a claim against others "not to be excluded from the use of the common materials needed to produce one's subsistence."[23] Where some persons are needy while others have a surplus (relative to their needs), a redistribution is morally required.[24]

Similarly, Christman maintains that Locke never intends to establish a right to "liberal ownership," understood as the right to "complete dominion" over one's goods.[25] Christman notes that considerations of the common good (and, no doubt, the fair share proviso) prohibit unlimited accumulation of the sort MacPherson takes to be permissible on Locke's view.[26] He further points to the spoilage proviso, citing it in defense of the claim that Locke thought possessions were justified only to the extent that they are necessary for the conveniences of life; possessions not meeting this condition necessarily violate the rights of others to appropriate from the common.[27]

Thus one can reasonably derive interpretations of Locke that span the political spectrum. The purpose of this chapter, however, is not to assess which interpretation is most defensible, but to determine which social policy among those offered by libertarians, egalitarians, and welfare liberals is morally most defensible according to the two rights theories. This amounts to an assessment of the strength of claims to property, and the purpose thus far has been to present an understanding of property that will be useful when examining the normative implications of the interest-based and goal-based theories of rights.

5.2 Rights of Redistributive Taxation:
The Interest-Based Theory

As noted in Chapter 1, the views of Rawls and Nozick have framed discussions of distributive justice over the past two decades. Rawls's view is seen as the archetype for socialist egalitarianism, prescribing first that basic liberties are to be distributed equally, and then that other primary goods may be distributed unequally only when such arrangements are to the advantage of everyone.[28] For Nozick, natural rights to one's (legitimate) holdings entail an entitlement theory of justice, the content of which (as described in the preceding section) is that a distribution is just if it accords with the principles of justice in acquisition, transfer, and rectification.

Neither Rawls nor Nozick utilizes the interest-based methodology. Rawls employs a hypothetical contractarian approach, although he[29] and others[30] regard the foundation as essentially Kantian in nature. Nozick, of course, relies on a theory of natural rights. The question before us is whether either of these extremes[31] will be supported by the interest-based theory of rights, or whether the compromise position—the welfare liberal position, according to which the free market should be supplemented with at least (and only) some redistributive programs—will follow from the theory. If this third possibility turns out to be morally preferable, something must be said about the degree to which such programs should exist, though a precise specification will in all likelihood not be possible.

We should first ease the potential worry that either "extreme" (libertarianism or socialist egalitarianism) might be immediately implausible on the interest-based approach, and thus should be ruled out of court. Regarding Rawls's principle of maximum equal liberty, the interest in political equality would ground the alleged right to equal liberty; such a right, according to the argument, would suffice to hold others under a duty, since disparities would allow for the possibility of political domination. Regarding the difference principle, a case could be made that a right to equality in economic holdings follows from an interest such as Raz's personal autonomy. Indeed, Kai Nielson goes further than Rawls: he proposes two principles of justice, the first mandating maximum equal liberty, and the second calling for equality of income and wealth (without a "difference" proviso).[32] Nielson claims that differences in economic power lead to differences in political power, which is unacceptable; his first principle therefore appears to entail his second. He then goes on to suggest that the corresponding duties associated with rights to equality of holdings would not (in a moderately affluent society anyway) be unduly burdensome. While this claim is debatable, it at least warrants discussion, in which case the conditions for an interest-based right to equality of holdings warrants discussion. Further, if, in accord with the interest of personal autonomy, the number of options (or as Nielson says, "whole life prospects") one has is tied to his income,[33] then the case is even stronger.

The libertarian can also focus on personal autonomy in making the case for strong private property rights. Employing the Lockean idea that fulfilling a life plan requires the use of at least some external goods, John Hospers claims that property rights are essential for carrying out the long-range planning necessary for designing and executing a certain course of life.[34] Similarly, Tibor Machan cites the right to private property as a "moral prerequisite" for the realization of self-development.[35] When property becomes conditional and can be appropriated from others without their consent, then the ability to formulate and carry out a life plan is lost as well. Property rights, therefore, must not be understood as conditional, even when competing interests are dire.

Is the libertarian position defensible on the interest-based theory of rights? Claims such as the ones made by Machan and Hospers establish the conclusion that some private property is indeed required if individuals are to retain personal autonomy, and we may thus accept that there is a right to some private property. But this conclusion only takes us so far;

if there is a right to some private property, then only Marxist theories are rendered unacceptable. Even egalitarian theories tend to allow for some private property; they just call for the amount of property owned by individuals to be the same. If the libertarian position is to be adequately defended, more support is required.

Machan attempts to provide the needed support by elevating property rights to the moral status of rights to life and liberty. For Machan and other libertarians, rights to life, liberty and property are basic and cannot be separated.[36] If this is the case, then Machan would be right to maintain that invasion of liberty (such as rape) and invasion of property (such as theft) are equally egregious transgressions.[37] But Machan's reasons for property rights being basic are unclear. On the interest-based approach with personal autonomy as the relevant interest, loss of property, perhaps unlike loss of liberty and certainly unlike loss of life, may correspond with degrees of loss of personal autonomy. If I am reasonably well off and am relieved of a small portion of my overall wealth, then the corresponding loss of personal autonomy would be quite trivial, perhaps even negligible. That small portion may, however, make a tremendous difference for the personal autonomy of someone else; it may enable her to achieve a reasonable number of life options when before she had few or none, without significantly affecting the scope of my available life options.

Indeed, something like personal autonomy is the very ground offered by Machan as the basis for his claims for strong property rights. The structure of his argument, essentially, is that we need control over external goods in order to formulate and execute a life plan, and his conclusion necessarily entails the premise that, within certain moral limits, we are morally entitled to what we need in this respect. The question is whether the state of affairs in which the needed goods are already owned constitutes a relevant moral limit. Machan claims it does, since violations of life and liberty are clear limits, and violations of property are analogous. The suggestion, though, is that violations of property are (or at least may be) less serious, since they (may) infringe on personal autonomy to a lesser degree.

Even Machan at one point admits to priorities among the rights to life, liberty, and property.[38] Though rare, conflicts, he says, may occur from time to time, in which case property rights are to be recognized only after the right to life first and the right to liberty second. The implication, then, is that property rights can be overridden more easily than liberty rights, which in turn can be overridden more easily than the right to life. The question posed to libertarians is whether competing interests (such as need) are sufficient to override property rights, and the response that virtually nothing is sufficient is, we are finding, suspect.

Loren Lomasky also attempts to justify the libertarian position. His version centers on the idea of persons as project pursuers, beings whose nature it is to formulate and pursue meaningful life projects; in this sense, his version does not differ from other formulations. Further, he justifies the basic rights (to life, liberty, and property) by appealing to persons as project pursuers, citing their needs to be alive, be free, and have control over the material means necessary for their pursuits. The justificatory process entails assessing the costs associated with ensuring that these needs are met; if the costs are too high, then no duty to meet these needs of life, liberty, and property can be said to exist.[39] In this way, the process is similar to that of the interest-based approach, where determining the existence of a particular alleged right entails assessing whether the interest on which the alleged right is based is sufficiently strong to hold others under a correlative duty.[40] Lomasky's conclusion is that in the case of life and liberty, the existence of the right is supported; each person (as project pursuer) possesses claims, held against others, of noninterference in these areas. This is the case even though fulfilling duties associated with the claims compromise liberty to some extent (e.g., your right not to be harmed is correlative with my duty not to harm you, which limits my freedom), since the cost of fulfillment is less than the moral weight of the interest on which the right is based. However, the cost of ensuring that others have the material means (i.e., property) necessary for their pursuits is greater than the moral weight of the interest, according to Lomasky.[41] Hence, we arrive at the conclusion that individuals retain strong rights over their own property, and that the competing (alleged) right to receive assistance from those of ample means turns out to be nonexistent.[42]

The challenge to Lomasky's libertarianism, and its stance that the moral weight of the interest in receiving certain external goods from others is less than the cost of supplying those goods, might begin with claims to minimal assistance. If certain people legitimately have no means available for providing for their most basic needs (those things required for a minimally decent existence), might those people have claims, held against others who possess surplus goods, to receive at least some assistance? Might there, in other words, be "subsistence rights"?[43] It has already been suggested (in the discussion of Machan's views) that such rights are, on the interest-based model, legitimate. For such persons, who are in destitute situations, the preservation of life itself is dubious. The interest is therefore strong and suffices to ground a right to receive assistance, provided there are no overriding considerations. Lomasky suggests that the existence of a right to property, understood as a privilege (at the core, to do what one wants with his property) protected by a periphery of claims to noninterference, is an overriding consideration.

However, employing personal autonomy (or even something more basic, such as life itself) as the relevant interest defeats this suggestion, since the degree to which the interest would be compromised for the "contributor" is far outweighed by the degree to which the interest would be satisfied (or, conversely, would otherwise remain unsatisfied) for the recipient.

Further, since Lomasky himself appears to be employing something very much like personal autonomy (the need for exclusive control of external goods in order to pursue projects) in establishing property rights, consistency dictates that he should be sympathetic to this conclusion. For persons of substantial means, it is unlikely that all of their possessions are being employed for project pursuit, in which case there may be no moral ground for control over the holdings above and beyond that being used for such pursuit.[44] Regardless, the degree to which project pursuit would be hindered is minimal for those who are quite well off. Therefore, the cost of fulfilling the duties associated with subsistence rights are, contrary to Lomasky's conclusion, less than the moral weight of the interests on which subsistence rights are based.

Lomasky does explicitly point to three concerns about the feasibility of needs grounding rights. The first is that need, in itself, is unable to ground a right if there is no ability on the part of others to provide what is required. In the context of redistribution of wealth, a claim to assistance does not seem reasonable if based simply on the person's being needy; a second component, the ability to perform the correlative duty to assist, must also obtain if the right is to have a chance of being legitimate.[45] But this concern can be accommodated rather easily, for it is already taken into account by the interest-based theory. The interest in having one's needs fulfilled, though morally significant, is insufficient to ground a correlative duty if fulfilling the duty would be impossible (or even cause significant hardship). Another way to view the scenario would be to recognize that the state of affairs in which fulfilling the correlative duty would be impossible (or very difficult) is an instance in which the general subsistence rights of the needy would be overridden.

His second worry seems almost redundant. Lomasky contends that the argument from need focuses exclusively on the magnitude of the need while ignoring the magnitude of the sacrifice required for ensuring the need is met.[46] The discussion in the preceding paragraph should make it clear that this is not the case; the degree of sacrifice plays a significant role in the assessment of whether an alleged right is legitimate on the interest-based theory.

His third concern pertains to the manner in which there is a duty to assist. Should there be a duty to provide conditions that are sufficient for basic needs to be met, or to provide only the necessary conditions? Lomasky characterizes the difference between welfare liberalism and classical liberalism in these terms: welfare liberalism calls for an affirmative answer to the sufficiency question, and classical liberalism calls for assent only to the necessity question.[47] Insofar as the legitimacy of subsistence rights has been endorsed for those who would otherwise be unable to meet their needs, the necessary conditions are being targeted. This renders inapplicable Lomasky's ensuing protest that the alleged right to receive what suffices for meeting one's basic needs is too stringent.[48]

One other point should be noted here. Machan makes the claim that the needy do, in fact, have opportunities and resources at their disposal other than appropriating what belongs to others.[49] This is, of course, a highly debatable empirical claim, but its truth or falsity does not bear on the argument at hand. The claim is that according to the interest-based theory, the needy hold subsistence rights against the well-off. As a conditional statement, the claim is that if there are persons in destitute situations, then they have subsistence rights against those who are well-off, and Machan's denial of the antecedent fails to affect its truth status.

Another objection worth noting here may be referred to as the "body parts problem." It has been advanced that when some individuals are in a position in which they cannot meet even their basic subsistence needs, and when there are others who can withstand the loss of their possessions to the degree necessary to provide aid without significant detriment to these others' project pursuit, then the former hold subsistence rights against the latter to receive what is needed. The objection is essentially a reductio ad absurdum involving body parts as property. My neighbor needs a kidney transplant in order to survive, and I have two kidneys that match his requirements in all relevant ways. It seems, according to the interest-based theory as it has been described, that my neighbor has a right to one of my kidneys; my life may continue as it always has (with perhaps very minor differences) and his life will simply continue. It seems, then, that the cost of fulfilling the duty is less than the moral weight of my neighbor's interest in acquiring my kidney.[50] But this is absurd, since forcing me to surrender a body part is clearly wrong. Therefore, since there is no morally relevant difference between owning one's body and owning one's external property, and since control over one's body overrides any prima facie right to assistance held by others, control over one's external property must override such a right to assistance.

An adequate response to the body parts problem begins with the recognition that my kidney, unlike my external possessions, is in every way a part of me. We have seen that in order to explain how something external can be one's property, a rather complex theory (such as Locke's) is required. Understanding what it means to own something external is a messy business. What it means for me to own a kidney, however, is not at all messy. Appropriating my kidney is necessarily appropriating a part of me in a way that appropriating my external property is not. If we add to this the plausible premise that appropriating other people (without their consent at least) is wrong, then the conclusion is that taking the body parts of others is wrong, even in situations of dire need. In this way, the prima facie subsistence right to receive that which is needed is overridden in cases where it is body parts, and not external property, at stake.

Even if this analysis is not accepted, it must at least be recognized that the risks to the "donor" involved in transferring body parts are not involved in the transfer of wealth. Forcing others to submit to bodily invasion risks their well-being, and thus their ability to pursue projects as well. This response differs from the previous offering in that it does not suggest that redistribution of body parts is per se wrong; in an advanced technological society, capable of both "beaming" parts from body to body without risk and of eliminating the inherent dangers of having only one kidney, the practice might be able to be defended. For the foreseeable future, however, the risk factor does exist and suffices to override the prima facie right to receive assistance.

At this point, we should accept that the libertarian position has been defeated. The right to receive at least that which is necessary for subsistence has been verified on the interest-based theory. The relevant question now becomes whether there are rights to receive more than what is required for mere subsistence, such as that required to have a reasonable number of life options. Might there, in other words, be "autonomy rights"?

It should be clear that an individual's being alive does not entail that the conditions for personal autonomy will, for him, obtain. In some cases, providing only "subsistence welfare" may in fact allow for the individual to go on and acquire personal autonomy, although this is not necessarily the case. We need only refer to certain inner-city environments, where simply remaining alive is the only feasible goal. Raz's example of the hounded woman who spends every moment of her life trying to escape an attacker is a more imaginative example.[51] The point is that a reasonable number of life options does not necessarily follow from being afforded the means of subsistence only.

In general, the interest of personal autonomy is sufficiently valuable to ground the right to receive assistance to the material goods necessary to achieve such autonomy. Recall from Chapter 3 that personal autonomy unproblematically passes the "value test," in that its attainment generally contributes positively to the quality of human life. Whether it passes the "all things considered" test, that is, the assessment of whether it is sufficiently strong to ground duties on the part of others, is a further question.

Christman makes the case for a positive answer by distinguishing between control rights, understood as rights to use and exclusive possession, and income rights, understood as rights to retain that which is received in trade or rent.[52] Christman agrees that an individual's material circumstances significantly affect the options and life opportunities available to him, but he rejects the inference, made by some thinkers, that income is the key factor. Rather, it is control over the material conditions that is meaningful for one's options and opportunities. Since personal autonomy is said to obtain when the agent possesses a reasonable number of acceptable options for formulating and executing a life plan, it can be seen that control rights, and not income rights per se, are crucial.

In this light, the prospect of autonomy rights passes the "all things considered" test; the cost of fulfillment, which is the loss incurred by the well-off in the forced transfer of some of their holdings to the poor, is reasonable. What they are losing is some of their income; loss of control over their material conditions is minimal, since a significant portion of their holdings will be retained. In other words, the income rights of the well-off are pitted against the control rights of the poor in this moral clash, and employing personal autonomy as the foundational interest (as do Christman, Machan, and many others on both sides of the debate) implies that control rights must win out, since they are what is crucial for personal autonomy.

At this point, the welfare liberal position (and maybe even an egalitarian position) appears to follow from an interest-based theory of rights. Referring once more to Christman, this position may be summarized as the view that "while markets and individual ownership should be utilized as a central economic mechanism in society, the state must also take positive action to secure for every citizen the basic goods necessary to an adequate life."[53] This entails redistributive taxation for the purposes of ensuring adequate housing, education, health care, and perhaps even an adequate social life.

Before proceeding to the question of egalitarianism, consideration of one additional protest is in order. The objection, advanced most notably by Nozick, is essentially a reductio ad absurdum equating redistributive taxation with forced labor (which is assumed straightforwardly to be impermissible).[54] According to Nozick, tax programs implied by welfare liberalism arbitrarily discriminate between those who are well off and prefer leisure, and those who are well off but prefer to work more in an effort to achieve even better material conditions. The latter will be assessed a tax for her incremental work effort, while the former, opting to refrain from additional work, will not be taxed. Nozick suggests that this result effectively discriminates on the basis of taste, which is morally impermissible. Since a portion of the "worker's" incremental work time is, in a welfare state, effectively seized by those who are needy, consistency requires that a portion of the "leisurer's" leisure time must be seized as well; only this can avoid the discrimination. But seizing leisure is clearly wrong, and therefore seizing the work time (i.e., redistributive taxation) is also wrong.[55]

The best response here is to accept that taxing those who prefer to perform additional work in exchange for additional compensation does amount to forced labor, but to reject the assumption that the concept of forced labor is necessarily wrong. It has perhaps come to be seen as wrong because of the numerous historical examples of its being used to exacerbate inequality; but if its purpose is to alleviate inequality, it is not clear why it is necessarily wrong. If personal autonomy is the interest in question, it has already been suggested that the autonomy loss of those being taxed is outweighed by the autonomy gain of those receiving benefits. Since at least some redistributive taxation is permissible (and even required), at least some forced labor is permissible as well. For those who choose additional work, taxation can be viewed as the cost of acquiring additional material goods.

Any other attempt to address Nozick's objection while maintaining the liberal welfare position is likely to fail. One such attempt, mentioned by Richard Arneson (though only in passing), is that taxes should be assessed on the basis of ability rather than income.[56] In addition to obvious administrative and epistemological difficulties, such a policy would have the consequence of forcing talented individuals into high-paying occupations—even if careers in charitable, nonprofit organizations are preferred—in order to ensure that their tax burdens can be met. This, too, would amount to discrimination based on taste, and would also have some unpalatable ramifications for the personal autonomy of those involved.

So the only additional question to consider in this section is whether the interest-based theory entails not merely some redistribution of holdings, but a radical redistribution, such that a policy of socialist egalitarianism should be adopted rather than one of welfare liberalism. It should be noted that the society in question may fall into one of three categories. First, it may be that an egalitarian distribution would entail that all members be below the "autonomy threshold," understood as the minimal point at which personal autonomy can be had. If this were the case, then a right to receive from the (initially) well-off what would equalize holdings does not seem legitimate. Assuming (as we are) that pre-tax earnings were legitimately acquired, then if we are to avoid Marxism and take the concept of property seriously at all, the aspect of Raz's theory stipulating that the interest be sufficient to hold others under a duty cannot be met. The duty, in this case, would require the (initially) well-off to

relinquish their belongings to the point of no longer meeting the autonomy threshold themselves, and it is difficult to see how the interest of
personal autonomy can require this.[57] Even egalitarians concede that in
societies of this sort, the cost of fulfillment is likely too great. Nielson, for
instance, allows that our moral philosophy must be for human beings
rather than saints, and that human nature "is not so elastic that we can
reasonably expect people to impoverish themselves" in order to equalize
holdings.[58]

Second, society may be such that an egalitarian distribution would result in every person being above the autonomy threshold. In this sort of
society as well, the egalitarian position cannot be supported by the interest-based theory of rights. There is no interest in equality of possessions
per se that can serve as the basis for the right to receive benefits from
those who have more; such an interest simply lacks the value required to
ground this right. Neither can it be justified by the interest of personal
autonomy. Once redistribution has occurred to the point where each individual has achieved personal autonomy, no further redistribution is
warranted. The fact that some individuals (those who have more) will be
more autonomous, in the sense that they will have more life options before them, is irrelevant; so long as everyone has at least a reasonable
range of such options, personal autonomy is had. This observation heads
off the potential objection that the earlier appeal seemed to be to something like diminishing marginal returns of autonomy, when it was noted
that, with redistributive taxation, the autonomy loss of those who are
wealthier (and will be taxed) will be less than the autonomy gain of those
who are poorer (and will receive benefits). The claim was, rather, that the
lack of personal autonomy is sufficiently valuable to override the otherwise legitimate right to private property. Once personal autonomy is
achieved, however, the value of enhancing an already adequate range of
life options by appropriating the property of the well off is insufficient to
ground any such right.

Another objection pertains to the alleged connection between economic power and political power. Assuming that equality of political
power is morally required, the claim is that this state of affairs can only
be achieved through an equal distribution of wealth. The idea is that any
initial economic inequality, when subjected to market forces, will necessarily increase and will do so to the point where the rich will "dominate
effective participation in government."[59] Two claims are inherent in this
position, the first being that the degree of economic disparity will indeed
increase, and the second being that there are implications for political
power. Regarding the first, the existence of economic inequality is not, in
itself, objectionable. So long as personal autonomy is had by all, the state
of affairs is morally acceptable. Regarding the second, its truth is ques-

tionable. Even Rawls makes a distinction between the two; he accepts the requirement of political equality, the first of his lexically ordered principles, but allows for some economic inequality in his second principle. Nielson, who argues for the connection, is unable to provide a substantive argument for it, and instead claims that, "Only an utter turning away from the facts of social life could lead to any doubts about this at all."[60] It seems reasonable that institutional safeguards could provide for political equality even when economic disparity exists. Regardless, even if the connection holds to some degree, some political inequality may be permissible, so long as personal autonomy is not unduly compromised as a result. In this view, personal autonomy likely entails at least rough political equality for all, but not necessarily strict equality.

The result, then, is that in a society in which an equal distribution of wealth would leave everyone above the "autonomy threshold," no right to equal holdings can be established on the interest-based theory. We have seen that the same is true of a society in which an equal distribution would leave everyone below the autonomy threshold.

One other possibility remains: a society may be sufficiently wealthy to leave everyone exactly at the autonomy threshold if its wealth were to be equally distributed. In this case, the interest-based theory prescribes redistribution to the point of overall equality. This is the only way to ensure that everyone enjoys personal autonomy, and the cost of fulfillment is not unreasonable, since personal autonomy is not wholly lost for those who will be taxed. While societal wealth in this case would be equally distributed, it would be inaccurate to describe the scenario as having an egalitarian basis. The interest-based theory (and personal autonomy as the relevant interest) is doing the justificatory work; it just so happens that this framework prescribes an equal distribution in the special case where overall societal wealth is precisely this amount. The accurate statement is that, like the other possibilities discussed above, the interest-based theory entails a welfare liberal position.

5.3 Rights of Redistributive Taxation:
The Goal-Based Theory

The task in this section is to apply the goal-based theory of rights to this debate and ascertain which policy is warranted. As indicated in Chapter 4, the first step is to select a goal to which proponents of all three policies would be agreeable; the one that most effectively achieves the goal will be the one prescribed by this theory.

It was also noted in Chapter 4 that the utilitarian goal of happiness is too broad to serve as the moral basis of a social policy. Some may believe that well-being ought to be the goal, but while egalitarians and welfare liberals would likely endorse this suggestion, libertarians would not. Rather, a reasonable goal suggested itself in the previous section, namely that of freedom. Libertarians are concerned with preserving freedom, in that they consider the right to liberty to be basic and violable only in extreme circumstances. Welfare liberals, we have seen, take the increase in the freedom of those who receive welfare benefits as justification for such programs. The connection between the egalitarian position and freedom may seem less direct, but it, too, can be viewed as based on considerations of freedom. All three positions have reason to endorse freedom as the goal to be pursued.

Libertarians hold liberty (which will be used interchangeably with freedom) as precious and among the basic rights held by individuals. Defenders of libertarianism, we have noted, typically rely on natural rights theory for support in their arguments against taxation for redistributive purposes. Meanwhile, a goal-based account, with freedom as the goal, can be sketched fairly easily. It would be designed to demonstrate that redistributive taxation is coercive, in that the wealthy are forced to relinquish a portion of their property to the poor (or to the government as an intermediary). To the wealthy, however, it would be the same if the recipient is a mugger; the consequences of failing to accede to the demands of either are unpalatable. The desired libertarian conclusion is that any degree of redistributive taxation, since it coerces the wealthy in this way, reduces the amount of overall freedom and thus is not called for by the goal-based theory. More precisely, the conclusion is that strong rights to retain one's property are entailed by the theory.

Of course, there is another premise on which libertarians are relying in reaching this conclusion. Not only must it be the case that a policy of redistributive taxation must decrease the freedom of the wealthy, it must, in addition, not increase the freedom of the poor—at least not to the same degree.[61] The truth of this additional premise follows from the conception of freedom employed by libertarians. Recall that this conception is what has been labeled "negative freedom" (or "negative liberty"), understood as the ability to act without interference from others.[62] On this understanding, the wealthy lose freedom and the poor gain none, since the poor are always free (i.e., uncoerced) to increase their wealth and therefore their opportunities in life. It is evident that negative freedom is indeed employed by libertarians. Hospers indicates that the right to liberty is the right to conduct one's life "in accordance with the alternatives open to him without coercive action by others,"[63] and Hayek explicitly defines freedom as "independence of the arbitrary will of another."[64] When Nozick writes that "liberty upsets patterns," and then uses this as an argument to resist distributions based on need, merit, or any other "patterned" principle, he is clearly relying on this same idea.[65]

   The notion of coercion associated with negative freedom, while not altogether clear, can be summarized in the statement that an individual is
coerced when his alternatives are limited by the intentional actions of
others, those actions being aimed (at least in part) at limiting the former's
alternatives. It is at least safe to say that coercion implies intentionality.[66]
The alternatives of the wealthy, when reduced through taxation, are reduced by other individuals; hence, the wealthy are coerced and their
freedom is therefore reduced. It is argued by opponents of libertarianism
that the alternatives of the poor are limited, but the libertarian response
is that they are limited by circumstances, not by other people. Hence
there is no coercion, and they are not "unfree," as welfare liberals claim.
Their freedom cannot, then, be increased through redistributive taxation.
   However, to the poor it makes no difference whether it is other individuals or general circumstances that limit their alternatives; they still
lack a certain freedom, namely "positive freedom." Welfare liberals insist
on the moral relevance of this sort of freedom as well, utilizing the reasoning embedded in such questions as, "What is (purely negative) freedom to those who cannot make use of it? Without adequate conditions
for the use of freedom, what good is freedom?"[67] If positive freedom is
indeed taken into consideration, the premise in the libertarian argument
stipulating that the freedom of the poor is not increased through redistributive taxation (at least not to the extent to which the wealthy lose
freedom) becomes highly questionable.
   So there are two notions of freedom on the table,[68] only one of which is
consistent with the libertarian claim that redistributive taxation decreases
the overall amount of freedom in society. Which of the two notions
should be adopted is unclear. Libertarians provide no substantive argument in favor of negative freedom, but this is not in itself a strike against
it. Additional investigation is required.
   When applied to property, the two notions of freedom entail two different conceptions of property rights. If negative freedom is taken seriously,
a picture of property rights as unconditional (or at least overridable only
in extremely rare circumstances) must be adopted. This is in line with the
libertarian position: property rights are basic, and coercive redistributive
taxation, even for the purpose of alleviating the needs of the poor, cannot
be justified. On the other hand, if positive freedom is taken seriously, then
a picture of property rights as conditional must be adopted. This is in line
with the welfare liberal (and perhaps the socialist egalitarian) position: A
policy of redistributive taxation for the purpose of increasing the (positive) freedom of the poor is at least morally permissible and may well be
required. The issue may then be redescribed as the question of whether
conditional or unconditional property rights are to be preferred.
   James Sterba uses the "ought implies can" principle to argue for property rights as conditional. The idea behind this principle is that persons

cannot be morally required to do what they are unable to do, or—and this extension is crucial for Sterba's argument—to do "what would involve so great a sacrifice that it would be unreasonable to ask them to perform such an action."[69] The extension of the principle should not be problematic. Libertarians also rely on something like it in arguing that it would be unreasonable to require individuals to be forced to surrender a portion of their property for redistributive purposes. That requirement would be unreasonable because of its negative impact on the self-development of autonomous agents,[70] and on the long-range planning, which is distinctively human.[71] Sterba's claim is that it would, in fact, be unreasonable to require the poor to accept property rights as unconditional, since it would require them to "sit back and starve to death" in extreme cases, or at least to endure meaningless, unhappy, poverty-level lives. Unconditional property rights, in short, would violate the "ought implies can" principle.[72]

Such is not the case, however, for conditional property rights, since all individuals, rich and poor, can reasonably be expected to accept this. Libertarian objections to Sterba's account have disputed this claim, questioning whether anyone can reasonably be coercively taxed. In doing so, they emphasize the Lockean idea that property is what makes long-range planning possible. Machan's complaint is that Sterba's argument "lacks any foundation for why the needs of some persons must be claims upon the lives of others."[73]

But if this is the strongest protest libertarians can muster, we must side with Sterba. Machan and others lean too heavily on the claim that conditional property rights are an assault on the "lives" of others, and that such rights would effectively prevent the sort of long-range planning characteristic of human life. This is simply false. It would be closer to the truth if all of one's property were subject to redistributive taxation, but the welfare liberal, at least, maintains that only a portion is so subject, and that the wealthy must retain sufficient property to ensure that their lives are not disrupted in this way. Further, when the rich are aware, in advance, of what portion of their holdings will be taxed, they can account for that loss in the planning process. (Presumably, this already occurs in the case of tax dollars that fund basic services provided by the government to all citizens; there seems to be no reason why redistributive tax dollars cannot similarly be accounted for.) Some degree of disruption is unavoidable in a welfare state, but empirical observation informs us that long-range planning of the sort referred to by Machan and others is still possible.

If we accept property rights as conditional, then we are indicating a preference for positive freedom over negative freedom. We should at this point formalize the claim that admitting positive freedom into consideration means that a policy of at least some redistributive taxation would increase overall freedom, which in turns yields the existence of a right, held by the poor against the rich, to receive at least some assistance through such taxation. This conclusion rests on the idea that the degree of freedom lost by the wealthy is outweighed by the degree of freedom gained by the beneficiaries of such a policy. If this is correct, then not only is it false that redistributive taxation decreases freedom, it is also false that such taxation merely redistributes it from some members of society to others.[74] If, for example, there is "no net loss of freedom for society as a whole," as Robert Goodin claims,[75] then we should be indifferent between libertarianism and some competing redistributive policy. Thus, an implicit appeal to something like diminishing marginal returns of freedom is being made here, and it can be defended via straightforward considerations of the alternatives available to both groups (the poor and the rich) before, and after, such redistribution.

Even if this conclusion is questioned, Sterba has a second argument, one in which he is willing to view the issue in terms of negative freedom only. While it is argued that the rich ought to have the (negative) freedom not to have their property subject to redistribution, the claims of the poor can be seen as a negative freedom not to be interfered with while taking from the surplus holdings of the rich that which is necessary to satisfy their needs.[76] Casting the freedom of the poor as negative in this way appears to admit virtually all negative freedoms into the calculations, including such counterintuitive examples as the freedom not to be interfered with while murdering and raping. Because these freedoms are being assessed in a goal-based framework, however, there is no non-question-begging justification for omitting them. Thus, this negative freedom of the poor is appropriately admitted into consideration. [77]

The strategy from this point on is similar to that of the previous argument. The conflict is redescribed as a clash of these negative freedoms, and the question of which is to be preferred is answered according to the "ought implies can" principle; since it would be an unreasonable burden on the poor to relinquish such an important freedom, that freedom must be preserved. Meanwhile, the freedom of the well-off to retain exclusive control of their holdings must therefore be compromised.

Libertarian responses to this second argument are also unpersuasive. Machan's complaints are largely empirical. "Normally," he writes, people "do not lack the opportunities and resources to satisfy their own basic needs."[78] While a strong case can be made that the poor are more numerous than Machan seems to think, his objection nonetheless fails to affect the truth status of the conditional claim that if there are such individuals in such situations, they ought to have the freedom to appropriate what is needed from those who have surplus resources. The same response can be given to his ensuing claim that even when there are such needy individuals, they have the ability to seek help, and to rely on the generosity of others, rather than "loot."

The foregoing has been intended to demonstrate that a picture of property rights as conditional ought to be adopted, which in turn entails accepting the notion of positive freedom (or, in line with Sterba's second argument, something very much like positive freedom), and allowing it to contribute to considerations of how the overall amount of freedom in society is affected by redistributive taxation. The conclusion, again, is that freedom is better achieved through welfare liberalism, or perhaps even socialist egalitarianism, than through libertarianism. On the goal-based theory of rights, therefore, the needy do have rights to receive assistance.

This may initially seem an odd result when compared with claims made by Mill, whose writings on freedom, rights, and (to the extent that it falls into Mill's category of charity and beneficence) redistributive taxation are substantial.[79] While it is not an absolute requirement, consistency with Mill is desirable, and it is therefore worth noting how the above conclusion does not necessarily clash with Mill's theory.

The apparent conflict pertains to Mill's use of freedom in his moral theory. His conception of freedom, delineated in the first chapter of On Liberty, seems in line with the notion of negative freedom. According to his so-called principle of liberty, the prevention of harm to others constitutes the only justifiable collective restriction on individual action. Freedom and happiness are tightly connected for Mill; he appears to believe that happiness will be better achieved in the long run if individual freedom is retained. This is consistent with his famous discussion in Chapter 5 of Utilitarianism, in which he maintains that legal sanctions cannot, on utilitarian grounds alone, be leveled against those who freely choose not to contribute to charity or otherwise aid the needy. The (simplified) reasoning is that legally enforceable programs of redistributive taxation would decrease individual freedom, thereby decreasing the overall amount of happiness, and are thus not justified.

The explanation for the alleged divergence is that Mill, in making his claims, is speaking only of the freedom lost by the wealthy in a welfare system. There is no denying that some of their freedom is indeed compromised. The claim, though, is that the freedom gained by those who benefit in such a system more than makes up for the freedom lost by the wealthy, and Mill does not address this point. In other words, Mill focuses on individual freedom (and on those who would lose some individual freedom if forced to aid the needy) while the argument suggested thus far in this section focuses on the notion of overall freedom. There is, therefore, no explicit inconsistency. A new question, to which I will return momentarily, is why this difference in approach should exist.

A second apparent conflict with Mill pertains to the issue of rights specifically. For Mill, the (imperfect) moral duties of aiding the needy, unlike the (perfect) moral duties of refraining from positively harming others, are not necessarily correlative with rights held by those to whom the duties are owed. Thus, there may be no rights held by the needy against the well-off to receive assistance. A right, according to Mill, is "something which society ought to protect me in the possession of. If the objector goes on to ask why it ought, I can give him no other reason than general utility."[80] The "general utility" justification operates in the following way. Mill, like Bentham, takes any policy of punishment to entail a certain utility cost. If the benefits generated by the policy outweigh its cost, then it is justified. The policy of legally enforcing perfect duties is justified on this analysis, but the policy of legally enforcing imperfect duties to give to charity is not.

First, Mill indicates that despite the lack of a right to receive charity or beneficence, there may be rights to assistance held by the defenseless.[81] Second, it must be remembered that Mill, in making his claims, is employing the goal of happiness (or utility), which for reasons already mentioned is problematic. Third, he may in any case be wrong about the comparative utilities; the broad, ill-defined nature of happiness makes such determinations especially difficult. Regardless, our concern is with the goal of freedom, and since overall freedom will be increased if there is at least some redistribution in society, the goal-based theory of rights entails the existence of rights, held by the poor against the wealthy, to receive assistance through taxation. Mill's approach, though slightly different, is therefore not necessarily inconsistent with ours.

Still, there remains an apparently significant divergence. Our conclusion is based on a notion of overall freedom: the claim is that the freedom (in the form of property) of some (the wealthy) can be appropriated and redistributed because the overall amount of freedom in society will increase as a result. Mill, on the other hand, denies the justifiability of such a move, and instead maintains that the freedom of some cannot be compromised for the purpose of an overall gain. It may appear, on initial inspection, that Mill's approach is closer to Sumner's goal-based rights framework. Recall that Sumner maintains that rights can, in Dworkin's sense, be taken seriously. This is because rights can be constraints against the direct pursuit of the goal. For Sumner, the good ought not be reallocated—such that some individuals will incur a loss—anytime an overall gain appears imminent. In this vein, Mill's analysis appears similar, in that he indicates a preference for not shifting allotments of individual utilities whenever a net societal gain is deemed likely; the better approach is to recognize individual rights not to have utilities appropriated. In the present analysis, the good of freedom is employed rather than that of utility, but the principle can be expressed in the same way; in accordance with Sumner's framework, it can be argued that respecting individual freedom (in the form of property)—that is, not reallocating it in such a way that some individuals will incur a loss—will, in the long run, help to better achieve the goal of expanding overall freedom in society.

However, it can't be the case that all constraints are to be recognized as rights. There must be some reason for thinking that a particular constraint, in the form of a right, is justified—that is, that it will, in the long run, lead to a more successful attainment of the goal. Reference to Sumner's specific example will be helpful in seeing this point more clearly. He discusses the protocol employed by his university for approving research (biomedical and social-scientific) in which human subjects are used. Approval demands the satisfaction of two requirements. According to the first, the proposed experiment must promise to yield a satisfactory overall ratio of benefits to costs; expected harms to the subject (or any other foreseeable negative consequence) must be outweighed by the experiment's anticipated benefits. If this cost/benefit analysis prescribes going ahead with the experiment, a second requirement, according to which the subject must be adequately protected, must be also satisfied.[82] Confidentiality, compensation, and disclosure of information are among the factors affected by this second condition. Because the second requirement appears concerned with human dignity, its justification might seem deontological, but if a goal-based framework is underlying the two requirements, the ultimate justification must appeal to consequences. Sumner's claim is that in the long run, the ratio of benefits to costs will be greatest if this second requirement, which in many individual cases will operate as a constraint (and in all cases as a right of the subject), is recognized. The reason is that mistakes in the cost/benefit analysis will be made, and the costs of such mistakes could be severe.

The ongoing suggestion is that a policy of redistributive taxation would, on the direct cost/benefit analysis, yield an overall increase in freedom. But are there reasons for thinking that constraints, in the form of strong property rights (i.e., libertarian-style rights of near-exclusive control over one's holdings) would in fact lead to a more successful attainment of the goal? One reason for thinking that it might pertains to the incentives of a wholly free-market system. The argument, roughly, is that taxation, or any other factor limiting market return, is a disincentive to effort, so much so that in the long run a net loss in freedom will be the result.[83] A worker is taxed and so is less motivated to put forth his best effort, thereby incurring a loss of wealth (and thus freedom) for himself, above and beyond the direct loss incurred through taxation. There is, in addition, a loss for others, since this decrease will mean fewer tax dollars available for redistribution. Moreover, the individuals who are taxed most (executives and managers) are often directly responsible for the employment of others; this "trickle down" effect of the disincentive serves to compound the problem.

In order to demonstrate that, in the long run, the disincentive effect is not a reason for thinking that constraints in the form of strong property rights are advisable, it is not necessary to deny that expected income is a motivational factor. More modestly, it need only be denied that income is the sole motivational factor. The above argument assumes that the decision of how hard to work is based exclusively on income considerations, but this is certainly false. Volunteers are motivated by factors other than economic gain, as are welfare lawyers and others who intentionally pursue lower-paying jobs. Further, a corollary of this view is that since worker A's salary is many times that of worker B, A must be working many times harder than B, and this is implausible.[84]

The disincentive effect may also be argued regarding the poor who benefit from redistributive taxation. To guarantee a certain minimum standard of living is to create a class of free riders, especially if that standard is at the "autonomy" level rather than the mere "subsistence" level (as described in the last section). While there are some legitimate concerns here, this claim underestimates the degree to which human beings value worthwhile projects. We need not resort to a full-blown Marxist (utopian) theory of human nature to make this claim. The idea is that human beings will, for the most part, want to improve themselves, and once they are in a position to do so will not be content to remain passive, unproductive recipients. Regardless, this claim is perfectly consistent with the egoistic nature of humans espoused by libertarians; once individuals are in a position to acquire more, they will do so. In the end, the foregoing concerns about disincentives do not constitute a reason for thinking that constraining the goal of optimizing freedom by recognizing strong property rights will in the long run lead to a more successful attainment of that goal.

A second reason for endorsing such constraints relates to the potential discontent of those whose property is appropriated. Those individuals may see themselves as an oppressed minority, subject to the will of a voting majority that rationalizes a policy of punitive taxes.[85] The wealthiest are most susceptible to this sort of voting, and the eventual consequence may be that this segment of society, along with others who may be especially resentful, will become hostile and even dangerous; the overall effects on freedom would be substantially negative.[86] This possibility, although unlikely, is alleged to justify constraints on the pursuit of freedom by recognizing strong property rights.

Again, while this consideration does raise some legitimate concerns, the conclusion is too strong. For decades, some redistribution, directed by government, has taken place in the United States, yet the response has not been hostile. Discontent over paying taxes generally is nearly universal, regardless of whether the taxes are redistributed; the reaction generated by the discontent, however, would have to be significantly higher for it to be a reason to constrain the goal.

Based on the reasoning employed so far, it may begin to appear as though no constraint should be recognized. The egalitarian position, which entails radical redistribution (as opposed to the moderate redistribution prescribed by welfare liberalism), may correspondingly seem more plausible. This is because an unconstrained direct cost/benefit analysis arguably entails strict equality of freedom (and thus strict equality of holdings). This result is based on considerations of diminishing marginal returns, to which I appealed earlier in claiming that the freedom gained (by those who benefit from redistributive taxation) would outweigh the freedom lost. Following this principle through to its logical conclusion entails a strictly egalitarian distribution and thus radical redistribution. This means that property rights would be reduced to an extremely conditional status; the rights of those who have less to appropriate from those who have more would override any property rights until the point of equality is reached.

However, there are reasons for thinking that this sort of radical redistribution, though appropriate on a direct cost/benefit analysis, would not be the most effective way of achieving the goal. It was mentioned above that disincentive and discontent are legitimate concerns, but insufficiently so for strongly constraining the pursuit of the goal (by allowing for strong property rights). They are, however, sufficient for creating moderate property rights of the sort entailed by welfare liberalism (as opposed to the very weak property rights entailed by socialist egalitarianism).

First, a social policy of distributing holdings equally may indeed decrease incentive to the point of decreasing overall freedom. Under a policy of moderate redistribution, there remains an opportunity for individuals to acquire more wealth. A certain range of wealth levels remains intact, with no theoretical maximum (although a lesser payoff as income increases is to be expected in a progressive tax structure). Under a policy of radical redistribution, there is no range of wealth levels, and the opportunity to acquire more disappears. With few exceptions, those who would otherwise work more, and (in addition to bettering their own situations) thus generate resources for others, would be disinclined to do so. Similarly, those who would otherwise have less would be unmotivated to work hard. The resulting society, it can be imagined, would have few dedicated workers, and in such a society, overall resources are likely to be diminished. Insofar as resources correlate with freedom (as we have been assuming), overall freedom would be diminished as well.

Second, it is reasonable to think that the factor of discontent warrants constraining pursuit of the goal in this way. We in contemporary American society take the notion of property very seriously—not so seriously that any degree of redistribution meets with widespread resistance, but seriously enough that radical redistribution would be so met. The backlash against a socialist egalitarian policy of taxation may indeed be extreme; little imagination is required, for instance, to envision the reactions of certain antigovernment militia groups. The claim that overall freedom may well decrease as a result is then easily established. In this picture, discontent is a contingent problem; our attitudes regarding property are a function of a cultural and social framework in which it happens to be significant. A different background framework might yield different attitudes. Regardless, discontent is currently a problem for egalitarianism in our society, and in any case the disincentive problem, which may be more deeply embedded in human nature, would be much more difficult to overcome.

The position at which we arrive, then, is welfare liberalism. The principle of diminishing marginal returns entails the conclusion that overall freedom increases as equality of holdings is approached; but constraints barring the radical redistribution required by socialist egalitarianism force the welfare liberal conclusion. The property rights implied by this conclusion are of moderate strength. They are conditional, unlike the strong, unconditional rights inherent in libertarianism, but they are not exceedingly weak, as would be the case if an egalitarian distribution were morally required. According to the goal-based analysis, then, the poor hold rights against the rich to receive assistance, and the rich hold rights not to have their property appropriated for the purposes of achieving an egalitarian distribution of holdings.

A remaining criticism might be based on empirical observation. The last several decades, according to the objection, serve to demonstrate that moderate redistributive taxation does not produce the result of increasing overall freedom. The wealthy and the middle class have lost out, and evidence suggests that the poor certainly have not gained. Political conservatives like to use such evidence to argue for the impracticality of the welfare state. This sort of objection, though, can be addressed on several levels. First, the "evidence" is not so conclusive. Without getting into the specifics, statistics of poverty levels can remain static while the level of comfort that constitutes the so-called poverty line can fluctuate. It may well be that welfare programs (and redistributive taxation generally) have helped, and have increased overall freedom in society, allowing those who would otherwise be in desperate situations to enjoy more options. Second, even if the statistics are representative, the objection may amount to no more than an instrumental criticism. The (goal-based) theory behind redistributive taxation can be sound while the details of implementation may need some reworking. Finally, using statistical evidence of continued poverty to claim that redistributive taxation violates the "ought implies can" principle (since history clearly teaches us that such taxation does not work) is also premature, and insofar as it, too, points to an instrumental rather than a moral difficulty, it is misguided as well.

Notes

1. Similarly, the duty of the wealthy to relinquish a certain amount of their holdings for welfare purposes is sometimes said to be owed to the state, and sometimes to the poor directly.

2. Locke, Two Treatises of Government, ed. Peter Laslett (Cambridge: Cambridge University Press, 1963), section 123.

3. Locke is concerned with original acquisition, i.e., individual appropriation of unowned (or, more accurately, jointly owned) property.

4. Alan Ryan, Property and Political Theory (Oxford: Blackwell, 1984), 28. See also Lawrence Becker, Property Rights (London: Routledge & Kegan Paul, 1977).

5. See Jeremy Waldron, The Right to Private Property (Oxford: Clarendon Press, 1988), 203–7.

6. Robert Nozick, Anarchy, State and Utopia (New York: Basic Books, 1974), 175.

7. Ibid., 174–75.

8. A. John Simmons, The Lockean Theory of Rights (Princeton: Princeton University Press, 1992), 271–77.

9. David Hume, A Treatise of Human Nature, ed. L. A. Selby-Bigge (Oxford: Oxford University Press, 1978), 505–6.

10. Waldron, The Right to Private Property, 184–88; "Two Worries About Mixing One's Labor," Philosophical Quarterly 33 (1983), 42.

11. See Isaiah Berlin, "Two Concepts of Liberty" in Liberalism and Its Critics, ed. Michael Sandel (Oxford: Blackwell, 1984), 22–25; C. B. MacPherson, "Berlin's Division of Liberty," in Democratic Theory: Essays in Retrieval, ed. C. B. MacPherson (Oxford: Clarendon Press, 1973), 108.

12. An ongoing assumption is that the fair share proviso is, in fact, a moral limitation on property acquisition, if only a mild one (as Nozick claims). This reading, though prevalent, is not universally agreed to; Waldron, for instance, sees Locke's "enough and as good" claim as merely "a fact about appropriation in the early stages of man." See Waldron, "Enough and as Good Left for Others," Philosophical Quarterly 29 (1979), 322; The Right to Private Property, 209–12.

13. Anarchy, State and Utopia, 175.

14. Waldron, The Right to Private Property, 215. Another appropriate summary of Nozick's position here is that he views the fair share proviso as satisfied as long as "no one is made worse off on balance than she would have been had the no-ownership situation persisted," Gopal Sreenivasan, The Limits of Lockean Rights in Property (Princeton: Princeton University Press, 1994), 123.

15. Anarchy, State and Utopia, 151.

16. Commentators seem to think that Nozick's lack of an attempt to improve on Locke, together with the general nature of his discussion, point to the same conclusion: that his own view is largely Lockean. See Simmons, The Lockean Theory of Rights, 321; John Christman, The Myth of Property (Oxford: Oxford University Press, 1994), 61–63; Justus Hartnack, Human Rights (Lewiston, NY: Edwin Mellen, 1986), 55–59.

17. Anarchy, State and Utopia, 161.

18. Ibid., 159.

19. See Simmons, 320.

20. Tibor Machan, Individuals and Their Rights (LaSalle, IL: Open Court, 1989), 99, 107.

21. MacPherson, The Political Theory of Possessive Individualism (Oxford: Oxford University Press, 1962), 221–31. MacPherson goes on to criticize Locke on this count, but his interpretation of Locke's property claims fits the libertarian picture. See also Rolf Sartorius, "Persons and Property" in Utility and Rights, ed. R.G. Frey (Minneapolis: University of Minnesota Press, 1984), 209.

22. James Tully, A Discourse on Property (Cambridge: Cambridge University Press, 1980), 158–65.

23. Sreenivasan, 141. (See also 48, 49, 143).

24. The force of his claims is partially diminished when he concedes that, for Locke, those who are to count as truly needy are limited in number. (In this way, there may actually be similarities with certain libertarian claims, e.g., those of Machan, 106–7.) See 41–43 generally.

25. Christman, The Myth of Property, 29.

26. Ibid., 52.

27. Ibid., 53.

28. John Rawls, A Theory of Justice (Cambridge, MA: Harvard University Press, 1971), 60–61.

29. Ibid., 140–41, 251–57.

30. See, e.g., Kenneth Baynes, The Normative Grounds of Social Criticism (Albany: State University of New York Press, 1992), 51–68; Rex Martin, Rawls on Rights (Lawrence, KS: University of Kansas Press, 1985), 11.

31. Rawls and Nozick are often taken to constitute the "extremes" of the debate, though this is certainly not the case. On the left, Marx and Engels advocated the elimination of private property; property rights for Rawls, however, while highly conditional, are not done away with altogether. See The Communist Manifesto (New York: Bantam Books, 1992), 34. On the right, remarks by Friedrich Hayek can be inferred as denying even the minimal proviso allowed for by Nozick. See The Constitution of Liberty (Chicago: University of Chicago Press, 1960), 86–88.

32. Nielson, "Radical Egalitarianism," in Justice: Alternative Political Perspectives, ed. James P. Sterba (Belmont, CA: Wadsworth, 1992).

33. See, e.g., James S. Fishkin, Justice, Equal Opportunity and the Family (New Haven: Yale University Press, 1983), 32–34, 48–50.

34. Hospers, "The Libertarian Manifesto" in Justice: Alternative Political Perspsectives, 44.

35. Machan, Individuals and Their Rights, 141.

36. See Machan, 99; Hospers, 48; Murray Rothbard, For a New Liberty (New York: Macmillan, 1973), 43–46.

37. Machan, 98.

38. Ibid., 99.

39. Lomasky, Persons, Rights, and the Moral Community (Oxford: Oxford University Press, 1987), especially Chapters 5 and 6.

40. The methodology is not, however, exactly the same. See note 42 below.

41. Lomasky, 94–96.

42. Lomasky's method of arriving at these conclusions differs from that of the interest-based theory in the following way. He is concerned with the rational motivation of project pursuers to conform to a system of basic rights. His derivation of basic rights is essentially conventionalist, in the tradition of Hume and somewhat similar to the contemporary picture sketched by Gilbert Harman in "Moral Relativism as a Foundation for Natural Rights," Journal of Libertarian Studies 4 (1980). Lomasky arrives at the conclusion, that coupled with a qualified egoistic picture of human nature, the rational motivation for acceding to a rights claim is present if the claim is to life or liberty, but not if it is a positive claim to the property of others, i.e., to being supplied with material goods by others. As the discussion proceeds, it will be suggested that the libertarian position is unstable even on Lomasky's picture of basic rights, as well as on the interest-based theory of rights.

43. The term, "subsistence rights," is borrowed from Henry Shue, Basic Rights (Princeton: Princeton University Press, 1980), 53.

44. The similarity to Locke's "spoilage proviso" should be noted here.

45. Lomasky, 86.

46. Ibid., 87.

47. Ibid., 88–92.

48. Perhaps the difference between the two types of liberals, more accurately, is that for welfare liberals, attainment of the conditions necessary for subsistence will, in most cases at least, be sufficient as well, since persons will not let themselves deteriorate if they can help it. (Further, it may be that at certain times and for certain people, supplying that which is sufficient is the only way of supplying that which is necessary.)

49. Machan, 107.

50. See Machan, 105; Lomasky, 140.

51. Joseph Raz, The Morality of Freedom (Oxford: Oxford University Press, 1986), 374.

52. Christman, 19–21.

53. Ibid., 171.

54. Anarchy, State and Utopia, 169–71.

55. This objection, as stated, operates against any degree of redistributive taxation.

56. Richard J. Arneson, "Property Rights in Persons" in Economic Rights, ed. Ellen Frankel Paul, Fred D. Miller, Jr., and Jeffrey Paul (Cambridge: Cambridge University Press, 1992), 206–7.

57. See David Copp, "The Right to an Adequate Standard of Living: Justice, Autonomy and the Basic Needs" in Economic Rights, 245–47.

58. Nielson, "Radical Egalitarianism," 105.

59. Ibid., 107.

60. Ibid., 107.

61. The very idea of a libertarian allowing for any such tradeoffs of freedom may seem implausible. However, the aim of the current section is to analyze which social policy, from among a pool of candidates that includes the so-called libertarian policy, follows from the goal-based theory of rights. The tension here results from the recognition that many self-professed libertarians reject the current moral methodology altogether. In itself, this is not problematic for the present project. Further, a case could potentially be made (though I will not do so here) that libertarians do allow for such tradeoffs, since the "freedom" (Hobbesian though it may be) to harm others is restricted in order to allow for individual "freedom" to be realized.

62. Berlin, "Two Concepts of Liberty."

63. "The Libertarian Manifesto," 43.

64. The Constitution of Liberty, 12.

65. Anarchy, State, and Utopia, 160–64.

66. See Nozick, Philosophical Explanations (Cambridge, MA: Harvard University Press, 1971), 49, 309, 520. The will of another agent is a necessary ingredient of coercion, according to Nozick; circumstances alone (i.e., absent the will of an agent) cannot amount to coercion. In the end, Nozick and others are hard-pressed to cite the morally relevant differences among the various ways in which one's alternatives can be limited.

67. Berlin, 17.

68. Although this may imply that a single goal has not yet been specified as the one relevant for this particular application of the goal-based theory, the upcoming discussion will reveal that if the goal is found within the scope of freedom generally, one notion recommends itself. Further, the conflict will be assessed in light of the other notion as well, and in this way all bases should be covered.

69. James Sterba, "From Liberty to Welfare," in Justice: Alternative Political Perspectives, 57.

70. Machan, 141.

71. Hospers, 44.

72. Sterba, 60–61. In making this claim, Sterba is departing from a somewhat standard interpretation of the principle, according to which "can" is assessed in terms of mere possibilities. On that reading, the poor "can" accept unconditional property rights. The extension of the principle, to include "what would involve so great a sacrifice that it would be unreasonable to ask them to perform such an action" (which, it was noted above, should not be problematic), allows for the desired conclusion.

73. Machan, 102. See also 105 generally.

74. See, e.g., Will Kymlicka, Contemporary Political Philosophy (Oxford: Oxford Universtiy Press, 1990), 147.

75. Robert Goodin, Reasons for Welfare (Princeton: Princeton University Press, 1988), 313.

76. Sterba, 57. See also Hospers, Libertarianism (Los Angeles: Nash, 1971), Chapter 7.

77. The lack of a right to murder or rape in the goal-based framework will therefore result from calculations that include even the freedom not to be interfered with while murdering or raping.

78. Machan, 107.

79. The upcoming brief aside purposely ignores Mill's lengthy Principles of Political Economy (London: Penguin Books, 1970). Not only are the details of that work well beyond the scope of the current discussion, but the notion of property Mill utilizes there may diverge from the one employed here. He writes, "The essential principle of property being to assure to all persons what they have produced by their labour and accumulated by their abstinence, this principle cannot apply to what is not the produce of labour, the raw material of the earth." (II, 2, 5) I therefore take the liberty of assuming that redistributive taxation, as described in the current chapter, is of the same status as charity for Mill.

80. Utilitarianism, 52.

81. On Liberty, Chapter 4.

82. Sumner, The Moral Foundation of Rights, 182–83.

83. Hayek, The Constitution of Liberty, 98–99.

84. Christman, 116.

85. Milton Friedman, Capitalism and Freedom (Chicago: University of Chicago Press, 1982), 174–75.

86. Hare, "Justice and Equality," in Justice: Alternative Political Perspectives, 193.

6

Affirmative Action

6.1 The Idea of Affirmative Action

This chapter's debate has been particularly intense, and the rhetoric surrounding it particularly astringent. A rudimentary definition of affirmative action is that, for members of minority groups, the fact of being in such groups must be considered as a positive factor in hiring decisions. The policy could be specific, requiring numerical quotas of minority employees, or general, requiring merely "good faith" efforts on the part of employers to positively consider minority applicants. While, in theory, compliance could be supervised directly by governments, individual businesses have typically instituted their own affirmative action programs (at least when advised by their lawyers to do so) in order to avoid more direct government involvement.

For our purposes, the focus will be on black individuals as the beneficiaries of affirmative action policies. The intention is not to exclude members of other minority groups who, on the condition that affirmative action (AA) ought to be adopted, would also have claims to preferential treatment. Focusing on one particular group, however, is convenient in that doing so serves to facilitate discussion; results of this analysis can (in all likelihood and to various degrees) then be applied to other groups. Further, focusing on blacks rather than, say, women as potential holders of the right to preferential treatment allows for an incorporation of a unique history of discrimination into the analysis. One other allowance will be that employment will be the focus, rather than academic admissions or some other context in which AA might be appropriate.

As was the case in the previous chapter, three main possibilities will be considered in the quest for the morally preferable social policy. First, AA may be required; businesses failing to take the fact of minority membership into account in the hiring process would be subject to legal action. Second, AA may be altogether impermissible; businesses taking race into account for any reason (i.e., failing to act in a race-neutral fashion) would be subject to the charge of discrimination.[1] Third, AA may be a permissible practice; businesses may, at their discretion, choose to favorably consider minority applicants in their hiring decisions, but doing so would be neither required nor prohibited by law.

When appeals to moral rights are made in the AA debate, the claim is made on the one hand that a right exists not to be discriminated against, and this right (typically alleged to be held by white persons) entails not being subjected to such social programs. On the other side, a right to be preferentially considered, possessed by disadvantaged minorities, is alleged to exist. This right will derive from a more basic core right, such as the right to equal opportunity, or to compensation for past or present injuries. A variety of justifications has been provided for these core rights, most of which can be understood in an interest-based or goal-based framework.

Affirmative action does not mean, as some have appeared to conclude,[2] that unqualified minorities are to be preferred over qualified nonminorities; AA reaffirms the necessity of hiring only those individuals qualified for the positions in question. What it does mean is that the most qualified applicant is not necessarily the person who ought to get the job.[3] So long as all members of a pool of applicants are deemed qualified for a certain position, the fact that nonminority applicant A is somewhat more qualified than minority applicant B should be irrelevant (or at least discounted). Moreover, according to the dictates of AA, applicant B (the only minority in the pool) ought to get the job (in the absence of any overriding factors). Exclusion of B on the basis of her being less qualified is justifiable only when the additional qualification is necessary for the job in question.

Regardless of the specific justification for AA, the underlying factor driving the pro-AA position is racism, most often "overt racism," understood as deliberate discrimination against blacks simply on the basis of race. But proponents of AA are often concerned with a more subtle variety, "institutional racism," which includes practices that are apparently unbiased on the surface, conceived in race-neutral fashion, but that have the effect of discriminating against blacks.[4] The United States Supreme Court expressed this idea in a unanimous decision that included the directive that "The Civil Rights Act proscribes not only overt discrimination, but practices that are fair in form but discriminatory in operation."[5] Examples include seniority-based promotions (or layoffs), since those most recently hired tend disproportionately to be black, and the practice (discussed above) of hiring the best qualified candidate, since blacks have often been denied the opportunity to receive an education equal to that of their job-seeking competitors. This background of institutional racism will help to frame the interest-based and goal-based analyses of rights pertaining to the AA debate.

Finally, it should be noted that the alleged rights associated with AA will be assessed in accordance with the policy in its current form; in other words, in a rights framework it is the fact of being black that establishes the right to be preferentially considered. The claims to be examined, then, are whether being black is a sufficient condition for possessing the right to be preferentially considered, and whether required or permissible AA can be justified through appeal to such rights.

6.2 Rights of Affirmative Action: The Interest-Based Theory

Grounding a policy of required AA in a right to be preferentially considered (which, in turn, is grounded in a more general core right which is then justified by the interest-based theory) requires clearing several hurdles. First,

(A) Is there a legitimate interest on which such a right may be based?

This is, essentially, just the "value" test. The question is whether there exists some valuable interest—one that accords with Joseph Raz's humanistic principle of increasing the well-being of those who possess the interest—and which can therefore get a potential right off the ground. Several candidate interests will be assumed to unproblematically pass the value test. Second,

(B) Would this right be possessed by all black persons?

In other words, would the interest be applicable to all blacks, such that all would be eligible for the right to preferential treatment? Since it is the policy in its current form (the fact of being black as sufficient for possessing the right) that is under consideration, an affirmative response to (B) is a necessary condition for the acceptability of the required AA policy. Third,

(C)Would AA be an effective means of attending to the interest on which the right is based?

Unless an affirmative response to (C) can be found, any right possessed by all blacks grounded by the interest established in (A) and (B) cannot serve as the basis for the derivative right to preferential treatment. Fourth,

(D) Are there any overriding considerations that would effectively cancel the (conditionally established) right to preferential treatment and thus the justifiability of the required AA policy?

This is essentially the "other things equal" test. Assuming that the existence of a right to preferential treatment, possessed by all blacks, can initially justify required AA, are there any competing moral factors sufficiently strong to override the right? Candidates for these factors will typically be the violations of the rights of individuals who would be adversely affected by such a policy. Recall from Chapter 3 that failure to pass the "other things equal" test indicates that a competing moral consideration effectively negates the existence of the right.[6]

The hurdles, then, pertain to (A) value, (B) universality, (C) policy effectiveness, and (D) competing moral factors.

One interest that could serve as the basis for the right to preferential treatment is personal autonomy.[7] According to this justification, the long history of discrimination against blacks has left them with inadequate options in life. Affirmative action, it is claimed, would allow for a "reasonable number of life options" to be achieved, since under such a policy blacks would have options not realistically feasible in a "colorblind" or race-neutral hiring process; the institutional racism would be too much to overcome.

As an interest, personal autonomy unproblematically passes the value test; the well-being of those possessing the right would no doubt be increased. Regarding (B), however, there is an immediate difficulty with the personal autonomy approach. The set of those who lack personal autonomy and the set of those who are black are not identical, although there is significant overlap. A policy of race-based AA would afford advantages to some who do not lack personal autonomy, and would fail to aid some who really do stand in need of some assistance. The suggestion here is that race is not the best indicator of the status of personal autonomy; in our society, wealth is likely to be a much better indicator. It was claimed in the previous chapter that an individual's degree of personal autonomy and her level of wealth strongly coincide. At best, therefore, rights to preferential treatment grounded by the interest of personal autonomy would be possessed by those who are poor, and not by those who are black. A policy of wealth-based AA thus looks more plausible than a policy of race-based AA.[8] Regardless, as long as personal autonomy is the focus, the latter appears to be stalled by this "correspondence problem."

A somewhat different approach would be to focus not on the interest of personal autonomy, but on equality generally, and equality of opportunity in particular. A core right to equality of opportunity is generally accepted (insofar as a rights vocabulary is accepted), and has, in various forms, been argued for by Rawls[9] and Dworkin,[10] among others. It differs from a core right based on personal autonomy, since it is not concerned with the issue of autonomy levels and the question of whether they are above a minimum threshold. According to this new interest and the line of argument it engenders, once the right to equal opportunity is established, a derivative right to preferential treatment, possessed by those who lack equality of opportunity, follows. Since blacks lack equality of opportunity, blacks have a right to be preferentially considered, and a policy of race-based AA is therefore justifiable.[11]

Of course, it appears that a correspondence problem similar to the one that plagued the personal autonomy approach to the right to preferential treatment obtains here: there is a poor fit between those who stand to benefit from AA and those who lack equality of opportunity. On the one hand, AA would leave out a number of nonblack individuals who lack equality of opportunity and would thus be arbitrary in its application. On the other hand, AA would include a number of black individuals whose opportunities are in no way inferior.[12] This is the more serious problem for (B). If there are black individuals whose interest in equality of opportunity is not being harmed by race-blind principles, then establishing a right to preferential treatment, possessed by all blacks, may not be possible.

The empirical question is whether there are, in fact, such individuals. Gertrude Ezorsky has argued that there are none, that it is unimaginable that any black person in contemporary American society has managed to escape the negative effects of racism, overt or institutional, experienced as deprivation of equality of opportunity. Even those blacks who appear to have done so are victims, though perhaps to a lesser degree.[13] Bernard Boxill, agreeing with Ezorsky, accuses those who believe there are such unaffected blacks of confusing the notion of being unharmed with the notion of being harmed to a lesser degree (less than other blacks). His claim is that all blacks are, in fact, being harmed (in the form of deprivation of equality of opportunity) by continued racism, and attempts to demonstrate otherwise invariably point to examples of blacks who are merely suffering less than others; but it does not follow that those blacks are not suffering at all.[14]

How can these claims be demonstrated? One way would be to argue that in the absence of any racial discrimination, blacks would certainly be occupying a significantly higher percentage of quality jobs. Although, of course, arguments utilizing statistical disparities are sound only on the condition that the discrepancies have been caused by discrimination, this additional claim can be defended reasonably well, especially when viewed as an inference to the best explanation.[15] Even so, a correspondence problem persists. This approach, at best, supports the conclusion that blacks as a group lack equality of opportunity, and that some sort of group right to preferential treatment therefore follows. This possibility will be addressed later, but on the individual level, it is virtually impossible to demonstrate that every black person (or even most) would, in terms of equality of opportunity, be better off if there were no racism. Indeed, common sense would indicate otherwise, since many blacks today are being offered desirable positions without regard to race. It is much easier to establish the claim that all (or most) blacks are in some indirect way being harmed by the continued existence of racism, but not by deprivation of equality of opportunity.

This latter claim, of course, is not easily (or at all) open to examination. The opposing view, equally resistant to testing, has been suggested as well. Because of discrimination, according to this line of thought, even today's "best-prepared" black individuals continue to suffer some degree of inequality of opportunity, and they would therefore be even better prepared if full equality of opportunity were realized.[16] This consideration gives rise to Boxill's claim that while blacks undeniably suffer various degrees of this sort of harm, it is false to conclude that some blacks therefore suffer no such harm. Again, this is not easily open to empirical investigation.

It should be clarified that the interest currently under consideration, equality of opportunity, is a case of present harm; it is the idea that blacks are currently being harmed by being denied equality of opportunity. The role of past harm to blacks should at this point remain distinct in the analysis. The interest of being compensated for past harm may also be a legitimate basis for the right to preferential treatment, and will be reviewed momentarily.

However, one other attempt to establish the right based on present harm relies on the notion of indirect harm. Boxill contends that, even if it were the case that some blacks escape the sort of direct harm considered above, all blacks suffer a certain indirect harm.[17] That the social and cultural environment in contemporary American society is unfriendly and even hostile to blacks is undeniable, and the claim is that the very existence of such an environment itself constitutes a harm to anyone who is black. This (indirect) harm can be of several main types. First, there exists a realistic threat of direct harm in the form of violation of security. Insofar as a threat is itself a harm, all blacks are therefore harmed. This threat is pervasive, and obtains for blacks in a way that it does not for other segments of society.[18] A consequence is that blacks suffer psychologically, since for any individual black person, the persistent "violence" done to other blacks, because they are black, "is a warning that (he) too may experience the same treatment."[19] Second, the current racist atmosphere contributes to a certain "judgmental injustice," since in such an environment, the fact of being black invariably enters into hiring decisions. If this were the case, the harm would be direct, and would fall under inequality of opportunity, already discussed and found to be somewhat problematic. Again, though, this is no doubt the case for some blacks, and inequality of opportunity will therefore be considered an instance of pres-

ent indirect harm for our purposes. Regardless, blacks suffer certain negative psychological effects knowing the very real possibility of being denied equality of opportunity, and this may be construed as indirect.
Third, the continuing racist atmosphere, in connection with the foregoing
two considerations and others like them, generates a lack of self-respect
and self-confidence that then serves to inhibit the ability to compete (ed-
ucationally, and ultimately for employment) on the same level as others
who are never victimized in this way.[20]

These considerations can be collected under the rubric of indirect
harm. The interest in avoiding indirect harm provides a more convincing
affirmative answer to (B) than the interest in equality of opportunity. Regarding (A), both are valuable in accordance with Raz's humanistic principle; but, the argument for the former grounding a right to preferential
treatment possessed by all blacks is much stronger, since it more plausibly incorporates the idea that the mere fact of being black entails suffering indirect harm.

There is another candidate for the interest that might eventually
ground a right to preferential treatment, namely the interest in being
compensated for past harm. The idea is that all blacks, at some point,
have been harmed by racial discrimination. The harm may have been direct or indirect, and the racism overt or institutional. This is, of course, a
departure from the interest in avoiding present harm, and may well be
an even more successful route to take; the claim that all blacks have, at
some point, been negatively affected by racism is quite plausible.[21] Such
was Thurgood Marshall's conviction:

> It is unnecessary in 20th century America to have individual Negroes
> demonstrate that they have been victims of racial discrimination; the racism
> of our society has been so pervasive that none, regardless of wealth or posi-
> tion, has managed to escape its impact."[22]

The core right, then, is a right to receive compensation for past injuries.
Boxill points to this idea when he questions the assumption that persons
who have overcome past injuries no longer have a right to compensation.[23] Since the (plausible) claim is that all blacks have been injured in
this way, all blacks would then have a derivative right to be compensated
for past discrimination specifically.

Therefore, the interest in being compensated for racial discrimination,
regardless of whether the harm has been overcome, is a sound candidate
and requires assessment under (C) and (D). For simplicity, this interest
will be referred to as "past harm." The other will be referred to as "present indirect harm."

Given these two candidate interests, the next task is to address (C), the question of whether AA would be an effective means of attending to the interest in question. To this point, the (as yet conditional) rights are, summarily, rights to compensation generally.[24] In addressing (C), we are addressing the question of whether either can serve as the basis for a derivative right to preferential treatment as a particular form of compensation.

The most obvious problem here is that those blacks who stand to benefit from AA are not those blacks whose interest (be it past harm or present indirect harm) has been compromised most severely. Qualified blacks would benefit, since being qualified for a job is still a necessary condition for being hired under AA. Unqualified blacks would not benefit. It is a reasonable assumption that those who are qualified tend to be those whose interest has been compromised least, and that those who are unqualified tend to be those who suffer (or have suffered) most. As William J. Wilson notes, those black individuals who suffer most from inequality of opportunity, for example, tend to be those who also lack education and job training.[25] Regarding present indirect harm, unqualified blacks are likely to be those who feel the negative effects (fear, lack of self-respect, and so on) most acutely. A similar claim can be made regarding past harm.[26] The suggestion here is not that those who benefit are wholly unentitled, since it has already been granted (in the discussion of [B] above) that the interests of all blacks have been compromised. The suggestion, rather, is that the degree to which the interests of unqualified blacks have been compromised is likely to be much greater than is the case for qualified blacks. Consequently, AA is ineffective in that it establishes a "reverse ratio" between those who have been (or are being) harmed most and those who stand to benefit from AA.[27] An affirmative answer to (C) would require that those whose interest is strongest be benefited by the policy (which is ostensibly intended to provide just this sort of benefit). It is being denied that the policy is effective in this way. In addition, the effect of benefiting those whose interest is comparatively weak further serves to hinder the most disadvantaged. Neither can it be said that the policy provides just the right kind of reparation to those who are in fact benefited; as their interest is relatively weak, they require little in the way of compensation.

To the extent that responses to this criticism deny the existence of the reverse ratio problem, the denial is lukewarm. Ezorsky claims that AA may be able to help even unqualified blacks, provided it is accompanied by other compensatory requirements, such as company training programs or probationary employment periods.[28] More often, the claim is accepted and attempts are made to justify it in some way. James Nickel, for instance, offers an "administrative justification" for AA. Pending consideration of (D), all blacks would have the right to compensation, even if the strength of the right varies on the individual level. Given the plausible claim that a case-by-case analysis of the degree to which the interest has been compromised is impractical, the question becomes what sort of policy would best attend to this right. Nickel contends that, while AA may be imperfect, it is preferable to (more effective than) a race-blind policy; under AA, it is at least the case that some who are so deserving will be compensated, in the form of preferential treatment.[29]

It is far from clear, however, that AA is indeed the best policy from an administrative standpoint. If present indirect harm is the interest in question, then a policy of wealth-based AA (as was suggested in connection with the interest of personal autonomy) appears more plausible than a race-based AA policy; the psychological difficulties and dearth of available opportunities correlate more accurately with those who are poor. This alternative policy can even be restricted to the category of black individuals, such that only poor blacks (as opposed to all poor individuals) would be preferentially considered. If past harm is the interest in question, then similar reasoning can be applied; those who have been harmed most will tend to be those who are poorest, and so a more restrictive policy, which affords benefits to poorer blacks, would be a much more effective means of attending to the interests. Therefore, AA should at least be revamped, or perhaps even rejected in favor of another policy. One such policy may be that of redistributive taxation aimed at benefiting poor black individuals. Regardless, AA in its current form does not appear justified on the basis of either past harm or present indirect harm.

A different objection to the reverse ratio problem questions the assumption that those who are harmed most really are those who would not benefit from AA. According to this claim, the fact that some blacks are more qualified (or, more generally, are better off) has no necessary connection with the degree to which they have been harmed by racism in the past or are currently being (indirectly) harmed by it. Rather, since the harms are solely a function of being black, all blacks are equally harmed. Thus, there is no reverse ratio of benefits and harms.

If this is the case, however, then AA effectively discriminates among blacks, in favor of those who are qualified and against those who are not. Even if all blacks are or have been equally harmed, AA affords advantages to those who are already better off simply because they happen to be better off. The policy is therefore ineffective because it attends to the interests of those who are less needy at the expense of those who are more needy. A possible alternative policy (though still focusing on past harm or present indirect harm as the relevant interest) would be compensation in the form of lump sum cash payments to all blacks. Those who are unqualified would thereby receive assistance in attempting to become qualified, and the qualified, having been equally harmed by racism in this scenario, would also be compensated. Further, cash payments seem to be an acceptable means of compensating victims of wrongdoing in our society. Of course, working out the details would be no small feat, and in accordance with (D), there would remain the question of who would be made to bear the cost, since there is no clear-cut wrongdoer.

In any case, when AA is considered in its current form, an affirmative response to (C) is not found, and the prospect of AA being an effective means of attending to the interest in question appears bleak. This result would effectively negate the existence of a right to preferential treatment.

One more attempt to affirm (C) warrants discussion, however. This attempt centers on the notion of a "group" right to preferential treatment. The idea is that blacks as a group have suffered past harm or are suffering present indirect harm. Unlike formal groups such as corporations or political states, blacks cannot be compensated through any organizational structure. The compensation must therefore be directly to the group's members, black individuals; but this does not mean that the individuals themselves possess the right. It remains a group right.[30] This picture eliminates the requirement of compensating individual blacks according to the degree to which their interests have been compromised, and also makes the problem of arbitrarily discriminating among blacks inapplicable. The right can be satisfied merely by affording advantages to some blacks.

It is not immediately clear just what it means for blacks as a group to have been wronged, or to have an interest in being compensated. It may just mean that all members of the group have been wronged. If this is the case, however, then the "group right" that is alleged to follow is merely a function of individual considerations, and is a product of the fallacy of composition. A more complete explanation than Boxill offers is in order.

One of the better explanations is provided by Will Kymlicka, who describes a culture-based approach to a group right.[31] According to Kymlicka, cultural membership is a good valued by all. A fairly strong cultural structure is necessary for autonomy,[32] since it is only through such a structure that persons can know the range and nature of life options available to them. Minority cultures, simply because they are minority, are forced to work much harder to preserve themselves than are majority cultures; the disadvantage is inherent. Therefore, providing minorities certain advantages is really a way of equalizing cultural stability. Building on this base, it need only be added that AA, being an effective means of preserving the African-American culture, ought to be one such advantage.

This sort of group right is not altogether implausible on the interest-based theory. A cultural group could count as an "artificial person" in

Raz's theory and thus be capable of possessing rights.[33] Furthermore, Raz himself devotes substantial time and space to the societal conditions that must obtain if personal autonomy is to be had. As a foundation for Boxill's group right, however, this will not do. First, Kymlicka views cultural stability as a means toward the end of ensuring the autonomy of the individual members of the culture. It is therefore autonomy (or, with minor adjustments, personal autonomy) doing the moral work in the analysis. Boxill's group right argument is thus reducible to the individual rights of the members of the group—rights to the conditions of personal autonomy generally, or, more specifically, to a strong cultural framework (which, for Kymlicka and also Raz, is a necessary condition for personal autonomy).

This problem aside, it is highly questionable whether blacks would constitute a culture in the sense necessary to possess any group rights. Kymlicka employs the example of the Inuit, a Canadian Indian tribe completely separated from the rest of society. Its culture is thus very well-defined, and its demise would indeed have immediate consequences for its members. That which associates all blacks in the United States as being in the same cultural group, however, is elusive. Alvin Goldman points to this problem, citing the requirement of actual interaction among members if the group is to have this sort of morally relevant status.[34] Although Boxill appropriately responds that common ideals or values may also serve to define a cultural group,[35] these, too, are missing in the case of most African-Americans. Were there a black culture that was needed by most members for their sense of identity, an analogue of Kymlicka's description of the Inuit might obtain. The claim is that the conditions for there being such an analogue are not met.

The appropriate conclusion is that the group right approach fails, and thus no plausible means of affirmatively responding to (C) can be found. What this means is that while all blacks may have various rights, based on past or present racism or the effects thereof (perhaps even rights to compensation), a right to preferential treatment cannot be established as a derivative of any of these. A social policy of required AA is therefore not justified on the interest-based theory of rights. Even so, exploring whether an affirmative answer to (D) can be found will help to determine the strength of this conclusion, and may provide some insight into which of the other policy options—permissible AA or required race-neutral hiring—is supported by the interest-based theory.

One competing factor may be the right of employers to hire the applicants of their choosing.[36] The right is a specific privilege and is a derivative of the more general core right to liberty, which may be grounded in a number of ways. For our purposes it is unimportant whether the employer is to be understood in a group or individual sense. The former is compatible with the interest-based theory, since Raz cites the corporation as an explicit example of an "artificial person" that may possess rights. The right may also be possessed by the individual (or individuals) who is, effectively, "the employer."

Whatever the details of how this right to "liberty of hiring" is grounded, it (like other derivatives of the right to liberty) is not to be taken lightly. It is not, however, absolute. While there has been much debate over the conditions that must obtain if liberty is to be overridden, it is widely agreed that prevention of harm to others is a legitimate justification for such limitation. It should therefore be clear that when present indirect harm is utilized as the relevant interest, it is likely to withstand the challenge of the employer's liberty interest. This consideration is what grounds the prohibition on overt discrimination in hiring, for example. It is also relevant in addressing institutional racism. The harm caused by unchecked hiring need not be intentional to be morally relevant. Neither must it be "direct" in the sense implied by Goldman, who maintains that "indirect psychological pressures," unlike instances of direct harm, are not morally germane.[37]

If, however, the interest in question is compensation for past discrimination, the case is not so clear. If the employer is not responsible for the past harm, there are questions of whether an imposed cost, in the form of compromised liberty of hiring, is appropriate. It is commonly thought that a necessary aspect of compensatory justice is that only the wrongdoer can be required to compensate the victim.[38] Assessing responsibility for past wrongs to blacks is difficult in any case, but especially so for employers. Can AT&T in its current 1990s form be held responsible for the discriminatory hiring practices of AT&T in the 1940s, even though no AT&T employees (executives or otherwise) remain from that era? Addressing this sort of question would require a more detailed investigation into the issue of artificial persons as potential rightholders in the interest-based theory. Rather than proceed down that path, I propose to bypass the matter of whether an employer "hiring liberty" overrides a right to preferential treatment based on past harm. The right (which, again, is being referred to conditionally, since the analysis of [C] rendered it unjustified) has already been seen to hold up against the employer liberty when based on the interest of present indirect harm. Allowing, then, that an employer's "hiring liberty" does not constitute an overriding moral consideration, we should proceed to another possible difficulty.

One of the more frequent objections to required AA is that it would unjustly violate the rights of those who would be adversely affected by such a policy. Typically, the rights of white persons are referred to in this context, and since we are focusing on black individuals as the beneficiaries of AA, referring to the competing rights of whites is an appropriate allowance.

It should perhaps be made clear that there is indeed a competing right that warrants attention. It is sometimes claimed that there is none, since no one can claim a right to any particular job. Boxill thus contends that AA proposes to "compensate the injured with goods no one has yet established a right to."[39] Even Dworkin appears to make this point. In discussing the Bakke case,[40] he examines possible rights to be judged on merit, to be judged as an individual, and not to be "sacrificed" on the basis of race—all of which are candidates for rights held by Bakke that may have been violated by the University of California's preferential admissions policy—and finds none of them plausible.[41]

However, none of these is the competing moral factor to be examined, which is what may be called a right to equal consideration, or equal treatment,[42] and has at times been referred to as a right to equal concern and respect.[43] It is, essentially, the right not to be discriminated against in the process of applying for jobs (or in the context of other formal procedures regarding life opportunities[44]), the right, in the case of black persons, that had been so frequently violated over such a long period of time. Dworkin, in his remarks, was focusing more specifically on constitutional rights rather than on moral rights, and Boxill may be correct that no one has a right to any particular job; however, if that were the only point of consideration, then discrimination would appear to violate no rights. The right to equal consideration presents a formidable challenge to the right to preferential treatment.

Attempts to discount this competing right to equal consideration can be made on several levels. Most basically, it may be claimed that whites are responsible for harm perpetuated against blacks, past and present. Whether whites are aware of the harm they are inflicting is irrelevant; what matters is that racism is harmful whether the racism is overt or institutional (not intentionally inflicted). Even if the harm is unintentionally perpetrated, and the racism is "merely" institutional, a charge of negligence can be leveled against whites, and such a charge is sufficient to ground compensatory payments. The result is that the competing right to equal consideration is softened to the point where the right to preferential treatment prevails.

The principle on which such an argument is based is sound; it accords with the moral requirement (if it is a requirement) that those made to bear the cost of compensation must also be responsible for the harm. The problem, rather, is an empirical one. It is implausible to think that all whites (or even most) are responsible, even inadvertently, for the discriminatory harm suffered by blacks. Some are no doubt guilty of engaging in the most overt acts of racism, including—but not limited to—the context of employment; but even Ezorsky, a strong proponent of required AA, claims that disentangling the guilty whites from those who are innocent is a practical impossibility, and that this attempt to soften the right to equal consideration (based on whites being responsible for the plight of blacks) fails.[45]

On another level, it may be claimed that all whites, while perhaps not responsible, have benefited from the effects of racism. The advantages of being white in contemporary American society, while perhaps not unjustly obtained (in the sense of wronging blacks), were unfairly acquired. This argument, too, applies to both interests (past harm and present indirect harm) as justifications for the right to preferential treatment. Whites have profited from discrimination practiced in the past, and continue to profit from present indirect harm suffered by blacks. In the former case, whites have garnered jobs that in a just society would have gone to blacks, and in the latter case whites continue to benefit psychologically, confident in their "full membership" in the community, a foundation of which is racist discrimination.[46]

There are two problems with this sort of approach to diluting the strength of the right of whites to equal consideration. The first is again empirical. Can it really be said that all whites have benefited in this way? If not, then AA would effectively compel some to bear the cost of compensation unjustly.[47] It seems more likely that whites who are already well-off and have comfortable jobs are the ones who have benefited, and that (predominantly younger) whites who are in the process of attempting to launch their careers or even find a first job are the ones who bear the brunt of AA.[48] If so, then another "reverse ratio" problem arises, this time between those whites who have benefited and those who will pay for the compensation. Further, there is evidence to suggest that a fair number of whites not only have failed to benefit, but have also suffered from the effects of racism. The willingness of blacks in the 1960s to accept inferior wages and working conditions, for example, effectively decreased the conditions for all workers and took jobs from some whites.[49] Thus, the claim that all whites have benefited from discrimination against blacks is suspect.

The other premise, the claim that having benefited from racism justifies being made to pay compensation, may also be questioned. Robert Fullinwinder points to the example of a construction company mistakenly paving A's driveway instead of B's.[50] A has benefited and B has lost out, but it hardly seems plausible that B is therefore justified in exacting some sort of compensation from A. The intuition suggested by Fullinwinder accords with the so-called "principle of fairness," according to which moral duties owed to others (and therefore perhaps correlative rights held against the duty-bearers) can be based on what is perceived to be fair.[51] The idea is that merely receiving a benefit, as opposed to voluntarily accepting it, cannot warrant compensatory payment. Traditional examples come to mind, such as the windshield washers at stoplights, who attend to cars before the drivers have a chance to decline, and then demand payment for their services. Further, even if the benefit is accepted voluntarily, coerced compensation may still be unjustified if it is not consented to.[52] On both counts, then, the "benefit" argument for the right to preferential treatment overriding the right to equal consideration is lacking.[53]

A third approach, if successful, would evade these criticisms. The idea is that whites are able to bear the cost of compensating blacks for past injustices (or present indirect harm), and exacting payment from them is therefore justified. On this approach there is no need to establish either any responsibility for the harm or any benefit that may have been incurred as a result. It is, more generally, an "ability to pay" argument, similar to the one endorsed in the previous chapter that justified the policy of moderate redistributive taxation.

Challenges to this third strategy, like the others, begin with empirical considerations. It can be objected that it is certainly not the case that all whites can pay. In the last chapter, a premise was that the rich could afford the reduction in personal autonomy, the interest grounding the right to retain control over one's property. If personal autonomy is the interest grounding the right to equal consideration, then poor whites are not in a position to have any portion of their personal autonomy seized. The assumption made in the last chapter was that anyone with a moderately high level of wealth enjoyed a moderately high level of personal autonomy, and thus anyone who was well-off could afford a reduction (in the form of taxation). In the present case, the assumption would have to be that anyone who is white enjoys a moderately high level of personal autonomy and can therefore afford the reduction, but this assumption is much more problematic. Of course, an interest other than that of personal autonomy may be employed as the ground for the right to equal consideration, but a different interest will not change the conclusion that the ability to pay among whites is not universal.

Assuming, however, that this problem could be overcome, and granting the other necessary assumptions (of which there are now several), it may be asked whether a policy of required AA, based on a right to preferential treatment, can be supported on the basis that whites, being able to pay the costs of compensation, should be required to pay. In other words, if all other considerations are put aside, how well does the right to preferential treatment withstand a head-to-head challenge from the right to equal consideration? Answering this question requires assessments of the moral weights of the interests on which the rights are based. The right to preferential treatment, we have said, may be based on two possible interests: compensation for past discrimination, or for present indirect harm suffered as a result of past and/or present discrimination. The right to equal consideration, we have said, may be based on the interest of personal autonomy.

Pitting first the interest of past harm against personal autonomy, the result is that the latter wins out. This is because the interest in being compensated for past injustice, in itself, is simply not as strong as one may at first think. Recall that Boxill prefers this interest because it satisfies the condition of universally applying to all blacks, and (more or less) to the same degree. His dispute was with the claim that "just because a person has overcome his injury, he no longer has a right to compensation."[54] This (prima facie) right was granted on the basis of Aristotelian corrective justice; until the wrongful act executed by the wrongdoer against the victim has been properly "equalized" in accordance with justice, the injustice remains, regardless of whether the subsequent advantage and disadvantage remains. But the party against whom this (prima facie) right is held is the perpetrator of the injustice, the violator of the victim's rights. The right is not held against "innocent bystanders."[55] Any case made for such a right held against innocent bystanders could not be justified. The very meaning of "compensation" breaks down when applied to a payment made by an innocent party simply because he is able to afford the cost. For the victim, a certain "equalization" has occurred; for the reluctant benefactor, however, things are now unequal.[56] As the injury may well have been fully overcome, the benefit incurred by the rightholder is mild and is inferior to the cost incurred by the bystander, even if some degree of reduction in personal autonomy can be afforded.

If, however, the injury has not fully been overcome, then the interest grounding the right to preferential treatment pertains to the present rather than the past. In other words, when present indirect harm (suffered by blacks) is stacked up against personal autonomy (of whites), a different result is likely to obtain. This is because (somewhat paradoxically perhaps) the sort of present indirect harm under consideration affects blacks much more directly than the mere failure to be compensated for past harm. In the case of redistributive taxation, property rights were pitted against autonomy rights. The conclusion was that those who can afford some reduction in personal autonomy, simply because they can afford it, may justifiably be relieved of some personal autonomy when the alternative would have severely detrimental consequences for others. In that discussion, both rights were based on the same interest (personal autonomy), and the analysis was thus somewhat less difficult. Even so, that analysis can be instructive for the current project of comparing a right to preferential treatment based on present indirect harm with a right to equal consideration based on personal autonomy. It does seem that some loss of personal autonomy for whites, in the form of diminished opportunities because of favoritism toward blacks in hiring decisions, would be justified when the alternative would have severely detrimental consequences for blacks. That such consequences would follow is reasonable. The present harm generated by racism (even institutional racism), though "indirect," is real. This has been granted. The general environmental conditions resulting from continued racism, while not devastating, are undeniably harmful. When compared to the cost of losing some personal autonomy, the conclusion must be that the right to equal consideration is overridden by the right to preferential treatment.

To this point, however, only one interest has been examined as the ground for the competing right to equal consideration. Could there be another? The right to equal consideration includes the right not to be discriminated against. Rephrased, the question might be whether this latter right can be violated even when personal autonomy is retained; if so, then some other value is serving as the foundational interest for the right.

The above question can be answered affirmatively. We can imagine a black individual who, for example, is discriminated against when inquiring about a certain piece of property that is for sale, the result being that he is never seriously in the running for the property. Now this may be of very little consequence to him; he may have many other options, and may view them as superior anyway. The effect on his personal autonomy would then be negligible. But it seems clear that a wrong has been done to him nonetheless, and it seems quite reasonable to express this wrong by saying that his rights have been violated, in particular his right not to be discriminated against. If this is correct, then what interest is grounding the right? Assigning a label is difficult. We might simply call it "equality," though the content is complex. The wrong done to the individual is that he is not treated as a "person" in the morally relevant sense; he is not treated as an "end in himself."[57] Despite the Kantian language, we might assert an interest in being treated as a person, which entails being treated as an equal and not being discriminated against. On this analysis, the abhorrence of the racial discrimination that has existed throughout the past several centuries has its source not so much in its denial of opportunities (or reduction of personal autonomy) per se, but in the violation of this new interest, "equality" as we are calling it, and the right to equal consideration that it grounds. Discrimination is despicable because it is the intentional practice of treating equals as unequals; the resulting depletion of opportunities (personal autonomy) is clear reason for additional condemnation but is not the source of the fundamental objection to it.

This interest may serve as the basis for the right to equal consideration possessed by whites that would be violated by required AA. This would amount to a right not to be made use of by others; for whites, it is a right not to be made to bear the cost of compensation simply because they are able to. This right, being based on the same interest that was continually violated by abhorrent racist practices, is substantial, and while linguistically capturing its content is not easy, its strength appears capable of overriding a right to preferential treatment.

Still, it may be objected that appropriating the property of the well-off (by levying disproportionate taxes) looks like another instance of violating this right, yet that practice was found to be justified on the interest-based theory. If there are no relevant differences between the two cases, it would follow that required AA would be justifiable as well. A relevant difference, though, is the following. When a person is relieved of a portion of his wealth, no specific good is taken from him. The loss might entail a deprivation of some luxuries, or less flexibility in the nature of one's preferences, but such losses are not personal in nature. However, when the deprivation is in the form of a specific career opportunity, the loss is personal. The career path a person chooses is a part of him in a way that money is not. While ineptitude or lack of merit may be legitimate grounds for prohibiting the pursuit of a particular job, the "ability to pay" (since the deprived individual is sufficiently competent to seek other careers) does not seem a legitimate constraint. With some (significant) allowances, it is analogous to the case of my wife, the woman of my dreams, being taken from me—or at least to my being deprived equal courting opportunity—simply on the basis of my ability to attract another spouse.[58] I do not want another spouse; spouses, unlike dollars, are not qualitatively identical and thus are not freely interchangeable. Neither are jobs.

This response also counters the suggestion, made by Ezorsky, that whites ought to bear the cost of AA but should then be compensated. Ezorsky contends that there is no way around the conclusion that the rights of (at least some) whites are violated by AA programs. The problem, she suggests, can be addressed by monetarily compensating those whites who are in fact adversely affected by the policy.[59] Ezorsky's proposal is problematic, however, not only because of the nonsubstitutability of jobs and dollars, but also because of the administrative difficulties associated with determining which whites have lost (and which have not) on account of AA. Further, the identities of these individuals become evident, creating undesirable situations.

The conclusion must be that on the interest-based theory, a right to preferential treatment cannot be justified, and thus neither can required AA. The argument to the contrary breaks down at several points. First, the interests of past harm and present indirect harm, while applicable to all blacks, cannot ground rights to preferential treatment specifically (although they could, pending further analysis, ground rights to some other form of compensation). Second, it is not the case that all whites are able to afford the cost. Third, the right to preferential treatment, when based on the interest of past harm, is overridden by the competing right to equal consideration; and the interest of present indirect harm suffers a similar fate, once it is realized that the interest of equality grounds equal consideration. Although several problems have been identified, only one suffices to deflect the argument for the right to preferential treatment, and thus required AA.

The possibility of permissible AA, though, remains open. If it is to be justified within the framework of the interest-based theory of rights, it must be the rights of the employer to which the appeal is made. The interest in liberty per se (that is, the interest in hiring exactly the person desired by the employer) has been found to be insufficient as a ground, due to the unwarranted leeway the right would grant (including the real possibility of legitimizing discriminatory hiring practices). Instead, we might look to an interest in creating a certain kind of workplace environment. It is reasonable, for example, that employers might view diversity as a good, and to that end may wish to take race into account when hiring. This principle is utilized by colleges and universities. Having an interest in maintaining a diverse student body, academic institutions take a variety of factors into account in the admissions process, including geography and extracurricular interests, not to mention gender and race. The interest seems legitimate, and without going into the details, admissions policies that are not strictly race-neutral appear to be morally permissible as a right of the institution.

However, two observations are in order. First, such policies do not fall under the guise of race-based affirmative action, any more than that of gender-based, geography-based, or extracurricular-based (high school newspaper-based?) affirmative action. Rather, race may be considered as one factor among several. Second, these same considerations cannot necessarily be extended to the employment context. Colleges have strong reasons for wanting to maintain diversity. Their main goal is education, the scope of which reaches beyond the classroom, and exposure to a diverse student body is seen by administrators as an integral part of "training young people for a multicultural habitat."[60] Thus, at the undergraduate level, admissions policies that deviate slightly from a strict race-neutrality standard are not unjustified.

However, in the workplace (and for that matter even at the graduate school level) such education is not the goal. Departures from race-neutral standards in hiring cannot therefore be similarly defended.[61] The result is that the rights of employers to initiate their own AA programs cannot override the rights of individual applicants to equal consideration. Exceptions will be rare, but not altogether absent. To take a most obvious example, the National Association for the Advancement of Colored People may have a well-founded interest in preferring black applicants. Such cases must be carefully scrutinized, however; a company may not prefer white applicants on the basis of higher projected sales to a (clearly racist) clientele, regardless of the accuracy of such projections.

Overall, then, a race-neutral hiring policy (with few exceptions) follows from the interest-based theory of rights. Whenever rights claims are made in this context, with interests as the moral ground, AA cannot be defended as a justifiable social policy.

6.3 Rights of Affirmative Action: The Goal-Based Theory

In the case of affirmative action, the decision of which goal to pursue should not be extremely difficult. It may, however, seem an initial worry. While those on both sides of the debate harbor ideals that on the surface appear very similar, disparities become evident after unpacking the underlying meanings.

We might, for example, take the ideal of equality of opportunity as the goal. Proponents of AA embrace equality; it is precisely because blacks lack equality of opportunity, they claim, that preferential hiring policies are justified. Of course, critics of AA also point to equality of opportunity in defending their position. The meaning they ascribe to equality of opportunity is more closely aligned with "equal consideration" (as described in the previous section), which is incompatible with preferential hiring. So this goal, in itself, will not do; while both camps may initially seem to agree to it, they would in reality be agreeing to very different aims.

These worries can be eased if we adopt the goal of achieving a race-neutral, or "color-blind," society. There is general agreement that racism is not to be tolerated, and that ridding society of its grip (and its effects) is desirable. The goal of eliminating racism, or achieving a "color-blind" society, would seem to pose no difficulties for those on either side of the debate. Skin color, which in theory is as morally irrelevant as eye color, ought to be just as irrelevant in practice.

The question, then, is whether AA hiring policies or race-neutral hiring policies would best achieve this goal. It may seem, straightforwardly, that if race-neutrality is the goal, race-neutrality ought to be the practice. But even on a direct cost/benefit analysis this is not necessarily the case. Doubtless there are AA factors that can reasonably be projected as positively contributing to the achievement of the goal, but there are also others that can be projected as negatively contributing to it. A review of these considerations is in order. The ensuing question will then be whether there are reasons for thinking that constraints on the direct pursuit of the goal are in order.

One factor apparently contributing to the AA position is the ongoing frequency and strength with which racism continues to be practiced. The frequency of the overt variety may be declining, but institutional racism, according to the argument, is so strongly ingrained in contemporary society that it can only be overcome through AA policies. This racism can take several forms, one of which is the method of hiring through personal connections. As of 1990, it was estimated that over 80% of executive-level positions were still being filled through a "networking" process.[62] Since these sorts of positions continue to be disproportionately held by whites, and since whites have the tendency (at least statistically) to network with other whites, the discriminatory effect on blacks is substantial.[63] Race-neutral hiring practices, it is argued, cannot overcome the severity of the problem. A second form of institutional racism is the race-neutral seniority systems used when decisions regarding promotions or layoffs must be made. Seniority-based preference systems, though "fair in form," are alleged to be "discriminatory in operation." They have tended to predominantly benefit whites at the expense of blacks, since in most instances whites have been hired ahead of blacks and thus enjoy more seniority.[64] The only way to break these sorts of cycles, according to the argument, is to implement a policy that affords advantages to blacks in the form of preferential treatment. Since AA would be a more effective means of achieving the goal of a race-neutral society, this consideration favors rights to preferential treatment over rights to equal consideration.

Another asset on AA's accounting ledger is found in the foreseeable "trickle-down" benefits the policy may have. For example, by placing representative numbers of blacks in quality positions, society can ensure that younger generations of blacks have role models. Black youths can grow up believing their opportunities are not diminished on account of race. The presence of role models can serve as a positive motivational factor for youths considering the additional education necessary to compete for quality positions in desirable professions.[65] In addition, increasing the number of blacks practicing law or medicine, to take two examples, is likely to help narrow the socioeconomic gap between the races by producing beneficial consequences for poor blacks. Black graduates of law school or medical school are more likely than white graduates to work in inner-city areas and aid the needy members of their own race. If the white applicant who would otherwise have been accepted to these schools would have ended up catering to affluent white neighborhoods, then the gap between the races would remain and even increase.[66] Of course, it is not the fact of a net decrease in overall suffering that, in the present analysis, is a positive consideration for AA; the goal is not that of general utilitarian happiness. The claim, rather, is that greater socio-economic parity would positively impact the pursuit of race-neutrality, since the effects of discrimination would be eased.

An associated consideration is the self-confidence of blacks, which is harmed by the effects of racism. The claim is that racism results in diminished opportunities for blacks, which in turn results in their having less self-esteem and self-respect than their white counterparts. The circle is completed when this effect disinclines blacks to pursue opportunities (in education, and ultimately in employment) that would enable them to compete for quality jobs currently held by whites. Thus, even when racism itself is removed, a self-fulfilling prophecy is left in its wake.[67] The result is continued disproportionate representation in such jobs, and thus no race-neutrality. AA, it is argued, breaks the circle by reinstating self-confidence. It may be objected that reduced self-confidence does not actually lead to reduced opportunities, and that the vicious circle described above is therefore a mirage. Reduced self-confidence may make pursuit of opportunities harder, but it does not actually reduce those opportunities.[68] This protest can be easily countered, however, by providing evidence that a correlation between self-confidence and available options does exist (and that the former, furthermore, causally influences the latter).

So, there are a number of potentially positive factors that should be taken into consideration in a direct cost/benefit analysis of AA. There are, however, several reasons for doubting AA as a superior means of achieving the goal of race-neutrality, beginning with a different sort of objection to the above claims regarding self-confidence. Rather than focusing on the connection between self-confidence and opportunities, one might focus on the connection between AA and self-confidence. Thomas Sowell takes this approach, and he reaches the conclusion that an effect of AA is that the advancements of blacks in the workplace (such as hirings, raises, and promotions) come to be viewed by the beneficiaries as suspect, as mandated entitlements rather than earned accomplishments.[69] When AA is in place, this possibility is always present, and blacks consequently come to doubt their abilities. This self-doubt affects all blacks, even those who would have attained their achievements without AA, since they can never be sure they have not benefited.[70] Again, the goal is not that of maximum self-confidence, but if blacks suffer in this way more significantly than whites, the effects are likely to hinder the achievement of race-neutrality.

Along the same lines, it may be argued that the negative effects on those disadvantaged by AA constitute a significant strike against the policy's effectiveness in achieving race-neutrality. At a minimum, it is claimed, the knowledge of being denied equal consideration causes whites to feel resentment toward blacks.[71] Since this strengthens race-consciousness, it is enough to hinder race-neutrality, but the resentment may well grow into more of a problem. It may reinforce racial prejudice in those who already harbor such tendencies, and in those who haven't it may cause prejudice to arise. Such feelings may not only be a function of increasing resentment, but may result from interpreting AA as being the only way that blacks can achieve parity with whites, a view that results in what Barry Gross expresses as the "permanent conferral of inferior status" on blacks.[72] A third-level reaction on the part of whites may be violence. Demonstrations on college campuses and even in the workplace can have dramatically negative results, and the ensuing consequence of reinforcement of racial identities obviously runs counter to our stated goal.[73] The claim that such reactions are impermissible and warrant social condemnation, although plausible, is irrelevant to the goal-based theory's application to AA in itself; so long as considerations of human nature support a certain possibility of such reactions, that possibility must enter into the calculations.

There is one other consideration that, although it will turn out not to be pertinent, is frequently discussed and so should at least be mentioned. It is often claimed that AA decreases overall societal efficiency, and so must be rejected by any forward-looking moral theory.[74] The argument is that required AA necessarily results in the hiring of less-qualified applicants, and when this occurs across a range of professions, society is worse off than it otherwise would be. But two things can be said about this concern. First, it is not clear that a reduction in efficiency does follow from required AA. The policy, recall, does not mandate hiring unqualified applicants, a fact that some writers tend to forget.[75] Of course, on those occasions when employees may be called on to carry out responsibilities above and beyond those required of the specific job, having the best qualified candidate in place would be beneficial. Corresponding gains in efficiency are likely to be minimal, though, and the positive trickle-down effects of AA, discussed above, may cast doubt on those gains altogether. Second, there is no apparent connection between efficiency and race-neutrality anyway. While it is a clear factor in utilitarian calculations of happiness, efficiency's effects on race-neutrality, if any, are negligible. It would thus be best not to include this consideration in the calculations.

To review, in the cost/benefit analysis of factors bearing on the goal of race-neutrality, several factors have been claimed as benefits. The first is the strong degree of institutional racism, a substantial hindrance to the goal, but one that can be overcome much more effectively by implementing AA. Second, there are so-called "trickle-down" benefits. The increased number of blacks in desirable positions would not only provide role models for black youths (and ultimately produce proportionate representation in those jobs), but would also contribute to greater overall socioeconomic equality. Third, AA is claimed to have positive psychological benefits for blacks in the form of restored self-confidence, which had been lost as a result of racist discrimination. On the other side of the ledger, the cost of alienating whites and the potential for increased racism must be taken into account, along with the claim that AA is in reality damaging to the self-confidence of blacks.

And these are not the only considerations. The number and variety of factors make a straightforward conclusion from a cost/benefit analysis an impossibility. This is not like the case of redistributive taxation, in which the principle of diminishing marginal returns of freedom entailed a theoretically clear result of the analysis. In the present case, too many complexities are involved. It would be of some help if the general effect of preferential treatment on the self-confidence of blacks could be assessed, since both sides claim this consideration as a point in their favor. Studies, though, have yielded conflicting results even on this score.

The suggestion here will be that it is unnecessary to determine which policy is more strongly recommended by the direct analysis. It dictates that AA either ought or ought not be adopted. If it is the former, then it will turn out that there are indirect considerations negating it. In other words, there are reasons for thinking that constraining the pursuit of the goal (by not affording rights to preferential treatment) would, in the long run, lead to a more successful attainment of the goal. Recall L. W. Sumner's reasoning for thinking such constraints might be in order. His worry was that we are fallible gatherers and processors of information, and that results of any direct cost/benefit analysis are therefore suspect. Along these lines there are several reasons for thinking that constraints ought to be implemented when required AA is, on the direct approach, thought to be the superior policy. First, the direct analysis prescribing AA makes use of the assumption that racial discrimination is ongoing. The fact of significant continued discrimination is generally accepted as straightforward; any challenge seems doomed. The question of just how the existence of discrimination is detectable, though, is relevant not only to the present but to the future as well. AA is designed to be a temporary solution to the problem of racism; once the goal of race-neutrality is achieved, its instrumental utility will cease. It is therefore necessary to have some way of knowing when the goal is reached. Implicit in the above discussion of factors in the direct cost/benefit analysis favorable to AA is the assumption that statistical parity is the relevant standard: If blacks do not enjoy proportionate representation in quality professions, then discrimination is presumed to be ongoing.

This assumption of a necessary connection between discrimination and statistical representation may be challenged. Redescribed, the supposition made by AA advocates is that were it not for discrimination, blacks would be proportionately represented across society. Knowing that this is the case is an impossibility; such calculations are well beyond anyone's abilities. Yet the (justifiable) observation that discrimination entails disproportionate representation has been, and continues to be, used as justification for its converse—that disparity entails discrimination. Further, sociological evidence suggests that, discrimination aside, uneven representation across racial, ethnic and cultural groups is the norm. According to Myron Weiner, "All multi-ethnic societies exhibit a tendency for ethnic groups to engage in different occupations, have different levels (and often types) of education, receive different incomes, and occupy a different place in the social hierarchy."[76] The notion of race-neutrality cannot entail proportionate representation. Such a standard is too severe. Consistent reasoning would point to the existence of discrimination based on hair color. The goal of race-neutrality must not be understood as outcome-based.

Of course, a case of dramatic disparity is strong prima facie evidence for the existence of discrimination. But current (and certainly future) statistical evidence is not "dramatic," especially when compared to mid-twentieth century statistics.[77] The current suggestion might be enhanced if some alternative explanation for the disparity could be put forth. One possibility might be age. Trends across the board indicate a positive correlation between age and income, which should be wholly unsurprising. The average age of black wage-earners is less than the average age of white wage-earners by roughly a decade.[78] It would follow that the average black income would be quite a bit less than the average white income. Another explanation might pertain to culture. Asians, for example, are disproportionately represented in science and engineering careers, a fact that can be traced to their statistically superior performance in mathematics and science classes.[79] Other possibilities that have been suggested include the desirability of attaining high-level jobs[80] and the manner in which individuals of different ethnic groups go about their work.[81] Some of these explanations perhaps warrant the criticism that they employ bias or stereotypes, and thus some are likely to be viewed as less acceptable than others. But no specific alternative explanation is needed in order to make the point, which is to question the assumption of a necessary connection between statistical disparity and discrimination. The burden of proof is certainly on those who limit the possible explanations of disparity to either discrimination or random accident (and then rule out the latter).

The claim, therefore, is that the knowledge upon which assertions of discrimination are made is imperfect, and when such assertions are improperly made as a result, the goal will be severely hindered, even if such errors are infrequent. The otherwise appropriate prescription—of recognizing rights to equal consideration as the superior means to achieving the goal—would be compromised for no good reason.

A second reason for thinking that constraining pursuit of the goal by not affording to minorities rights to preferential consideration pertains to the idea that AA is necessary if racism is to be overcome (and race-neutrality achieved) within a reasonable time period. The claim in the cost/benefit analysis was that the ongoing existence of discrimination, and the degree to which it has become entrenched in our society, make the attainment of the goal virtually impossible without the implementation of some positive steps (i.e., without some "affirmative action"). However, examination of the trends prior to the implementation of AA do not bear this out. Despite the fact that blacks were immeasurably behind the rest of society a hundred years ago in terms of socioeconomic status, gains were made, even in the face of appalling overt discrimination and deliberately erected barriers. The progress was, understandably, slow at first, but it continued to accelerate as the twentieth century wore on, and by the 1960s the velocity in gains had reached an all-time high.[82] As Richard Freeman wrote in 1973, "While black-white differences have not disappeared, the convergence in economic position in the fifties and sixties suggests a virtual collapse in traditional discriminatory patterns in the labor market."[83]

If discrimination causes socioeconomic disparity, then decreasing disparity is prima facie indication of decreasing discrimination, as well as of positive movement toward the goal of race-neutrality. These facts therefore contradict the idea that without the implementation of positive steps designed to increase the standing of blacks, progress would stall, and race-neutrality would be an impossibility.

Perhaps the claim that AA is necessary for the attainment of the goal (within a reasonable time period at least) is too strong, and the claim is not, in fact, underlying the considerations of the cost/benefit analysis. More modestly, so long as AA is a superior means of achieving the goal, it appears to be justified on the goal-based theory of rights. The question, then, is whether AA does, in fact, facilitate the achievement of race-neutrality more effectively and efficiently. If it were indeed superior, then we would expect to see an increase over the rate of improvement that obtained prior to the implementation of the policy. However, this was not the case. Taking 1971 as the starting date for AA,[84] the overall economic advances for blacks as a group seemed to slow considerably at that point. The best-educated and most experienced blacks continued to make inroads into the ranks of professional and high-level occupations, but at a rate less than had been the case during the previous decade.[85] Meanwhile, the status of the most disadvantaged blacks began to retrogress shortly afterward, a phenomenon unknown during previous years.[86]

We might speculate on the reasons for these results, although again, specifying the actual causal factors is unnecessary; citing the evidence is enough to cast doubt on the claim that the goal of race-neutrality is more effectively achieved with AA than without it. One possibility is that the result of AA discriminating within the class of blacks (as proposed in section 6.2) really does occur. The claim was made that the most disadvantaged blacks are not helped and are in fact harmed by the policy. In the context of the goal-based theory, if (as the evidence suggests) the decline of the most disadvantaged blacks, contemporaneous with the implementation of AA, occurs with no rate of change in the improvement in the status of the most advantaged blacks, then the overall effect will be negative.

A second possible explanation for these results has been advanced by Charles Murray, who describes a perhaps frequent chain of events that may occur in educational and employment contexts alike.[87] By its nature, AA induces companies to hire according to different applicant pools, and the "goals and timetables" aspect of AA means that a certain percentage of the black pool must be hired. This does not necessitate the hiring of unqualified persons; due to the gap in education and abilities caused by generations of racism, however, those blacks who are hired tend, statistically, to be among the least qualified of all of those hired. One result is that tremendous pressure is put on blacks to keep up with the rest of the group. When disparities in abilities begin to emerge, the practice of "opting out" of the competition game has become a popular method of coping; the response is often to simply stop putting forth much effort. Another result is that employers are hesitant to push the less qualified as hard as they do others; not only must those employees' major difficulties be addressed (and thus minor ones go unchecked), but the pressure to get blacks through to the next rung on the corporate ladder (or to the degree in education) motivates the employers (or teachers) to tolerate more errors from this group, and thus, intentionally or not, a different standard is effectively set. The problem is that those who achieve on lesser standards tend to be hurt in the long run, since others are achieving against higher standards. According to Murray, for those blacks who are pushed through the process and receive several promotions as a result of AA, the observation tends to be that they are "bright but unspectacular" employees, and an unfortunate perception emerges: Many blacks who have achieved are simply commodities. Murray refers to this phenomenon as the "mascot syndrome."[88]

Speculation on the precise reasons for the negative impact of AA on race-neutrality could continue indefinitely. It may simply be the case that the best we can do in the way of achieving race-neutrality is to continue the moral education that began in earnest in the 1950s and 1960s. As Ezorsky and others have pointed out, the racist attitudes harbored against blacks are deeply felt and widely held. However, this might be a reason for thinking that such feelings cannot be overcome through any such policy as AA. Once a racist attitude is adopted, expelling it is difficult if not impossible. It may just take several generations to reach the goal, with each new generation clinging to racism less widely and less deeply. If there is such a natural limit on the velocity with which the goal of race-neutrality can be approached, the belief that AA or any other social policy can be effective is illusory. Again, continuing to point out the moral irrelevance of skin color—the approach taken by many civil rights leaders in the 1950s and 1960s—might just be the most effective way of achieving a race-neutral society; it would certainly explain the difference in the rate of improvement for blacks prior to, and after, the implementation of AA.

There is one other factor that lends credence to the suggestion that rights to equal consideration (rather than rights to preferential treatment), even if uncalled for on the direct cost/benefit analysis, ought to be protected as a constraint. This factor pertains to the alleged control society has over the scope of the policy. First, all sides agree that AA was designed to be a temporary solution. (The idea that some are to be permanently preferred because of skin color is, of course, indefensible.) The problem is knowing when the temporary period has ended. Neither a specific time constraint nor a specific social goal has been put forth as the marker. With a general goal, such as that of race-neutrality, the policy is apt to continue indefinitely, as disputes over whether the goal has indeed been achieved are inevitable. Such problems ultimately hinder the goal. Second, the scope of those benefiting from the policy, though initially confined to blacks, now encompasses enough minorities to include roughly two-thirds of the population. Again, though not originally foreseen by the framers of the policy, the result has been an inability to maintain control. Third, the nature of the benefit has expanded as well. Although the "affirmative action" referred to by Presidents Kennedy and Johnson was not of the numerical variety, by 1971 the policy had taken on a form neither was endorsing. That form itself, along with the ongoing possibility of continued expansion, constitutes a significant threat to the goal of race-neutrality rather than a facilitation of it.

We may once again speculate on the reasons why the expansion of AA in these ways has continued. Perhaps the sense of entitlement created by the policy is the culprit. History has demonstrated that once a social policy benefiting certain citizens is created, its revocation occurs only on the rarest of occasions. It is human nature to come to depend on a continued benefit, and also to view those who would seek to remove it as cruel and heartless. This is perhaps the most likely explanation of the expansion, but it is certainly not the only possibility. To reiterate, a specific cause need not be demonstrated in order to make the point. The bottom line is that, for whatever reason, AA has gone on longer, has encompassed more beneficiaries, and has changed in form to the point where it is likely to postpone the goal of race-neutrality rather than to hasten it.

The unforeseen consequences discussed over the previous several pages are not unique to the United States. The counterproductive effects of preferential policies have been observed in a variety of countries, with their own unique histories and cultural backdrops.[89] This would suggest the existence of something about the very nature of such policies that makes them socially undesirable. Whether or not this is indeed true depends on making a sociological case for a causal connection between the policy itself and its unintended negative impact on the very goal it is designed to expedite. While some speculation regarding such impact was provided, a conclusive argument of this sort certainly was not. Nonetheless, these observations serve their purpose by providing reasons for thinking that rights (held by minorities) to preferential treatment, if called for on the direct cost/benefit analysis (which was examined from a "pre-AA" perspective temporally and conceptually), ought to give way to rights to equal consideration. If, on the other hand, the direct analysis yields rights of the latter sort from the outset, there are no reasons for thinking that constraints would be appropriate; indeed, the historical findings discussed above serve to bolster the plausibility of the anti-AA factors.

The goal-based theory affords little room for the compromise position of permissible AA. In the context of undergraduate college admissions there may be reasons for allowing race to be taken into account; the plausible claim is that race ought not to be treated differently from such factors as geographical location. However, if the goal is race-neutrality, then perhaps race, like eye color, should not come into play at all. Regardless, since such policies would count race as one factor among several, under the "goals and timetables" doctrine they are not, strictly speaking, affirmative action policies. In the context of hiring, there is no reason to think that affording businesses the liberty of instituting their own AA policies would not have the same negative effects of required AA. The prescription of the goal-based theory of rights, then, in accordance with a right to equal consideration (recognized directly or as a constraint), is mandatory race-neutrality in hiring.

Notes

1. The term "discrimination" tends to have a negative connotation, but as Louis P. Pojman has noted, this need not be the case. For example, "the ability to

make distinctions" in certain contexts, such as in wine tasting, can be commendable. See Pojman, "The Moral Status of Affirmative Action" in Morality in Practice (5th ed.), ed. James P. Sterba (Belmont, CA: Wadsworth, 1997), 239. Nonetheless, for present purposes the term "discrimination" will refer to unjustified discrimination, the morally (and logically) problematic practice of treating similar entities differently.

2. William T. Blackstone, "Reverse Discrimination and Compensatory Justice" in Social Justice and Preferential Treatment, ed. Robert D. Heslep (Athens, GA: University of Georgia Press, 1977), 74; Sidney Hook, "Discrimination, Color Blindness and the Quota System" in Reverse Discrimination, ed. Barry R. Gross (Buffalo: Prometheus Books, 1977), 86; Thomas Sowell," 'Affirmative Action' Reconsidered," in Reverse Discrimination, 125.

3. See Gertrude Ezorsky, Racism and Justice: The Case for Affirmative Action (Ithaca: Cornell University Press, 1992), 41–44.

4. Ibid., 1, 14.

5. Griggs v. Duke Power Co., 401 U.S. 424 (1971).

6. The test is not necessarily incompatible with the other interpretation of "overriding" a right, which is that the right is retained except when the competing consideration obtains. If it is asserted that the consideration currently obtains universally, this reading is not untenable. It does require some maneuvering, however, and we will therefore adhere to the former reading (which is more in line with Raz's framework, anyway).

7. Recall that personal autonomy pertains to the range of adequate options available to an agent, rather than to the Kantian sense of autonomy.

8. Blackstone similarly suggests that if anyone has claims to preferential treatment, it is the lower class generally ("Reverse Discrimination and Compensatory Justice," 77–78.) Such a policy would be justified on the interest-based theory only if the right to preferential treatment possessed by the poor were clearly established (i.e., if personal autonomy were a sufficiently strong interest to ground the relevant correlative duties on the part of others). There may also exist the question of whether some other sort of social policy (such as redistributive taxation, which in the last chapter was found to be justified on either foundational theory of rights) might be a superior means of restoring personal autonomy to those who lack it.

9. John Rawls, A Theory of Justice (Cambridge, MA: Harvard University Press, 1971), 83–89.

10. Ronald Dworkin, A Matter of Principle (Cambridge, MA: Harvard University Press, 1985), 214–18.

11. This is roughly the argument offered by Tom L. Beauchamp, "The Justification of Reverse Discrimination," in Social Justice and Preferential Treatment.

12. For further discussion on this point, see Blackstone, 67; James S. Fishkin, Justice, Equal Opportunity and the Family (New Haven: Yale University Press, 1983), 91–97.

13. Ezorsky, 77–79.

14. Bernard Boxill, Blacks & Social Justice (Lanham, MD: Rowman and Littlefield, 1992), 148–49.

15. The causal connection is not, however, universally accepted. Contrary views are offered by Nathan Glazer, Affirmative Discrimination: Ethnic Inequality

and Public Policy (Cambridge, MA: Harvard University Press, 1975), Chapter 2; Barry R. Gross, "Is Turn About Fair Play?" in Reverse Discrimination, 380; and Sidney Hook, "The Bias in Anti-Bias Regulations" in Reverse Discrimination, 89–90.

16. Boxill, 150–51; Fishkin, 92.

17. Boxill, 152. Boxill himself does not apply the term "indirect," since he thinks the force of his claims would consequently be diminished. I apply the term to distinguish the current consideration from the previous one; its designation should in no way imply that it may carry less moral weight than the direct harm of inequality of opportunity.

18. This addendum effectively negates the protest that a variety of social groups are adversely affected in this way, or that this sort of (less direct) harm is inadequate as a basis for a right to preferential treatment. See, e.g., Alan H. Goldman, "Affirmative Action" in Equality and Preferential Treatment, ed. Marshall Cohen, Thomas Nagel, and Thomas Scanlon (Princeton: Princeton University Press, 1977), 206. Goldman views the plight of the black American as comparable to that of the Jewish American.

19. Boxill, 152.

20. This point is addressed by Judith Jarvis Thomson, "Preferential Hiring," in Equality and Preferential Treatment, 36.

21. This claim is argued for by Louis Katzner, "Is The Favoring of Women and Blacks in Employment and Educational Opportunities Justified?" in Philosophy of Law (2nd ed.), ed. Joel Feinberg and Hyman Gross (Encino, CA: Dickinson, 1975), 91–96.

22. Regents of University of California v. Bakke, 438 U.S. 265 (1978).

23. Boxill, 149.

24. I will speak of "compensating" blacks for present indirect harm as well as for past harm, even though in the former case the interest is in avoiding harm as much as having present harms redressed.

25. William J. Wilson, The Truly Disadvantaged, (Chicago: University of Chicago Press, 1987), 8.

26. See, e.g., Thomas Nagel, "A Defense of Affirmative Action," Report from the Center for Philosophy and Public Policy 1 (1981), 7.

27. Goldman utilizes the term "reverse ratio," and does so specifically with respect to those who have been harmed by past discrimination. The basic idea can be extended to include (what I am calling) present indirect harm and equality of opportunity as well. See Goldman, "Reparations to Individuals or Groups?" in Reverse Discrimination, 322. The problem may also be described as violating the "Proportionality Principle," a component of compensatory justice according to which those who are harmed most are deserving of the most compensation. See Robert Simon, "Preferential Hiring: A Reply to Judith Jarvis Thomson," in Equality and Preferential Treatment, 43–44.

28. Ezorsky, 66–69; 80.

29. James W. Nickel, "Should Reparations Be to Individuals or to Groups?" in Reverse Discrimination, 315–16.

30. Boxill, 153–54.

31. Will Kymlicka, Liberalism, Community and Culture (Oxford: Clarendon Press, 1989), Chapters 8–10. While Boxill does not develop the details of the concept of

a group right, he gestures toward culture as playing a significant role in establishing the group right, possessed by blacks, to preferential treatment. He should
therefore welcome Kymlicka's discussion. (See Blacks and Social Justice, 156–58,
generally.)

32. Here, the meaning of "autonomy" for Kymlicka is, with minor differences,
relevantly similar to Raz's "personal autonomy," in that it focuses on available
options, particularly "long-range" options. See Kymlicka, 164–66; Raz, The Morality of Freedom (Oxford: Oxford University Press, 1986), 373–77.

33. This is just Raz's so-called "principle of capacity for possessing rights." See
The Morality of Freedom, 166.

34. Goldman, "Limits to the Justification of Reverse Discrimination," Social
Theory and Practice 3 (1975), 292.

35. Boxill, 158.

36. Nozick, Anarchy, State and Utopia (New York: Basic Books, 1974), 236–38.

37. Goldman, "Reverse Discrimination and the Future: A Reply to Irving Thalberg," The Philosophical Forum 6 (1974–75), 324.

38. See, e.g., Blackstone, "Reverse Discrimination and Compensatory Justice,"
52–54; Gross, "Is Turn About Fair Play?," 384–87; Lisa H. Newton, "Reverse Discrimination as Unjustified," in Reverse Discrimination; Simon, "Reply to Thomson," 45–47.

39. Boxill, 167.

40. Regents of University of California v. Bakke, 438 U.S. 265 (1978). This was the
case of a white applicant (Bakke) who was denied admission to the medical
school at the University of California at Davis. Because of his relatively high test
scores, he believed he would have been admitted if not for the school's policy of
admitting a predetermined number of minority applicants. His claim was accepted by the California Supreme Court, but that decision was reversed by the
U.S. Supreme Court, which upheld the permissibility of such quotas.

41. Dworkin, A Matter of Principle, 298–300.

42. Nagel, Introduction in Equality and Preferential Treatment, xii.

43. Hare, Moral Thinking (Oxford: Oxford University Press, 1981), 154; Raz, The
Morality of Freedom, 220.

44. Purely private acts of partiality toward one's friends and family members,
of course, do not violate the rights of others. When equality of opportunity in formal contexts is recognized, the opportunities of others should not be substantially diminished as a result of partiality; when they are so diminished, policies of
redistributive taxation (discussed in the previous chapter) are the appropriate
remedy.

45. Ezorsky, Racism and Justice, 82–84.

46. Thomson, "Preferential Hiring," 38–39.

47. George Sher, "Justifying Reverse Discrimination in Employment," in Equality and Preferential Treatment, 59–60.

48. This point is made by Hardy E. Jones, "On the Justifiability of Reverse Discrimination" in Reverse Discrimination. Jones goes on to consider the feasibility of
a "beneficiary of justice" tax, levied against successful (i.e., secure in employment) white persons only. I have occasionally suggested that a policy of taxation
(with the proper benefactors and beneficiaries) would be a much more justifiable

form of compensation than a policy of preferential treatment, and Jones's recommendation may be a worthy candidate. Germans born after World War II, for instance, though in no way responsible for the injustices against Jews during the Holocaust, nonetheless pay taxes that go toward reparations to Jewish victims; attempts to justify this sort of policy, which employs a completely different sort of compensation, are much more likely to be successful. (See Ezorsky, 85.)

49. Victor Perlo, Economics of Racism U.S.A. (New York: International Publishers, 1975), 172.

50. Robert Fullinwider, "Preferential Hiring and Compensation," Social Theory and Practice 3 (1975), 16–17.

51. See, e.g., H. L. A. Hart, "Are There Any Natural Rights?" in Rights, ed. David Lyons (Belmont, CA: Wadsworth, 1979); Rawls, "Legal Obligation and the Duty of Fair Play" in Law and Philosophy, ed. Sidney Hook (New York: New York University Press, 1974), 9–10.

52. For discussions regarding the distinction between consent and voluntary acceptance, see Nozick, Anarchy, State and Utopia, 90–95; A. John Simmons, Moral Principles and Political Obligations (Princeton: Princeton University Press, 1979), 118–36.

53. For additional problems with the principle that benefiting justifies payment, see Newton, 377; Simon, 46–47.

54. Boxill, 149.

55. The application of this terminology to the present context is from Simon, 46.

56. Recall that the assumption is that he is neither responsible for nor has benefited from racial discrimination.

57. A gesture is made toward this idea (though vaguely so) by Lloyd L. Weinreb, Oedipus At Fenway Park: What Rights Are and Why There Are Any (Cambridge, MA: Harvard University Press, 1994), 187.

58. Perhaps the most significant allowance (aside from bracketing empirical doubts about my alleged ability) is that my wife would have to be indifferent between myself and competing suitors.

59. Ezorsky, 86–88.

60. Dinesh D'souza, Illiberal Education (New York: The Free Press, 1991), 14.

61. Appeals to the desirability of black role models in the workplace might be made at this point, but this consideration is more appropriately applicable to the goal-based theory. The inference (from the previous paragraph) that it was relevant in the case of colleges is unfounded, since the relevant interest was that of the colleges and not of the minorities themselves.

62. Kathleen Parker, Executive Edge (Emmaus, PA: National Center for Career Strategies, 1990), 19.

63. Ezorsky, 15–16.

64. Ibid., 24–26.

65. Ibid., 69.

66. Boxill, 168.

67. Boxill, 151; Thomson, "Preferential Hiring," 37.

68. Barbara Baum Levenbrook, "On Preferential Admission," Journal of Value Inquiry 14 (1980), 258.

69. Sowell, " 'Affirmative Action' Reconsidered," 130.

70. See Nagel, "Equal Treatment and Compensatory Discrimination," 17.

71. Ibid., 17.

72. Barry Gross, "Is Turn About Fair Play?," 383. This is why, according to Gross, "Discrimination in any form is invidious."

73. See Sowell, Preferential Policies: An International Perspective (New York: William Morrow, 1990), 124–25.

74. Boxill, 162.

75. Whether the best qualified applicant is likely to perform better even in an "ordinary" job is debatable. The additional qualifications would not typically come into play. Further, an argument can be made that more qualified individuals are more likely to become bored in such jobs, and thus not perform as well as lesser qualified applicants.

76. Myron Weiner, "The Pursuit of Ethnic Inequalities Through Preferential Policies: A Comparative Public Policy Perspective" in From Independence to Statehood, ed. Robert B. Goldmann and A. Jeyaratnum (London: Frances Pinter, 1984), 64.

77. See U.S. Commission on Civil Rights, The Economic Progress of Black Men in America (Washington: U.S. Commission on Civil Rights, 1986).

78. Sowell, Markets and Minorities (New York: Basic Books, 1981) 130.

79. Lucy W. Sells, "Leverage for Equal Opportunity Through Mastery of Mathematics," in Women and Minorities in Science, ed. Sheila M. Humphreys (Boulder, CO: Westview Press, 1982), 12.

80. Gross, 381.

81. Sowell, Civil Rights: Rhetoric or Reality? (New York: William Morrow, 1984), 46–47.

82. As measured in terms of earned income. See Sowell, Ethnic America (New York: Basic Books, 1981), 210–13; U.S. Commission on Civil Rights, 11.

83. Richard B. Freeman, "Changes in the Labor Market for Black Americans, 1948–1972," Brookings Papers on Economic Activity 1 (1973), 118.

84. It was on December 4, 1971, that the Department of Labor amended its directives in accordance with the Civil Rights Act, and called for the implementation of "goals and timetables" in the hiring of minorities. Commentators generally agree that AA in its current form (as going beyond mere "good faith" requirements on the part of employers) was born at this point. See, e.g., Glazer, 47–49.

85. Sowell, The Economics and Politics of Race (New York: William Morrow, 1983), 187.

86. Finnis Welch, "Affirmative Action and Its Enforcement," American Economic Review (May, 1981), 132.

87. Charles Murray, "Affirmative Racism," in Morality in Practice (4th ed.). (Indeed, when both contexts are taken into consideration, Murray sees the negative effects on blacks as expanding exponentially.

88. Ibid., 277.

89. Sowell, Preferential Policies: An International Perspective. Sowell discusses a variety of examples throughout the book, including preferential policies in Sri Lanka, India, Russia, New Zealand, Israel, China, Canada and Britain.

7

Pornography

7.1 Assigning a Definition

The degree to which pornography ought to be restricted is typically assessed in light of the First Amendment, or the moral right to freedom of expression more generally. Because this freedom is held precious by the general population, any proposed regulation has been forced to demonstrate a compelling justification for limiting the right. Whether this is the proper approach will be assessed in this chapter, along with implications of the interest-based and goal-based theories for the various rights alleged to exist in this context.

Currently, the pornography industry faces a number of regulations. It is illegal, for example, for children to be connected with pornography in any way. Sales to minors are forbidden, as is the use of children in the production process; even the consumption of child pornography by adults is unlawful. Aesthetic considerations have grounded limitations on public displays and advertising. However, an outright ban of the industry, called for by members of such disparate camps as feminism and conservatism, has been found to be unjustified; some freedom to produce and distribute pornography has been protected under the First Amendment. One of the more recent attempts to institute complete prohibition was an ordinance, authored by Catharine MacKinnon and Andrea Dworkin, that was originally adopted by the Indianapolis City Council. It was later found to be unconstitutional by the Court of Appeals, a decision summarily affirmed by the U.S. Supreme Court.[1]

Determining the morally appropriate social policy requires at least a cursory understanding of just what pornography is, although that can be difficult, given the wide array of definitions offered in the philosophical and legal literature.[2] One problem is that obscenity is sometimes equated with pornography, despite its traditional meaning as that which is indecent, lewd, or offensive in general. Another problem is that definitions tend to be offered by those with definite views on the moral permissibility of the industry, and the definitions therefore tend to be not only descriptive but also saturated with normative content. Given all of the potential difficulties, the aim here should be rather modest. If a general understanding of what constitutes pornography can be agreed to, one that is (as far as possible) normatively neutral, then the tasks of assessing the various rights involved and subsequently determining the morally suitable policy can be facilitated.

While pornographic materials tend to be sexually graphic, we would do well to avoid thinking the converse is true. With very few exceptions, the debate over pornography is not about whether fine art or literature, even if sexually explicit, should be censored.[3] These items are thought to make a cultural contribution in a way that more mundane films and magazines, which frequently function as nothing more than "masturbatory aids," do not. In addition, it is not the case that all sexually explicit pictorial depictions involving actual persons as "actors" are deemed unacceptable by anti-pornography lobbyists. There exist portrayals of so-called "egalitarian" encounters in which women are in no way demeaned, humiliated, abused, or in general degraded. These sorts of images ought not to count as pornography, according to Gloria Steinem, but should instead fall under the category of "erotica."[4] Feminists do not object to erotica, she claims, but to the inequality and even violence that are frequently part of sexual imagery.

Here we have a reasonable standard for delineating the boundary of pornography: consisting of explicit characterizations of nonegalitarian sexual activity in which the female (typically) is depicted as a means of enjoyment for males (the viewer(s) and/or the actor(s) in the scene). A brief survey of other pornography opponents makes it clear that Steinam's stipulation that inequality is the key ingredient in pornography is generally accepted. MacKinnon and Dworkin, in drafting the Indianapolis ordinance, defined pornography as:

> The graphic sexually explicit subordination of women through pictures or words that also includes women dehumanized as sexual objects, things, or commodities; enjoying pain or humiliation or rape; being tied up, cut up, mutilated, bruised, or physically hurt; in postures of sexual submission or servility or display; reduced to body parts, penetrated by objects or animals, or presented in scenarios of degradation, injury, torture; shown as filthy or inferior; bleeding, bruised or hurt in a context which makes these conditions sexual. Erotica, defined by distinction as not this, might be sexually explicit materials premised on equality.[5]

According to Helen Longino, pornographic materials are those

Verbal or pictorial explicit representations of sexual behavior that . . . have
as a distinguishing characteristic 'the degrading and demeaning portrayal
of the role and status of the human female . . . as a mere sexual object to be
exploited and manipulated sexually.'[6]

Andrea Dworkin, in other work, has described pornography in terms of
"male power,"[7] and Catherine Itzin also points to inequality as pornography's defining characteristic, writing that

In pornography women are treated as sexual objects/sexually objectified/
subordinate/sexualized/reduced to sexual parts/as objects of sexual use
and abuse/pieces of meat/objectified for male desire.[8]

The understanding of pornography as the explicit depiction of nonegalitarian sexual activity is appropriate for our purposes. It is agreeable not
only to opponents such as those noted above,[9] but also to defenders of
the right to consume pornography, who view the prohibition of the private use of (almost) any such material, no matter how violent, as unacceptable. Since the disagreement seems to focus on nonegalitarian images, the area of dispute is highlighted by this definition.

Of course, it should be noted that this understanding diverges from
others traditionally employed. Again, on the present definition, pornography is not to be understood as material that is (merely) sexually explicit, or, following the so-called "Miller Test,"[10] as material that appeals
to a prurient interest in sex and that is "patently offensive." Such traditional conceptions make no use of the notion of inequality. Thus, even
that which is extremely offensive to the average member of society may
not count as pornography for our purposes if it retains the principal egalitarian element.[11]

Even with this definition in hand there will be specific examples that
are difficult to classify as either pornography or erotica, but in itself this
is not an objection to the general definition. Further, this conception allows for a wide range of images to count as pornography. Minimally,
portrayals of encounters in which a male simply initiates and directs the
various activities will fall into this category, as will many instances of
simple posing by females, since feminists in particular often take these
events to be examples of male domination, of men using women for their
own pleasure. The degree of inequality can increase from here to include
the extremely violent imagery described in some of the above definitions.

7.2 Rights of Pornography: The Interest-Based Theory

As noted in Chapter 1, the debate here essentially focuses on the question
of whether pornography should be altogether prohibited by the law, or

whether it merely warrants certain restraints. The freedom to produce and distribute pornography is typically defended via reference to freedom of speech. In the framework of the interest-based theory, the right to produce and distribute pornography can be viewed as a derivative of the core right to freedom of expression (though it will be seen that this is not the only plausible conception). In order to understand the strength of this right, its underlying justificatory interest(s) must be examined.

A temptation here is to refer to Mill's marketplace of ideas. According to Mill, the public is best served when there is exposure to the ideas and beliefs of others, regardless of how bizarre or extreme they seem. All speech should be admissible, since—perhaps contrary to initial appearances—it may turn out to be true.[12] Of course, that which constitutes "truth" will vary according to context; scientific truths are subject to empirical assessment in a way that ethical truths are not. Nonetheless, the freedom in the nineteenth century to condemn slavery, for example, is a fitting illustration, since the wrongness of slavery ultimately became accepted in the marketplace of ideas as "truth."

While Mill's intention was for all speech (at least when privately conducted) to be protected in this way, it is unclear how the (private) production and distribution of pornography can contribute to the discovery (or generation[13]) of moral truth. A better approach would be to accept Cass Sunstein's suggestion that political speech ought to be distinguished from nonpolitical speech. According to Sunstein, political speech is that which "is both intended and received as a contribution to public deliberation about some issue."[14] The determination of the appropriate category for any particular instance of speech will not always be clear; there will be hard cases, and the existing circumstances must be taken into account. However, if we apply the standard of reasonableness to the question of speaker intention, and the standard of a "sufficient minimum" to the question of when speech is received as political,[15] this difficulty can at least be minimized.

Mill's remarks are most acceptable when they are understood as pertaining to political speech in this sense, since only that which is intended or received as a contribution to public deliberation can really contribute to the public discovery of "ethical truth." This brings into question the belief that a right to produce pornography, insofar as it is understood as a derivative of the right to freedom of speech, can be grounded by any interests stemming from Mill's marketplace of ideas.[16]

For confirmation that this doubt is well-founded, we might look to other justificatory differences between the two types of speech. It has already been implied that all individuals have an interest in not being shielded from the political or social views of others. This has also been described as a "listener autonomy" interest by T. M. Scanlon, who claims that persons ought not to be prevented from using their deliberative capacities to sort through the various beliefs in the public arena and to arrive at their own conclusions.[17] This is an interest of the "audience," and so is more accurately a right of the audience rather than of the speaker.

An interest that does ground the speaker's right directly is that of contributing to the political processes of one's state. This idea rests on the plausible claim that persons ought to have a say about the policies that affect their lives. A third interest underlying freedom of political expression, one held by all citizens, is that of denying government the opportunity to regulate speech in contexts in which its own objectives may consequently be adversely affected. When speech is political, government objectives are almost always at stake. The possibility that persons may, to the detriment of government, actually be influenced by speech provides the motivation to implement restrictions, but history has demonstrated that citizens are best served when such restrictions are resisted.

Collectively, these factors suggest that the case against limitations on political speech is very strong indeed, although declaring the right to be absolute would be problematic. The important point here is that the right to freedom of nonpolitical speech is not supported by these interests, and is thus somewhat less immune to government regulation. This is relevant to the case of pornography, which is most appropriately classified as nonpolitical, since it fails to meet the criterion of being intended and received as a contribution to public deliberation. Even Ronald Dworkin, one of the more vocal defenders of the right to pornography, sees no political values at stake in this context.[18] MacKinnon is therefore at least partially justified in accusing pornography rights advocates of hiding behind the "All speech is equal" interpretation of the First Amendment.[19] Thus, the strength of the right to produce and distribute pornography depends on the strength of the right to freedom of nonpolitical speech.

This more general right is grounded, I suggest, in the moral value of personal autonomy. Recall that personal autonomy, simply put, is had when the agent possesses a reasonable number of adequate options. Thus, personal autonomy is about the positive freedom of individuals to pursue their own life plans, but it is also about the negative freedom to be unrestrained in doing so from the restrictive actions of others. This interest, again, can be understood in terms of Locke's doctrine of natural liberty. The (negative) core right that follows is a general right to be free, that is, to be left alone, and thus to be able to engage in the activities of one's choosing, within certain limits (to be discussed shortly). Hence, it should be understood as a Hohfeldian privilege at the core, with a periphery of claims to noninterference. The right to freedom of nonpolitical speech can be viewed as a derivative right, and a notion of "speaker autonomy"—a counterpart to Scanlon's "listener autonomy"—adds more substance to this derivative right. Disallowing nonpolitical speech is an especially personal sort of invasion, conflicting with such values as freedom of association and conscience.[20] The right to produce, consume, or otherwise use pornography is a further derivative. Ronald Dworkin's discussion is relevant here, since he sees pornography rights as deriving from the more general right to moral independence, which is quite compatible with personal autonomy. According to Dworkin, "People have the right not to suffer disadvantage in the distribution of social goods and opportunities, including disadvantage in the liberties permitted them by the criminal law, just on the ground that their officials or fellow-citizens think that their opinions about the right way for them to lead their own lives are ignoble or wrong."[21]

Given this picture of the right to pornography, the question relevant to the issue of its prohibition is when this freedom may justifiably be overridden. A principle of legal moralism would allow for restriction when the activity is contrary to community norms. Patrick Devlin's defense of moralism-based regulation is perhaps the best known.[22] According to Devlin, there exists (and there ought to exist) a "public morality," understood as the basic ethical beliefs that unite individuals into a community. Commonality of ideas is the very basis of a society; as Devlin writes, "Without shared ideas on politics, morals, and ethics no society can exist."[23] The claim, then, is that a public morality is necessary for the continued existence of society. Assuming that it is permissible for a society to take actions essential for its continued existence, it may prohibit those activities contrary to the public morality. Assuming further that the production or use of pornography is such an activity, the moralistic justification for prohibition is complete.

There are several problems with this approach. First, ascertaining just what the public morality consists of is a difficult business. Devlin's most explicit guideline is that of "the reasonable man" or "the man in the jury box, for the moral judgment of society must be something about which any twelve men or women drawn at random might after discussion be expected to be unanimous."[24] Such unanimity requires the view to be prevalent among an extremely high statistical percentage of the population. In a pluralistic society, the scope of such beliefs is likely to be extremely small, and it is reasonable to think that the private consumption of pornography will not be found so widely objectionable. Second, as H. L. A. Hart points out, moralism presumes the existence of a static moral code that should never be altered; but the prescription that the current morality ought to obtain for eternity is a dubious one to say the least.[25] Third, moralism is just what Dworkin's right to moral independence is supposed to counter. This right "trumps" considerations of a public morality (except, perhaps, in the most extreme of circumstances). These results line up with the interest-based model nicely. Individuals do have an interest in resisting the collapse of their societies, but the likelihood of such a collapse as a result of private pornography usage is almost nil.[26] Also, the interest in pursuing one's own course of life (and the specific activities it includes) in accordance with one's moral convictions appears sufficiently strong to resist moralistic challenges. Hence, the right to pornography, grounded in the interest of personal autonomy, cannot be overridden on this basis.

A corollary to this discussion pertains to the role of offensiveness in limiting conduct. It is hard to deny that a principle of offensiveness is sometimes sufficient for restricting certain activities. Rules against public nudity are typically justified in this way, and other, much more offensive exhibitions can be imagined as well. Prohibition of these in public or on network television is defensible.[27] (Of course, the activity must be generally offensive, and not just offensive to some.) It is for this reason that restrictions on public displays of, or advertisements for, pornographic materials are permissible (assuming that pornography does, in fact, meet the standard of being generally offensive). Private consumption, however, is an altogether different matter. Whether or not the offensive activity is reasonably avoidable is a workable standard for assessing limitations; if it is reasonably available, then it is best classified as private and should not be regulated for reasons of offensiveness.[28]

Another justification occasionally offered for limiting individual liberty is paternalism. Protecting women from entering into situations that may be unhealthy, coercive, or worse is not an unreasonable aim. It may be suggested that men, too, suffer from exposure to pornographic materials, since they may become addicted in some way,[29] or, more mildly, may become confused about the nature of sex. Demonstrating the prevalence of these sorts of evils is difficult, but the real problem is that paternalism is simply insufficient as a justification for prohibiting pornography. It allows the state to treat its citizens as children, which is in direct conflict with personal autonomy. After all, "government" is only a collection of persons, and the claim that it may dictate to another group of persons what is in the latter's best interest is not defensible. Personal autonomy allows for persons to engage in even those activities that may not be in their best interest. Of course, the idea of advance consent or precommitment (individuals freely consenting to have some of their future options restricted because of, say, weakness of will) is plausible, but such consent must be actual rather than merely hypothetical;[30] the assumption that everyone values his health and well-being cannot be extended to justify the prohibition of pornography.

Instead, we should look to harm as a basis for restriction. There is substantial agreement that the scope of liberty is limited to those activities that do not harm others (at least not without their consent). The question is whether even the private consumption of pornography can be said to cause the harm necessary to justify its prohibition.

This discussion will occupy the rest of this section. For organizational purposes, direct harm will be distinguished from indirect harm, the former being any evil intentionally visited upon the victim. Two types of direct harm that could potentially warrant prohibition will be examined, followed by four types of indirect harm.

The most direct form of harm alleged to be caused by the pornography industry is the harm to women that occurs in the process of producing the material. It is often claimed that women are physically abused in this process, especially in making films. In the extreme, examples are presented where women have actually been raped and even murdered in order to manufacture the material.[31] Even in the mildest pornography, which is "merely" nonegalitarian, some harm is still said to befall women. This point in particular is emphasized by MacKinnon, who objects to the claim that the acts in pornographic films, because they are in films, are in some sense not "real." For the women involved, the experience is real, and has to be real for the film to be effective. "In pornography," she writes, "the penis is shown ramming up into the woman over and over; this is because it actually was rammed up into the woman over and over."[32] In this sense, according to MacKinnon, rape is an element in all pornography. In addition, coercion and blackmail come into play, for once women have appeared in pornography, they are much more vulnerable to the demands of the producers.[33]

There is no denying that these sorts of things do happen in the industry. The specific examples offered by MacKinnon and others should not be simply brushed aside. Anecdotal evidence, however, advances an argument only so far. If the mistreatment of women in the production process were a necessary element of pornography, then prohibition on this basis would be in order. But production harms are not as widespread as pornography opponents tend to believe.[34] If there were even a strong connection (rather than a necessary one) between making pornography and harming the women "actresses" in the process, a strong prima facie case for prohibition could be made, but even this lesser standard is likewise not met. Perhaps this particular job involves a higher risk of harm than many others, but surely this is no reason to ban the industry. The more defensible approach would be to pursue the individual cases where mistreatment has occurred. The sorts of bodily harm described above ought to be addressed in any context. The interest of personal autonomy, grounding a prima facie right to make, consume, and participate in pornography, is therefore not overridden on this basis.

The second type of direct harm is the causal connection alleged to exist between the consumption of pornography and the commission of sexual and violent crimes against women. Reference to this causal link is made by virtually all anti-pornography lobbyists in their arguments. The idea is that exposure to pornography causes the acknowledgment of otherwise latent yearnings that are sexually violent in nature; or implants in males a desire, formerly absent, to commit crimes against women; or, in cases where such desires are already held and recognized, the exposure desensitizes those men to the point where any inhibitions are effectively removed. MacKinnon in particular chooses to point to anecdotal evidence to support this claim, citing examples that implicate movies, magazines, and video games, among other media.[35] Others rely more strongly on studies suggesting that exposure does indeed alter men's attitudes toward women. The perceptual changes may be general. It may be, for instance, that men consequently come to believe that violence against women is not as serious as they previously thought. The changes may also be specific. Some studies report an increase in the acceptance of the "rape myth," the perception that women, contrary to outward appearances, actually enjoy being raped.[36] Others report that more men reveal a desire to commit rape and a claim that they would do so if evasion of the law were guaranteed.[37]

Pornography rights advocates sometimes respond to this argument, and to the studies suggesting the causal link, by asserting that the totality of evidence is inconclusive. This is only partially correct, for the claim that men's attitudes and beliefs are affected by the exposure is, by and large, supported by the evidence.[38] However, the proposition that exposure directly harms women in the form of substantially increased instances of sexual violence requires more than this; it requires evidence that the behavioral patterns of men are affected in the same way. On this count, there is indeed much disagreement. The existence of a positive correlation between pornography consumption and subsequent criminal violence against women is sometimes denied altogether,[39] and when it is acknowledged it is often said to be a very mild connection.[40] Even those whose findings indicate changes in attitudes caution against extrapolating to the conclusion that behavior must therefore also be affected.[41] Some even go so far as to suggest that pornography benefits women, since it provides a harmless outlet for men who might otherwise act on their aggressive tendencies.[42]

If the right to consume pornography, grounded in an interest in personal autonomy, is to be overridden on the basis of direct harm, there must exist a fairly clear connection between the exposure and the harm. The conflicting conclusions of the various studies indicate that this is not the case. Even so, a causal connection cannot necessarily be inferred from a statistical correlation. In particular, the claim that pornography consumption is a symptom of the socially deviant behavior, rather than a cause of it, is supported equally well.[43] Of course, a strong correlation is good prima facie evidence of a causal connection. It is unfair, though, to compare the current context to that of smoking and its relationship to lung cancer, as Catherine Itzin does;[44] the smoking/lung cancer correlations are much stronger, and a causal link between them has been clearly established. In any case, the correlations associated with pornography consumption are not strong enough to warrant even the prima facie conclusion.

The best that can be said for this anti-pornography argument is that exposure to pornography can, in some instances, be a causal factor in the commission of sexually violent crimes against women. Exposure is neither a necessary nor a sufficient condition; some offenders act even without exposure, and many consumers never commit any transgressions.[45] (We cannot take seriously MacKinnon's claim that many men who use pornography "do rape women (but) they just never get caught."[46]) To label exposure a "causal factor" is to say that, in specific cases, the sexual offense would not have occurred but for the exposure. In these cases, it makes some sense to say that the pornography "caused" the harm.[47] However, it is an open question whether the pornography exposure should be designated as the relevant cause (or, in legal jargon, as the proximate cause). If a causal factor is understood as one of several factors that are individually necessary and jointly sufficient for a given effect,[48] then there is no prima facie reason for selecting any one causal factor as the culprit. The strategy of banning pornography on the basis of it being a causal factor is thus not only logically unsound, but would license the prohibition of most R-rated movies (as well as many PG-rated movies), a variety of television programs and advertisements, a majority of cartoons, and countless other presentations that have been found to be causal factors in the commission of violent crimes from time to time.

The conclusion here must be that while some of the claims regarding the "link" between pornography and violence are not unfounded, the prohibition conclusion is not called for. The interest of personal autonomy is of sufficient weight to require a much stronger connection if it is to be overridden on this basis.

The above harms were classified as "direct" because they are immediate results of intentional behavior. In the end, nothing rides on the direct/indirect distinction; it is employed for ease of discussion only. The next four harms may be labeled as "indirect," since they are not results of actions that are themselves intended to have the harmful effect. All of these are in some way related to the central idea of discrimination. Even so, each should be addressed separately; the foundational interest, or the right that is alleged to follow from it, varies in each case, and thus the possibility for varying prescriptions exists.

First, it may be suggested that personal autonomy is the relevant interest, grounding a core right to liberty in the same way that the right to consume pornography was said to be justified. In the current reasoning, women's personal autonomy is negatively affected, since their options are reduced as a result of the pornography's existence. This is because pornography is alleged to provoke, or at least contribute to, a generally negative perception of women that is often not even recognized by the men who harbor it. Thus, the evidence cited above regarding changes in men's attitudes toward women (which was acknowledged to be widespread) is the core of the support for this argument; no subsequent criminal actions by those men need be discussed. Rather, a different claim is asserted, namely that these attitudes ultimately have concrete effects in the form of diminished opportunities and options for women.[49] Continuing economic disparities, such as those in hiring, promotion, and compensation in the workplace, are typical examples.

An analogy to environmental pollution has occasionally been employed to make this argument clearer. It is rare that a single piece of pornography ever causes a particular instance of harm. Over time, however, the cumulative effects can plausibly be argued to have negative consequences for women. Regulation, and indeed prohibition, of various environmental practices have their foundations in the aggregate (rather than any specific) effects that result from them.[50]

There are several reasons for thinking that the right to produce and distribute pornography should not be overridden by a right, grounded in personal autonomy and in the form of a claim, held against others that they not use pornography. First, there is prima facie evidence that the alleged relationship between exposure and concrete negative effects does not obtain. As the pornography industry has grown over recent decades due to technological advances, women have continued to make progress, and they have in fact increased the options available to them. It may be argued that such growth would have been even greater had pornography not been concurrently legal. This is unlikely, since the growth rate has remained relatively constant even in the face of great expansion in the production and circulation of pornography.

Further, even if these considerations are bracketed, it will turn out (for reasons to be addressed shortly) that the right to have pornography banned cannot be sustained. First, however, it should be noted that the strategy for defending this claim should not be the one recommended by Ronald Dworkin. Dworkin points out that speech explicitly advocating the economic (and even the social and political) subordination of women should not be restricted, even though such speech likely would have some negative effects on them. Because of this, he claims, private consumption of pornography cannot be restricted, even if pollutive effects

could be demonstrated.[51] However, Dworkin's approach here is somewhat misguided, because it places pornography on the same moral level
as political speech, although pornography has been acknowledged to be
an instance of nonpolitical speech and thus more susceptible to regulation.

The better approach to assessing the viability of any right based on this
first type of indirect harm is to correctly line up the competing rights and
their justificatory interests in order to see which is of greater moral
weight. When this step is taken, then even on the condition that some
correlation exists between exposure and actual negative effects on
women, rights to produce and consume pornography (Hohfeldian privileges with peripheries of claims to noninterference) appear to win out
over the right to deny others the freedom to consume it (a Hohfeldian
claim). This is because the personal autonomy of women, while perhaps
negatively affected by the existence of pornography, is not effectively diminished to the point that it falls below the "minimum threshold" discussed in Chapter 5. In that chapter, it was argued that mere differences
between two groups in levels of personal autonomy are insufficient to
justify infringement on the freedom of those with more; the "needy"
must be below the minimum. It was further argued that the poor, having
limited means, are indeed below this threshold, and thus can be said to
lack personal autonomy. The class of women, however, cannot legitimately be said to lack personal autonomy. Therefore, their alleged right
is insufficiently strong to ground a correlative duty on the part of men
not to use pornography.

It may be objected that the personal autonomy of pornography users is
illicitly being granted pride of place here. After all, denying pornographers this particular freedom does not relegate their personal autonomy
below the all-important threshold, either. The difference is that this
would be a denial of a specific liberty, one that is not a direct assault on
any specific liberties of others. The claim here is that denial of a specific
liberty for some, for the sake of what is at most a risk for others that some
options may be closed off, is impermissible. What is permissible is denying a specific liberty to infringe on others' specific liberties; hence the justifiable restrictions on the freedom to discriminate against women.

More of the reasoning behind this claim can be seen when we consider
the potential implications of allowing for the success of this argument.
Any number of elements in society can be said to reduce the personal
autonomy of women in the same way pornography allegedly does. As
noted above, many television, magazine, and billboard advertisements
can plausibly be said to have the same effects, even though the sexual
connotation is less explicit. Movies and soap operas are other examples.
Consistency requires that, if the above feminist argument against

pornography is accepted, then the specific liberties involved in producing and viewing these other sorts of images must similarly be prohibited. But the problem is even more substantial, for the factors affecting men's attitudes toward women are likely to include even such mundane items as clothing, general public discourse, and modes of private interaction. Humans are psychologically oriented in such a way that virtually all input affects attitudes. It is wholly impractical to prohibit all activities that might have certain psychological effects on the basis that those effects may be causal factors of certain behaviors (except perhaps those activities for which a very clear correlation has been established). It is not merely the case that the implementation of such prohibitions would be difficult; the claim is that the myriad rules would make for an unmanageable society. This worry can be accommodated on the interest-based theory by pointing out that far too many important interests would be compromised if such actions were taken. Therefore, the conclusion regarding this first type of indirect harm is that prohibition is too severe a measure in the context of pornography; the denial of specific liberties requires more than the existence of a risk of autonomy loss if it is to be justified.

The second type of indirect harm differs in the following way. In the previous case, the alleged right that followed from the interest of personal autonomy was based on a conception of positive liberty. Pitted against the right to pornography, as a negative liberty, it was at a disadvantage from the outset; as was argued in Chapter 5, positive claims against others to that which enhances one's personal autonomy are, on Raz's model, sufficiently strong to ground legitimate rights against others (override their negative claims) only when one's lack of autonomy is dire, that is, is below the "minimum threshold." Portraying the issue as a conflict of negative liberties, however, puts it in a different light. Personal autonomy cannot be used to ground a right to nonpolitical speech (or any of its derivatives) that effectively denies others their (negative) right to freedom of speech, be it nonpolitical or, even more strongly, political. It may be argued, though, that this is exactly what pornography does. MacKinnon, who seems to leave no anti-pornography argument untouched, points to this line of reasoning also.[52] The effects of pornography are alleged to cause "audience" perceptions of women speakers to be altered to the point where the women are no longer taken seriously,[53] and to subsequently cause women to become disinclined to speak at all.[54]

This is a novel approach to the case for prohibition, but it is ultimately unsuccessful. There is no doubt that some activities (or speech) do have certain silencing effects, but, contrary to the claims of MacKinnon and others, they do not deny women the negative liberty to speak. Implicit in the argument is an illicit expansion of the notion of negative freedom.

However, it is more in line with the traditional distinction (engendered by Isaiah Berlin) to specify the denial as that of a positive liberty to be provided with the conditions that encourage women to speak and to be heard. Once this move is made, the debate is once again seen as being between a positive liberty on the one hand and a negative liberty on the other, and the prescription will thus be as it was before. On this matter, I am therefore in agreement with Ronald Dworkin[55] and in disagreement with Sunstein, whose strict Madisonian interpretation of the First Amendment entails even a positive right to at least some of these conditions, since, he claims, this is what is required in a properly functioning deliberative democracy.[56] In sum, the right grounded by the interest in contributing to the public debate can only be negative (in this case a Hohfeldian privilege), since a positive right (a claim) would come into conflict with specific (negative) liberties of others—liberties that, I have argued, are of greater moral weight, since they are not in conflict with interests that are acutely absent.

The third type of indirect harm employs a completely different justificatory interest. It may be argued that the analysis, to this point, has missed the mark altogether, for it is not the negative effect of pornography (in terms of personal autonomy loss) that constitutes the harm; rather, the discrimination itself is problematic. The debate over prohibition is not a conflict of liberties, or, on the interest-based model, a conflict of rights resting on the same interest of personal autonomy. It is instead a conflict of two separate values, namely, liberty on the one hand and equality on the other. In this light, the fact of subordination of women, regardless of its degree, is sufficient to warrant prohibition. The observation that the subordination does not result in an unacceptable loss of personal autonomy is irrelevant.

MacKinnon and Langton each put forth strong versions of this argument. Looking first into Langton's views, she claims that women do not in fact enjoy a socioeconomic status equal to that of men. This should be readily accepted; while women have made advances in recent decades, clear disparities continue to exist. Second, Langton claims that the existence of pornography contributes to the ongoing subordination of women. This is based on the notion that pornography, which portrays women as nothing more than a collection of body parts to be exploited by men, has at least some negative effects on the freedom of women. The moral difficulty is not this loss of freedom per se, but the fact that it serves to keep women on a socially inferior level relative to men. Thus, again, it is inequality that serves as the crux of the argument.[57] We might appropriately refer to the right to equal consideration, discussed in Chapter 6, as the one violated by the existence of pornography according to this argument.

This idea is expanded by MacKinnon in her version of the argument. She, more than Langton, constructs the case as a legal one in which the conflict is between the First and Fourteenth Amendments, and then claims that the latter must win out. Nonetheless, the respective moral values of freedom (either freedom of speech or freedom generally) and equality are appealed to. In essence, her claim is that the government, in the name of equality, may justifiably prohibit discrimination. This means that the freedom to engage in discriminatory actions (including speech) may be forbidden. Her second premise is that pornography contributes to the pervasive inequality between men and women; it is at least a case of defamation, resulting in harm to women's reputations (and perhaps much more), since it depicts women as inferior and servile, as nothing more than sexual objects. This is the case even when it is privately consumed. These attitudes, which are inevitably adopted by the male users, ultimately play out in the form of discrimination.

The equality argument against pornography is perhaps the most novel of those offered by the feminist camp, and it deserves thoughtful consideration. The question of whether it can withstand potential problems might begin with another gesture toward the intuition that women today seem to be approaching, rather than retreating from, parity with men. In itself, of course, this is inconsequential to the argument; the claim is that the status of women cannot reach that of men, regardless of its current trend. Second, it is sometimes pointed out that other feminist writers disagree with the premise that the very existence of pornography contributes to the subordination of women.[58] This sort of superficial complaint, too, will have minimal impact.

The truly damaging flaw in the equality argument begins to emerge as MacKinnon describes her view of its implications. She argues that pornography should be legally actionable for the same reasons as hate speech: both have the same damaging effects on equality. The analogy holds insofar as nonpolitical speech is at stake in both contexts. The difference, however, is in the type of harm. Unlike hate speech, the alleged harm of pornography does not consist in a direct assault on a designated individual (or group of individuals).[59] MacKinnon has overextended the premise that government may prohibit discrimination, for it may not go so far as to prohibit activities (particularly private activities) that happen to have certain diffuse discriminatory side-effects. Yet again, certain mass media images come to mind (such as beauty pageants and beer commercials) as also having such side-effects. Most troublesome, though, is the implication that even private speech may be prohibited; consistency would require MacKinnon to disallow even personal communication among friends or family members that would result in the violation of her equality standard. This degree of government intrusion is intolerable.

MacKinnon's claims demonstrate an overzealousness to assure that any conflict involving equality is resolved in its favor, as well as a failure to treat equality as one consideration among several in a proper analysis of specific rights conflicts. The personal autonomy interest grounding the right to pornography overcomes this particular challenge.

This error can also be seen in Langton's formulation of the argument, which is not valid as it stands. In addition to her claims that the status of women is currently unequal to that of men, and that pornography contributes to the ongoing inequality, she must, if the prohibition conclusion is to be reached, add the claim that anything contributing to the ongoing inequality may be banned. This is just what I have been arguing is unacceptable.

The fourth and final type of indirect harm is based on a very slight adjustment of the previous argument. The premise that pornography contributes to the subordination of women is sometimes altered so as to be the claim that pornography is itself subordination. In this view, the consumption of pornography constitutes sexual discrimination rather than causes it, and as such is morally equivalent to harassment and can thus be prohibited.[60] Here, too, Langton provides a similar argument, pointing to the authoritative nature of pornography as the key; because it is the vehicle through which many young males in particular learn about sexual violence, coercion, and inequality in general, it "tells its viewers what women are worth."[61]

The brief response here is that pornography is not authoritative in the way argued for by Langton. If it were, no other societal factors would be required ingredients in the subordination of women; pornography, being authoritative, would by itself suffice as subordination. Given the range of other suggested contributing factors, however, this seems unlikely.

It should perhaps also be noted that this argument does at least succeed in casting doubt on the moral relevance of the speech/conduct distinction. This has already been accounted for, however, within the implications of the interest-based model presented in this section. For nonpolitical speech such as pornography, the question of whether it should count as speech or conduct does not affect the findings; the interest of personal autonomy grounds both freedom of speech and freedom of conduct, and so the right to consume pornography is of the same moral weight in either case.[62]

The conclusion, then, is that on the interest-based theory of rights, the call for an all-out ban on pornography is not warranted. The method of beginning with the prima facie right to pornography and then bringing potential challenges to it (which failed), does not affect the outcome of the analysis. We might have begun with the prima facie right to have pornography banned, and then brought against it the challenge of violation to individual liberty, which would have negated that right. Private production, distribution, and use, though based on a somewhat weaker interest than the one grounding political speech, must still be allowed. It may, of course, be regulated in various ways, but any regulation is grounded in considerations of offense, which do not obtain in matters of privacy.

7.3 Rights of Pornography: The Goal-Based Theory

Various effects of pornography have been considered in connection with the interest-based theory of rights, and those findings will be assumed to obtain for the remainder of this chapter. However, previous discussion suggests a problem in trying to find a single goal agreeable to the various participants in the debate. Defenders of a right to pornography are disturbed over restrictions of liberty accompanying prohibition. While feminist anti-pornography advocates are also somewhat concerned with this good, they appear to be at least as worried about pornography's effects on equality. The arguments offered by MacKinnon and Langton above in particular make it clear that equality can clash with liberty, hence MacKinnon's claim that "the law of equality and the law of freedom are on a collision course in this country," and that equality must be upheld.[63] In order to account for both goods, each will be examined in this section, beginning with liberty.

The feminist arguments make evident exactly whose liberty is allegedly compromised by the continued existence of the pornography industry. It is the liberty of women, most directly those women who become victims of sexually violent offenders inspired by exposure to pornography. Of equal moral relevance is the indirect loss of freedom discussed in the previous section: pornography contributes to a "polluted" environment in which men's perceptions of women are altered by exposure, and these more negative perceptions ultimately have concrete discriminatory effects.

On the other side of the accounting ledger in a direct cost/benefit analysis of prohibition's effects on freedom, there are several parties who would be negatively affected. First, consumers would be denied an entertainment option, one which by all estimates is utilized more frequently than we might care to think.[64] Of course, personal attitudes are irrelevant in the goal-based framework (unless they genuinely affect the goal). What matters is the effect on liberty. It should be added that not all consumers are men; women, too, would lose an option under prohibition, even though they tend to exercise the option less frequently.[65] Second, the "actors" and "actresses" in the industry would lose their jobs under prohibition. In response to feminist arguments, some have pointed out that females who make pornography would be denied an opportunity to improve their economic situations. This point is made by Ronald Dworkin, who emphasizes that the fact of being an unpleasant option does not (in itself) distinguish it from certain other unpleasant employment options (such as working in fast-food restaurants) which furthermore are economically inferior.[66] Third, the (typically male) producers would similarly be denied an opportunity to pursue their chosen careers.

In the assessment of which rights (and thus which policy) are recommended by the direct analysis, the feminist case would be much stronger if a causal link between pornography consumption and subsequent violence against women were more firmly established. If it were, or even if a strong correlation existed, the substantial loss of freedom endured by the victims of such crimes would likely be decisive. However, the evidence, as discussed in the previous section, does not support the alleged link. The fact that pornography consumption is a causal factor (or is even the relevant causal factor) in a few cases of severe deprivation of freedom appears outweighed by the widespread deprivation that would result from prohibition.

Evidence is also lacking in respect to the indirect loss of freedom that, according to feminists, occurs as a result of perceptual changes in men who use pornography. Women continue to make inroads socially, politically, and economically, and these are accompanied by increases in liberty. Of course, there is a chance that such gains would be even more considerable but for the existence of pornography. When pitted against the actual losses that would occur under prohibition, however, this "chance" is outweighed. With respect to both the direct and indirect losses of freedom, then, the right to consume pornography prevails.

An objection to this finding is likely to be based on the claim that the pornography users' losses of freedom are trivial. For consumers, pornography is merely one form of entertainment, and its demise would leave intact numerous other options. The producers, photographers, computer programmers, actors, and actresses (and others in the industry) would be able to remain in the entertainment business, even if this specific business is no longer an alternative. Meanwhile, the competing deprivations of liberty suffered by women that coincide with continued permissibility of pornography are substantial. Even if the instances of violence incited by pornography are rare, the loss of liberty on those occasions is severe. Thus, it may be argued that very few such instances are needed for prohibition to be recommended by the liberty approach to the goal-based theory. When the detrimental effects of the indirect harms are added to the mix, the objection is complete.

For each individual whose liberty is negatively affected by prohibition, the consequence may indeed be somewhat trivial. However, when those consequences are summed across all relevant parties, the total liberty loss is considerable. When compared to the few instances of direct harm and the various diffuse indirect harms, a strong case against prohibition remains intact. To see this more clearly, imagine that all areas of entertainment that have similar effects are banned. It has been suggested more than once in this chapter that many nonpornographic movies have the same sorts of effects, as do many advertisements, television programs (from beauty pageants to situation comedies), and even some books. It would be difficult to maintain that the deprivation of the freedom to partake of these kinds of entertainment results in an overall increase in freedom in society. At the aggregate level, this seems clear. Thus, there is no reason for thinking that the prohibition of any individual contributor to this aggregate conclusion (including pornography) itself produces an overall increase in freedom.[67]

At this point, we see a familiar problem with consequentialist arguments. The relative utilities, or in this case freedoms, can be manipulated in order to guide the theoretical considerations toward a desired conclusion. The prospect of arriving at a meaningful conclusion may therefore seem dubious. In order to strengthen, then, the initial finding that prohibition is unwarranted on the goal-based theory with freedom as the relevant goal, an additional claim will be put forward; it will be suggested that even if prohibition is assumed to be called for on the direct cost/benefit analysis, constraints in the form of rights to consume pornography would, in the long run, lead to a more successful attainment of the goal.

A primary worry is the "slippery slope" concern that censoring pornography would increase the scope of materials subject to censorship. In the United States, this is the basis of the American Civil Liberties Union's anti-prohibition position, the concern being that art, literature, and even political expression may ultimately be censored if the government is allowed to ban such material as pornography. There does seem to be good reason for this apprehension. Historically, government censorship has tended to result in the quelling of dissent. Even merely sexual (but not pornographic) works, such as James Joyce's Ulysses, have been suppressed once the state has been given any such power. Conceptually, it makes sense that those in the sexual entertainment industry generally, and not just pornography specifically, would not want to take chances with the law, and thus would cease dealing with any item that could be in the "gray area" with respect to what is proscribed. This is because the wording of any ordinance cannot precisely delimit what counts as pornography, and it would therefore be very difficult to know whether a particular piece of "pornography" is indeed pornography until it is tested by law. Some of the initial attempts to prosecute violations of the Indianapolis ordinance (prior to its repeal) make this clear.[68] In short, the concerns are in some ways similar to those expressed in the case of affir-mative action; regarding certain legislation, it is very difficult—much more so than one might think—to know in advance what its effects will be. Controlling the scope of its effects afterward is at least as difficult.

Of course, a protest might be made that slippery slope worries are un-founded. First, it may be argued that historical examples of the above sorts of difficulties are inappropriate, since we tend to learn from past mistakes and so are unlikely to encounter those same sorts of problems. Second, there are already a number of speech restrictions, putting us in some sense already on a slope; yet there seem to be relatively few con-cerns about it being slippery enough to cause the sorts of problems de-scribed above.[69] Examples of such restrictions include bans on hate speech and harassment, yet complaints about these limitations causing slippery slope problems are minimal. While lines may be difficult to draw in certain situations, attempts to draw them should not cease.

Reasonable attempts to draw lines should indeed be undertaken. The real nature of the slippery slope problem, though, is illustrated by the suggestion that pornography is relevantly similar to the sorts of cases noted above. The harm (in terms of deprivation of liberty) in those cases is much more clearly established. Whereas harassment (and hate speech, for that matter) is itself an assault on liberty, the most that can be said of pornography is that it may be a causal factor in some cases of assault, or that it may lead to some instances of discrimination. Susan Easton's ob-jection itself exemplifies how slippery the slope can be, since she sees no difficulty in extending already-existing limitations (which are restrictions on assault and are thus justified) to cover pornography and cases like it, where the harm (to liberty) is very questionable indeed.

The conclusion, then, is that more liberty is had in society under poli-cies that permit rather than ban the production, distribution, and con-sumption of pornography. It has been claimed that this result follows from a direct cost/benefit analysis; but even if it doesn't, constraints in the form of pornography rights ultimately lead to a more successful at-tainment of the liberty goal.

The remaining task, before taking up discussion of the goal of equality, is to consider whether, on the assumption that a direct analysis prescribes pornography rights, constraints in the form of women's rights might be warranted. If this were the case, the goal-based analysis with liberty as the relevant goal would be guilty of generating contradictory conclu-sions. Some of Langton's remarks can be construed as suggesting that women's rights should be recognized even in the face of straightforward consequentialist considerations.[70] The claim is that in a sexist society such as ours, in which practices of discrimination remain prevalent, the standard of proof for liberty loss endured by women should be more moderate. It has been assumed throughout that the liberty loss, if it is to be pertinent, must be clear, present, beyond a reasonable doubt, or some combination of these criteria. However, Langton suggests that in the current sexist culture it makes sense to err on the side of caution, and she implies that doing so will ultimately better serve overall societal liberty.

Again, though, the willingness to adopt a relaxed standard of proof is precisely what the slippery slope worry is concerned with. If the standard is relaxed in this way, and to this extent, then there appears to be no barrier to potential censorship of most anything in society. Langton cites (and supports) the recommendation of a British study that indicates that when there is no strong evidence either way, so that it may be the case that some harm is caused by a certain practice, then it is sensible to be cautious and restrict the practice.[71] Following such advice in the context of the current framework would generate the implausible conclusion that freedom is augmented when all such practices are prohibited. When it is prohibition of even private consumption that is under consideration, the standard of proof of harm (deprivation of freedom) ought to be fairly strict, and on the goal-based theory must be strict. Even Langton, in the end, concedes that the recommendation of prohibition does not easily follow from the considerations she offers.[72]

At this point, then, the conclusion with respect to liberty should be accepted. Consequences of pornography for the goal of equality, endorsed by many feminists, must now be considered. In this context, the overall amount of liberty in society is irrelevant. So long as equalization between the genders is achieved, the goal is met—and thus morally justifies the measures—even if it comes at the expense of liberty.

On a direct analysis, it makes sense that a policy of prohibition would be more effective in achieving the goal of equality than would a more permissive policy. It is indeed the case that women continue to be subordinate to men in today's society, and it is reasonable that the existence of pornography, understood in terms of its nonegalitarian content, contributes to the general nonegalitarian environment. Despite the fact that gains have been made in recent decades, reason dictates that such gains would be greater if not for nonegalitarian influences. The reasons for this claim are those discussed in the previous section: men who consume pornography tend to adopt (or to enhance already existing) discriminatory attitudes toward women, and while those attitudes may translate into actual practices of discrimination only infrequently, at least some inequality results. The goal of equality would thus be better served if rights, held by women against others that the others not produce, distribute, or consume pornography, were granted (and if a policy of prohibition were thus adopted).

The ensuing question is whether there is reason to believe that recognition of constraints in the form of rights to produce, distribute, and consume pornography would ultimately be a more successful strategy. Once again, slippery slope worries serve as the basis for the claim that such constraints are warranted. Since society is already sexist, as Langton, MacKinnon, and others claim, legal prohibition of pornography may be turned around and used against the very group the ban is supposed to protect. This concern is expressed by Carol Smart, who emphasizes the need to account for the already existing nonegalitarian nature of society when considering prohibition.[73] First, because of the "patriarchal" nature of the state, legal measures may be interpreted by the predominantly male judiciary in such a way as to hinder, rather than enhance, the goals of the feminist movement (equality in particular). Second, she feels that since prohibition is endorsed by the staunchly conservative religious "Moral Right" as well as by feminists, other less attractive policies called for by the "Moral Right" would consequently become more viable. These worries are shared by other feminists (such as the Feminist Anti-Censorship Task Force) and they ground the claim that legal measures are not, in the long run, the best way of achieving the goal of equality.[74]

Smart's point is well-taken and is supported by observation. In the wake of the Indianapolis ordinance in the United States and the Obscene Publications Act in Britain, a number of feminist and lesbian items were seized by authorities.[75] The problem is not only the existence of a patriarchal judiciary, but also the inability to draft legislation precise enough to include just the materials targeted by such a measure while excluding the other materials. It bears repeating that in this and other contexts (affirmative action, for example), legislative measures intended to guide society in a certain direction have often taken on lives of their own, and the degree and scope of their influence have often come to exceed, by far, the intentions of the original lawmakers. In this particular case, then, the better strategy might be to refrain from disrupting the current trends toward equality, which are quite favorable to women, even if there is reason to think, on a direct analysis, that such trends could be accelerated.

Easton suggests that one way of stopping the slide down the slippery slope would be to focus on mens rea and actus reus, the elements typically necessary for conviction under the criminal law. She claims that neither of these is present in the cases of art, literature, or other works of "redeeming value," including (presumably) feminist and lesbian works of the sort with which Smart is concerned. In the context of pornography, however, Easton argues for the existence of both a mens rea (in this case the intention to sexually arouse) and an actus reus (in this case the act of creating degrading depictions of women).[76] The presence of these elements allows for pornography to be distinguished from other materials and thus subject to legal prohibition without worry that other materials will come to be within the scope of censorship.

This response, too, illustrates the real worries associated with the slippery slope. Traditionally, the purpose of the mens rea requirement has been to ensure that the act was performed either with the intention of committing a transgression or with reckless disregard for the potentially harmful (foreseen) consequences. It can hardly be argued that producers of pornography intend to discriminate against women in various ways. Perhaps the claim is that producers are reckless (in that they are aware of the risk of harm they cause to women, but disregard it) or even negligent (in that they fail to fulfill a duty of care, which is not to harm women even indirectly). The negligence option is particularly problematic, since mens rea is not found in negligent acts. The real difficulty, though, is the assertion that pornography producers and distributors, on the basis that their activities happen to generate some inequality, are indeed reckless or negligent. If this allegation can be maintained, then there is no barrier to sustaining a charge against certain feminists that they, too, contribute to inequality, since some of their writings can be seen as emphasizing the inferiority of males.[77] Thus, Easton's suggestion does not fulfill its purpose of creating a stopping point along the slippery slope, and the prospect of prohibition backfiring—and damaging the push toward equality—remains.

Easton attempts a similar, but slightly more complex, argument later in her book. She frames pornography production, distribution, and consumption as instances of the general transgression of inciting sexual hatred, which she then claims is analogous to the case of incitement to racial hatred. This latter wrong is recognized by the law (as in hate crimes), and since the law in that context is acceptable, there is no reason for thinking that incitement to sexual hatred ought not to be a crime as well. In this respect, her strategy is somewhat similar to the one MacKinnon employs at times. By appealing to the broader justificatory base of incitement to sexual hatred, Easton apparently believes pornography can be kept separate from other sorts of materials, the banning of which would harm the feminist pursuit of equality.

However, when Easton's argument is applied to the forward-looking, goal-based framework with equality as the relevant goal, several problems become evident. It may be argued that enacting hate legislation has not helped racial minorities, and in fact it has backfired in just the way feared by Smart.[78] Such legislation was used in the 1960s to convict members of Britain's Universal Coloured Peoples' Association; despite the fact that their intention was to generate racial awareness through dialogue (some of which made reference to injustices perpetrated by whites), they were found to have contributed to hatred between the races. Michael X, a leader of the civil rights movement in Britain, was jailed for several months for some of his comments. Again, two main factors appear to contribute to these sorts of unfortunate and unintended results: the already existing nonegalitarian nature of society, and the inability to draft sufficiently specific legislation. Society continues to be racist, and minorities are at risk when the nonminority authorities apply general legal statutes.

These sorts of concerns are present in the case of feminism as well, and in this sense, at least, the analogy holds. Some of MacKinnon's remarks, for example, could indeed be construed as inciting hatred against men,[79] and, unfortunately, it is reasonable to think that a hate-based restriction of the sort described by Easton would not only be used by someone in the citizenry in an attempt to censor MacKinnon, but would also be used by someone in the judiciary as a basis for ruling against MacKinnon.

There are other difficulties with this approach, including problems with the analogy (such as the historical differences between women and racial minorities) and epistemological problems of ascertaining just when a particular instance of speech (or action) incites hatred. The preferable strategy is to accept that prohibition poses risks to equality, since, in accordance with the glide down the slippery slope, the scope of materials affected by legal prohibition may well expand.

This implies the existence of rights to produce, distribute, and consume pornography, which in turn implies that a social policy banning pornography ought not to be adopted. Instead, it should be recognized that the speed with which society is approaching equality between women and men (economically, politically, socially, and otherwise) is notable; we are on the right track. Certainly, decisive action is called for when progress toward a goal is stagnant or negative, but when progress is positive (and considerably so), intervening in an attempt to increase that speed may prove detrimental. As in the case of affirmative action, there may just be a natural limit to the velocity of progress toward equality.

Thus, the prescription of the goal-based theory is the same whether liberty or equality serves as the relevant goal: pornography should not be legally prohibited.

Notes

1. American Booksellers v. Hudnut, 475 U.S. 1001 (1986). In Canada, however, a similar statute was upheld in accordance with the new Canadian constitution, the Charter of Rights and Freedoms. (See Butler v. Regina, 2 W.W.R. 577, 1992.)

2. Frustration with the inability to arrive at a workable definition led Justice Stewart to issue his well-known statement that he could not provide a definition

of pornography, but simply knew it when he saw it. Jacobellis v. Ohio, 378 U.S. 184 (1964).

3. For a discussion of the possibility of pornographic art, see Susanne Kappeler, "No Matter How Unreasonable," Art History 2 (1988).

4. Gloria Steinem, "Erotica and Pornography: A Clear and Present Difference," in The Problem of Pornography, ed. Susan Dwyer (Belmont, CA: Wadsworth, 1995).

5. See MacKinnon, Feminism Unmodified (Cambridge, MA: Harvard University Press, 1987), 176.

6. Helen E. Longino, "Pornography, Oppression and Freedom: A Closer Look" in The Problem of Pornography, 35. Longino incorporates into her definition some of the language employed by the United States Report of the Commission on Obscenity and Pornography (New York: Bantam Books, 1979), 239.

7. Andrea Dworkin, "Power," in The Problem of Pornography, 48–49.

8. Catherine Itzin, "A Legal Definition of Pornography," in Pornography: Women, Violence and Civil Liberties, ed. Catherine Itzin (Oxford: Oxford University Press, 1993), 439.

9. Following MacKinnon and Dworkin, feminists will call for the prohibition of all inegalitarian material, and following Steinam, will call for the prohibition of only such material (leaving erotica unaffected). Conservatives will encourage the prohibition of at least sexually inegalitarian material (as well as erotica and other items that are more generally offensive). There is general agreement among these groups regarding the preferred policy on pornography as defined here, and this agreement is a key factor in proceeding with this definition.

10. Miller v. California 413 U.S. 15 (1973).

11. Steinam implies that, so long as the material is not inegalitarian (and thus not pornography on the current view), it retains an element of value, be it literary, artistic, cultural, or otherwise. It is clear from its decision in Miller that the Supreme Court does not share this conviction.

12. Mill, On Liberty, ed. John Gray (Oxford: Oxford University Press, 1991), Chapter 2.

13. The qualification is added to account for J. L. Mackie's views on morality, expounded in Ethics: Inventing Right and Wrong (London: Penguins Books, 1977).

14. Cass Sunstein, Democracy and the Problem of Free Speech (New York: Macmillan, 1993), 130.

15. So long as a sufficient portion of the audience takes the speech to be a contribution to public deliberation about an issue, this second criterion is met.

16. The additional assumption is that pornography is properly classified as nonpolitical speech.

17. T. M. Scanlon, "A Theory of Free Expression," Philosophy and Public Affairs 1 (1972), 204.

18. Ronald Dworkin, "Do We Have a Right to Pornography?," in The Problem of Pornography, 78.

19. MacKinnon, Only Words (Cambridge: Harvard University Press, 1993), Chapter 3.

20. See Sunstein, 139.

21. Ronald Dworkin, "Do We Have a Right to Pornography?" 79.

22. Devlin, The Enforcement of Morals (London: Oxford University Press, 1965), especially Chapters 1 and 5.

23. Ibid., 10.

24. Ibid., 15.

25. See H. L. A. Hart, Law, Liberty, and Morality (Stanford: Stanford University Press, 1963), 51–52.

26. Devlin would no doubt contest this claim, since he allows that even private actions can contribute to the disintegration of society; hence his rejection of the private/public distinction in morality. See The Enforcement of Morals, 13–14.

27. The stipulation that such exhibitions are properly classified as nonpolitical speech is crucial to this claim.

28. Some may claim offense at the mere knowledge that the pornography industry exists. However, it is a reasonable assumption that more viable interests come into play only when there is actual exposure to the offensive material.

29. Corinne Sweet, "Pornography and Addiction," in Itzin, ed., Pornography: Women, Violence and Civil Liberties, 83–86.

30. It is on this point that I break with Gerald Dworkin in his defense of paternalism. See "Paternalism," in Philosophy of Law (5th ed.), ed. Joel Feinberg and Hyman Gross (Belmont, CA: Wadsworth, 1995), 215–16.

31. See, e.g., Andrea Dworkin, "Against the Male Flood: Censorship, Pornography and Equality," in Itzin, ed., Pornography: Women, Violence, and Civil Liberties, 522–23; Susan Easton, The Problem of Pornography (London: Routledge, 1994), 19–20.

32. MacKinnon, Only Words, 27.

33. Easton, 19.

34. On this point see Duggan, Hunter, and Vance, "Feminist Antipornography Legislation" in Morality in Practice (4th ed.), ed. James P. Sterba (Belmont, CA: Wadsworth, 1994).

35. Feminism Unmodified, 180; Only Words, 37.

36. Edna F. Einsiedel, "The Experimental Research Evidence: Effects of Pornography on the 'Average Individual'," in Itzin, ed., Pornography: Women, Violence and Civil Liberties, 265–66; James Weaver, "The Social Science and Psychological Research Evidence: Perceptual and Behavioral Consequences of Exposure to Pornography," in Itzin, ed., Pornography: Women, Violence and Civil Liberties, 293.

37. N. M. Malamuth and James V. P. Check, "Sexual Arousal to Rape Depictions: Individual Differences," Journal of Abnormal Psychology 92 (1983), 55–67.

38. This assertion on my part is made on the basis of a limited number of studies. However, since similar conclusions in this respect were found across the range of examined studies, I take the claim to be substantiated.

39. See Berl Kutchinsky, "Legalized Pornography in Denmark," in Men Confront Pornography, ed. Michael S. Kimmel (New York: Meridian Books, 1990), 244–45, who cites evidence from both Denmark and the Netherlands in support of this claim. See also William A. Linsley, "The Case Against Censorship of Pornography," in Pornography: Research Advances and Policy Considerations, ed. Dolf Zillman and Jennings Bryant (Hillsdale, NJ: Lawrence Erlbaum, 1989), 350.

40. Edward Donnerstein, Daniel Linz, and Steven Penrod, The Question of Pornography: Research Findings and Policy Implications (New York: The Free Press, 1987), 171.

41. Ibid., 133–36. There are, of course, studies that affirm the alleged causal link, such as Diana E. H. Russell, "Pornography and Rape: A Causal Model" in Itzin, ed., Pornography: Women, Violence and Civil Liberties.

42. See Patricia Gillian, "Therapeutic Uses of Obscenity," in Censorship and Obscenity, ed. Rejeev Dhavan and Christie Davies (Lanham, MD: Rowman and Littlefield, 1978).

43. For discussion see Deborah Cameron and Elizabeth Frazer, "On the Question of Pornography and Sexual Violence: Moving Beyond Cause and Effect," in Itzin, ed., Pornography: Women, Violence and Civil Liberties; R. T. Rada, Clinical Aspects of the Rapist (New York: Grune and Stratton, 1978) who suggests that a childhood of violence and sexual abuse is the more relevant cause of socially deviant behavior; and R. Langevin, D. Paitich, and A. Russon, "Are Rapists Sexually Anomalous, Aggressive, or Both?" in Erotic Preference, Gender Identity and Aggression in Men: New Research Studies, ed. R. Langevin (Hillsdale, NJ: Lawrence Erlbaum, 1985), who intimate, more specifically, a causal connection between a child's having an abusive, alcoholic and/or neglecting father and his exhibiting antisocial behavior well into adulthood.

44. "Pornography and Civil Liberties," in Itzin, ed., Pornography: Women, Violence and Civil Liberties, 559.

45. W. L. Marshall, "Pornography and Sex Offenders," 189.

46. Feminism Unmodified, 185.

47. This is the case, for instance, on Joel Feinberg's analysis of causation in the law. See Harm to Others (Oxford: Oxford University Press, 1987), 237.

48. This is roughly the picture set out by J. L. Mackie in The Cement of the Universe: A Study of Causation (Oxford: Oxford University Press, 1974), 35–36.

49. This point is made by Rae Langton, "Whose Right? Ronald Dworkin, Women and Pornographers" in The Problem of Pornography; MacKinnon, Only Words, Chapter 3; and Sunstein, 219.

50. H. Patricia Hynes, "Pornography and Pollution: An Environmental Analogy" in Itzin, ed., Pornography: Women, Violence and Civil Liberties, 387–89. I am also indebted to Larry May for his views on this matter. The analogy sometimes makes use of the concept of "group harm," which in the previous chapter was found to be problematic. However, if it is understood merely as reducible to violations of the individual rights of the members of the group (in this case women), no such difficulties should arise.

51. Ronald Dworkin, "Liberty and Pornography," in The Problem of Pornography, 118.

52. Only Words, 6, 77.

53. On this point see Frank Michelman, "Conceptions of Democracy in American Constitutional Argument: The Case of Pornography Regulation," Tennessee Law Review 56 (1989), 303–4.

54. Sunstein, 219–20.

55. "Liberty and Pornography," 120; "Women and Pornography," New York Review of Books (October, 1993), 36.

56. Sunstein, 46–48.

57. Langton, "Whose Right?", 100–1.

58. Ronald Dworkin, "Women and Pornography," 38.

59. For this reason, restrictions on hate speech seem permissible; the interest of equality outweighs its rather weak opponent, which is an interest, grounded in personal autonomy, in intentionally harming others (if only verbally). If, however, certain groups happen to be adversely affected as a result of political speech

(the right to which is grounded in interests of political participation, listener autonomy, and denying government the opportunity to censor), this result does not obtain. MacKinnon's apparent unwillingness to yield her equality standard even in cases of political speech compounds her problems. (Only Words, 82–86.)

60. Only Words, 99–100.

61. Langton, "Speech Acts and Unspeakable Acts," in The Problem of Pornography, 214–15.

62. The idea seems to apply as well to the political context. The right to make a contribution to public deliberation is grounded by the same interests, whether it is made via speech or conduct. The broader "freedom of expression" seems to be the more appropriate reference.

63. Only Words, 71.

64. The recent expansion of media in which pornography can be consumed has contributed to its increased usage. In addition to books and magazines, pornography can be consumed via telephone, home video, cable television, computer programs, and interactive computer networks. Because of the nature of the industry, annual sales figures are difficult to ascertain, but the conservative estimate several years ago was $10 billion. See Dwyer, The Problem of Pornography, introduction; Itzin, "Sex and Censorship: The Political Implications," in Feminism and Censorship: The Current Debate, ed. Gail Chester and Julienne Dickey (London: Prism Press, 1988).

65. See Hawkins and Zimring, Pornography in a Free Society (Cambridge: Cambridge University Press, 1991), 54–56. It should be noted that statistics of women pornography users may be exaggerated by counting sales of erotica, gay pornography, and other materials that do not fit the "nonegalitarian" definition specified in section 7.1.

66. "Women and Pornography," 37–38.

67. Incorporated into this claim is the ongoing assumption that all such types of entertainment have very similar effects, such that the aggregate conclusion results from a number of equal contributors, rather than from several with disparate effects on liberty.

68. See Duggan, Hunter, and Vance, "Feminist Antipornography Legislation," 328–33.

69. Easton, 69–70.

70. Langton, "Whose Right?," 102–4.

71. British Home Office, Report of the Committee on Obscenity and Film Censorship (London: Her Majesty's Stationery Office, 1979), 59. See also Hawkins and Zimring on the issue of burden of proof, 128–30.

72. Langton, "Whose Right?," 104.

73. Carol Smart, Introduction to Feminism and the Power of Law (London: Routledge, 1989).

74. See Lisa Duggan, "False Promises: Feminist Anti-Pornography Legislation in the U.S.," in Feminism and Censorship: The Current Debate.

75. See Easton, 66, 71.

76. Ibid., 69.

77. This charge has been made, e.g., by a number of reviewers of MacKinnon's Only Words. Carlin Romano's statement is representative. Romano writes,

"MacKinnon's scenario . . . reeks of exactly the dehumanizing attitude toward men that she accuses men of exhibiting toward women. It radiates the kind of hostility, resentment and contempt toward men that MacKinnon skewers men for expressing toward women, and perhaps prompts them to express more hostility in return." See "Between the Motion and the Act," The Nation (November 15, 1993), 564.

78. This is roughly the position taken by Pratibha Parmar, "Rage and Desire: Confronting Pornography," in Feminism and Censorship: The Current Debate.

79. For example: "The message of these (pornographic) materials, and there is one, as there is to all conscious activity, is to 'get her,' pointing at all women, to the perpetrators' benefit of ten billion dollars a year and counting. This message is addressed directly to the penis, delivered through an erection, and taken out on women in the real world." (Only Words, 21.)

8

Abortion

8.1 Moral Standing

The final application of the interest- and goal-based theories of rights will be to the issue of abortion. As discussed in Chapter 1, some parties to this debate in particular have been unyielding in their claims, each appealing to alleged rights that in the context of the debate seem to verge on being absolute. Those who oppose abortion point to a "right to life" possessed by the fetus,[1] which renders abortion impermissible. A few of these opponents think the right is absolute and thus that abortion is consequently never permissible. Others, however, offer the right as defeasible, subject to being overridden, but only in certain rare circumstances, such as when the life or health of the mother is in danger. Meanwhile, those who endorse the permissibility of abortion typically point to a "right to choose" possessed by the mother, which renders prohibition of abortion impermissible.

These two positions constitute the "extremes" of available policy options. The former may be referred to as the conservative position, understood as the claim that abortion ought not to be permitted. Doctors and mothers who engage in the practice violate the fetus's right to life, and thus commit a serious moral transgression for which they ought to be legally liable. The latter may be referred to as the liberal position, understood as the claim that abortion at any time during pregnancy ought to be available to women. For liberals, abortion violates no right to life; on the contrary, denying the opportunity to abort violates the woman's right to choose. Between these, there is room (nine months' worth of room) for a moderate policy that would allow abortion up to some point during pregnancy, but restrict (or even deny altogether) abortion availability thereafter. Such a position faces theoretical challenges; the moderate must pick out a certain point during the very gradual process of fetal development and indicate why abortion prior to, but not after, that point is permissible.[2] Neither the conservative nor the liberal faces this difficulty.

For the conservative the critical point—the one at which the right to life overrides or cancels the right to choose—is at conception. For the liberal, the critical point is at birth.[3]

A key aspect of the conservative argument, and also of certain liberal arguments, is the concept of moral standing. One might be tempted to think of legal standing as an analogue, especially since this route has been taken earlier in this book with respect to moral rights and moral duties. In the analogue approach, since legal standing is had by anyone (or anything) who has legal rights or legal duties, moral standing would be had by anyone (or anything) who has moral rights or moral duties. But this would not be the most useful understanding in the context of the abortion debate, in which the moral standing of the fetus is a primary point of contention. The dispute between liberals and conservatives is often a dispute over whether the fetus has a right to life; upon further inspection it often turns out to be a dispute over whether a fetus is the sort of thing that can have any rights at all. Disagreement over moral duties possessed by the fetus is nonexistent; no one is claiming that the fetus has (or even can have) duties. Applying terminology popular in the literature, the debate is not over the question of whether the fetus is a moral agent, understood as one who is capable of owing moral duties, but whether the fetus is a moral patient, understood as one to whom moral duties can be owed (and thus, on the Hohfeldian scheme, one who has moral rights).[4] Thus, for purposes of the discussion in this chapter, moral standing will be understood as the capacity for having moral rights.

Often underlying the discussion of the moral standing of the fetus is the debate over whether the fetus is a "person." The concept of personhood frequently plays a prominent role in simple arguments for or against the permissibility of abortion. Conservatives have appealed to some version of the argument that since the fetus is a person and since killing innocent persons is morally wrong, abortion is morally wrong. Liberals have responded by denying the initial premise.

Thus, since understanding what constitutes personhood is of some importance, only a few brief observations on this issue will be made at this point. First, persons are not to be understood as human beings. The latter designates a particular species, homo sapiens, and is appropriate only in biological contexts. Personhood, however, is a moral concept, and there is no necessary connection between being a person and being in the biological class of human beings. Thus, it may well turn out that some humans are not persons, or that some persons are not human. Second, it is clear from discussions in which the concept of personhood has been employed that the term has been used to designate those things that have all the moral rights of the prototypical normal adult human being, the prototypical person. Because the abortion debate is often a comparative disagreement over whether the mother possesses more moral standing than the fetus, specifying a particular set of rights is unnecessary (although a "right to life" is certainly among the set). It is enough to stipulate that there are some rights that all persons necessarily have; the question is whether the fetus has these rights as well. To persons should be attributed "full" moral standing. Things that can have no rights correspondingly have "no" moral standing. Straightforward conservative arguments attribute full moral standing to the fetus, while certain liberals attribute none to it. The concept of "some" moral standing should also be recognized, since it is conceivable that there exist certain things that have some rights but not the full scope of rights possessed by normal adult humans. Certain nonhuman animals (hereafter simply "animals," as distinguished from "humans"), for instance, may have some moral standing. Third, whether or not a particular thing has at least some moral standing, understood as the capacity to have at least some moral rights, will be a function of the underlying theory of rights. Thus, the implications of the two theories employed in this book will now be examined.

8.2 Rights of Abortion: The Interest-Based Theory

This section will first consider the liberal position, interest-based arguments for which are typically of two sorts. First, it is sometimes claimed that the fetus has no moral standing, from which it follows that aborting a fetus is no more morally problematic than, say, removing a tumor. Second, it is sometimes claimed that the unique relationship between mother and fetus is such that the mother possesses a right to an abortion regardless of the moral standing of the fetus; even if it has full moral standing and is thus a person, the fetus's claims are outweighed by those of the mother.

Arguments of the first sort are relatively straightforward. The fetus has no moral standing, and so no wrong can be done to it. A woman, on the other hand, has a wide variety of rights, and among the most important is the right to control her body. On the Raz model, this right is easily understood as based on the interest of personal autonomy and grounds the derivative rights to limit one's reproduction and to have abortions at any point during pregnancy.[5]

What is the reason for thinking that the fetus has no moral standing? An adequate answer to this question requires specifying a criterion for moral standing and then demonstrating that it is not met by the fetus. In the interest-based theory, a being has moral standing if and only if it has interests, but without unpacking what this means, this claim alone will not answer the question of whether the fetus has moral standing. Thus,

on the interest-based theory, the question of the criterion for moral standing is equivalent to the question of the criterion for possessing interests.

According to Michael Tooley, this criterion is self-consciousness.[6] In
support of his claim, Tooley first observes that possession of a right is
correlative with the obligations (or duties) of others. Such obligations,
however, are contingent upon the desires of the rightholder. From his
later comments, it is clear that Tooley intends this to mean that the
would-be beneficiary must be able to waive the performance of the duty
he is owed, and the failure to waive it indicates that the requisite desire
is retained.[7] The capacity to possess these sorts of desires is therefore a
necessary condition for the possession of rights. The so-called "right to
life," according to Tooley, is more accurately a right to continued existence, and more specifically to the continued existence of one's experiences and other mental states. Thus, the right to life, understood in this
way, is contingent upon the would-be rightholder's desire for this continued existence.

The final aspect of the argument is the stipulation of a necessary connection between desiring some good and possessing the concept of that
good. Tooley claims that an entity cannot have a right to life, understood
as a right to continued experiences, unless it possesses the concept of a
self as a continuing subject of experiences. Applied to the context of abortion, a fetus is not the sort of thing that can have this concept. Working
backward, it therefore cannot desire its own continued existence, and so
is incapable of possessing a right to life. (In order to classify this argument as one that denies any moral standing to the fetus, it need only be
added that if a being is not a candidate for possessing a right to life, it is
not a candidate for possessing any rights at all, and thus is devoid of
moral standing.)

The two key steps in the above argument are both problematic. The
first claims that rights are dependent upon the desires of the rightholder.
The assumption is that rights are alienable, and that the rightholder is to
be understood as an active manager of the various normative relations
over which he has a power. In other words, the choice conception of
rights is implicitly being appealed to by Tooley. This move should not be
allowed. First, this runs counter to the plan, set out in Chapter 2, to employ the benefit conception of rights in conjunction with the interest-
based framework. Second, the benefit conception is indeed appropriate
in the case of abortion, since the conservative, in claiming the existence of
a right to life held by the fetus, is clearly committed to that conception, as
a fetus lacks altogether the managerial abilities required of a rightholder
on the choice conception. This move by Tooley thus begs the question in
his favor.[8] Third, when the benefit conception of a right is employed, a
fetus retains its status as a candidate for having interests and thus for

having rights and moral standing.[9] Assuming that the right to life is a claim, held against others, not to be killed, it is perfectly plausible that a fetus can have such a claim without also having the ability to make the claim.[10] Of course, this consideration is not decisive in favor of the fetus; it merely rebuts Tooley's opposing claim, which would be decisive against it.

The second step in the argument—the claim that possession of desires necessarily assumes the possession of concepts—can also be questioned. Tooley appears to utilize a Kantian notion of concepts. According to Kant, concepts refer to universals; they are generalizable terms, applicable to an indefinite number of entities, and as such they allow for rationality. Without concepts, we would be limited to isolated, momentary particulars.[11] When Tooley writes that "the desires one can have are limited by the concepts one possesses," his rationale is that one cannot desire that a certain proposition be true unless she understands it, and such an understanding requires the possession of these sorts of universalizable concepts.[12] It is the introduction of propositional content into the explanation that is problematic. This seems to suggest the requirement of linguistic abilities. Tooley later denies this,[13] but then it is unclear what the possession of concepts amounts to. A different approach would be to allow for so-called "simple desires" (for which the possession of concepts is unnecessary) to enter into the considerations.[14] For example, studies show that the typical fetus will react negatively to bright lights or loud noises. The commencement of negative reactions to such stimuli is contemporaneous with the development of the corresponding organs for sight and sound. Thus, it seems perfectly appropriate to attribute to the late-term fetus, at least, a desire, even a "simple desire," not to be harassed with bright lights or loud noises, or other phenomena noxious to its senses. Therefore, even if Tooley's first step is permitted, such that rights are connected with desires, the sense of "desire" need not be one that necessarily relies on the possession of concepts, and thus the liberal position is not necessarily supported.[15]

One other potential problem warrants a mention at this point. The above objections aside, it may be suggested that Tooley's argument proves too much and can be rejected through a reductio ad absurdum. The concept of a self as a continuing subject of experiences and other mental states is not generally obtained until persons reach at least the age of two years, and perhaps later.[16] This implies that until that age, children cannot have rights, including the right to life. The ensuing implication is that infanticide is as permissible as abortion in Tooley's view, and surely this is not acceptable. In itself, however, this is not a decisive reason for rejecting Tooley's argument. This conclusion certainly conflicts with most commonsense intuitions, but to his credit, Tooley is consistent in allowing for infanticide nonetheless. Unless a more defensible criterion for moral standing can be recognized, the implications may have to be allowed (although given the above difficulties with the argument, a superior alternative can most likely be found).

A somewhat different liberal argument is offered by Mary Anne Warren, who focuses on denying that the fetus is a person.[17] According to Warren, various elements contribute to the concept of personhood. The most central are consciousness, reasoning, self-motivated activity, the capacity to communicate, and self-awareness. While she is not committed to the thesis that these are individually necessary conditions for personhood, Warren does suggest that personhood might be a matter of degree, and that a being lacking any of these conditions certainly cannot count as a person. Applying this reasoning to the case of abortion, she claims that even a late-stage fetus is no more "personlike" (in terms of these criteria) than a very early fetus or even a fish.[18]

Several responses can be made here. First, it is simply assuming too much to claim that a late-term fetus is, in the respects Warren delineates, no more personlike than an early fetus. It is entirely reasonable to believe that the late-term fetus is conscious, and also has a corresponding ability to perceive pain, since the brain is well developed by the end of the second trimester.[19] From all indications, there is also no reason for denying that it is capable of self-motivated activity, self-awareness, and some (simple) ability to communicate. In these respects, a late-term fetus is not appreciably different from an infant; certainly, there are no intrinsic differences between the fetus hours before birth and the infant hours after birth. Perhaps Warren intends more complex understandings of her elements of personhood, such that no fetus would be a person. If so, however, then infants would not be persons either, and infanticide would seem perfectly permissible.[20] (Again, this objection is backed only by intuition until a more specific alternative criterion for personhood can be provided.) Finally, Warren may not be denying that fetuses lack moral standing altogether, as demonstrated by her willingness to make personhood a matter of degrees. Rather, she may be denying that fetuses are full persons, possessing full moral standing. If fetuses can be said to have at least some moral standing, however, then more discussion is required before the liberal position can be established. It does not follow from women having full moral standing and fetuses having merely some moral standing that abortion is necessarily permissible.

In sum, the foregoing two arguments are prima facie problematic because of their inability to explain why late-term fetuses lack moral standing (or, in Warren's case, personhood) and why infants do possess moral standing (or personhood). Both have attempted to retain consistency by denying (some or full) moral standing to the infant as well. This move remains a possible solution, since the only objections to it are at this point merely intuitive.[21] The second type of argument for the liberal position focuses not on the moral standing of the fetus but on the relationship between mother and fetus, which may seem, on initial inspection, to be a more effective route.

On this second view, the moral standing of the fetus is irrelevant to the permissibility of abortion. A well-known version of the argument is provided by Judith Jarvis Thomson.[22] It should be noted at the outset, though, that Thomson allows that abortion is impermissible in certain cases, and thus does not take herself to be defending the strict liberal position. Even so, her remarks can easily be employed as such a defense, and a fairly substantial one.

Thomson considers the "right to life" invoked by conservatives and finds that it cannot be absolute.[23] Her suggestion is plausible, in that conflicts of absolute rights generate unhappy dilemmas. This observation, though, means that the right to life is more complicated than some conservatives (namely those who assert it as the sole basis for their view) seem to think. The question, then, is whether the fetus does have this right, and here Thomson argues by analogy.

She asks us to consider the case of a woman who awakens one morning to find herself back to back with a famous violinist who is suffering from a serious kidney ailment. While she was sleeping, the woman's kidneys were hooked up to those of the violinist. This arrangement sustains the violinist's life, and if it is continued for a period of nine months, he will have recovered completely and can be safely unplugged. The woman is able to disconnect herself, but then the violinist will die. The relationship between the two, who are both "persons," is thus parasitic, involuntary, and burdensome to the host.[24]

The claim that the woman has a duty to remain in bed, connected to the violinist for a period of nine months so that he may live, is unfounded according to Thomson. There is nothing grounding any such duty to remain connected. It follows that she possesses a Hohfeldian privilege to disconnect; she has, in other words, a "right to choose." Further, because she has no duty to remain connected, the violinist cannot possess a correlative claim that she remain connected. Thus, any "right to life" possessed by the violinist is not violated. The final step in the argument is to assert that pregnancy is an analogous situation.

This argument carries a good deal of plausibility on the interest-based theory of rights. The privilege possessed by the woman is a privilege to disconnect herself rather than a privilege to kill the violinist. If it is to carry any weight, the right to life must instead be conceived positively, and its content must be the receipt of positive assistance from the woman.[25] In this conflict, the right of the violinist to be assisted, based on an interest in continued existence, does seem to be outweighed by the right of the woman not to do so, based on an interest of personal autonomy (including bodily integrity). To claim otherwise would be to demand a great deal of the woman, to the point where no room would remain for supererogation. In Thomson's words, one cannot have a right that others act as Good Samaritans; to remain in bed connected to the violinist for nine months would indeed be an act of Good Samaritanism on the part of the woman, and the violinist cannot hold a right against her that she do so.

While persuasive, these considerations cannot, ultimately, support the liberal position on abortion. First, and most directly, not all pregnancies, and indeed very few, exhibit the characteristics of being burdensome to the extent portrayed in the case of the violinist. Women tend not to be bedridden, and in most cases are not adversely affected, physically or psychologically, to a degree anywhere near that of a woman who suddenly finds herself facing a nine-month imprisonment in bed.[26] The ensuing suggestion is that in many cases personal autonomy is not unacceptably compromised, and thus may well be outweighed by the interest of the fetus (who, recall, is assumed to be a person) in continued existence. The prima facie right to life would then override the prima facie right to choose abortion.

Thomson may respond that this approach is wrongheaded in two ways. First, the argument is supposed to suggest that rights to bodily integrity (in the form of claims against others) are the ground for the woman's more specific right to an abortion, and since bodily rights are very strong indeed, they cannot be overridden when pitted against claims to positive assistance. Rights (claims) to the use of another's body, which entail correlative duties to allow one's body to be used, require consensual acceptance of such duties. To deny this appears to endorse certain practices of slavery. Second, and more generally, Thomson feels uncomfortable with the idea that the existence of a right can be contingent upon the ease with which a correlative duty can be performed.

Beginning with the second of these, there is no reason why, as Thomson puts it, "the question of whether or not a man has a right (should not) turn on how easy it is to provide him with it."[27] Indeed, this contingent aspect is part of the interest-based theory as it has been delineated. Recall that in the Raz model an interest grounds a right if and only if it is sufficiently strong to ground the performance of the duty to honor the right, and whether or not this is the case is partly a function of the prevailing conditions. The implication for the abortion context is that the answer to the question of whether or not a particular fetus has a right to life is partly a function of whether the circumstances in that particular pregnancy allow for the mother to execute the duty.

Regarding the first criticism—that rights to bodily integrity are sufficiently strong so as to require consent if they are to be overridden by the
rights of another—Thomson appears to be begging the question here as
well. This protest bears a certain similarity to the so-called "body parts
problem," leveled by the libertarian against the welfare liberal in the debate over redistributive taxation. According to that problem, the fact that
one person has, say, two healthy kidneys and can part with one of them
does not mean he has a moral duty to do so, even when another person
will die without a transplant. Thomson's violinist scenario seems clearly
analogous in its commitment to rights to bodily integrity. However, the
response to the libertarian was that the lack of a duty to surrender a kidney is only contingent, and that if a safe means of doing so (and of overcoming the risks of living with one kidney) were one day discovered, the
duty would be had. In other words, the fact of bodily integrity is not the
overriding condition; rather, it is the contingent medical risk. It follows
that in the case of pregnancy, considerations of bodily integrity itself cannot suffice to block the duty of the mother not to abort.[28] Since pregnancy
is often relatively safe, the duty may often persist. Of course, a variety of
medical complications may cancel the duty, but this fact only counters
the conservative position; it does not establish the liberal position.

A final liberal protest would be to once again point out that in an abortion procedure, the mother (or doctor[29]) is not killing the fetus, any more
than the woman in Thomson's example is killing the violinist. She is,
rather, "disconnecting" herself from it. Thomson is careful to emphasize
this,[30] and it may be claimed that the above objections to her argument
have missed this important point. But the point has not been missed. The
claim is that there are times when the mother has a duty not to disconnect, and that the fetus, correlatively, possesses a right against her that
she not disconnect. Such times will include at least those pregnancies that
are not involuntary and unduly burdensome to the mother, since in such
pregnancies the interest underlying the mother's right to an abortion can
plausibly be said to be outweighed by the interest underlying the fetus's
right that she not abort.

The liberal position is not supported by Thomson's argument insofar
as the abortion of late-term fetuses, at least, does not in general appear to
be permissible. It remains open to the liberal to suggest that, contrary to
Tooley's claims, the fetus does have some moral standing, but that, contrary to Thomson's assumption, it is not yet a person. If so, its level of
moral standing might be similar to that of an animal. Since animals that
are inconveniences may be destroyed, it seems the same is true of fetuses.
More about this suggestion will be said later, but for now, the intuitive
objection noted earlier may be offered against the claim that all fetuses
are not persons. Were this the case, then infants, who are not significantly

different from late-term fetuses, are also on a par with animals, and may be destroyed if they are found to be inconvenient. Surely this is wrong. Of course, Tooley (and to some extent Warren) deny that infanticide is wrong. Whether or not their seemingly counterintuitive position can be refuted on the interest-based theory will be seen momentarily.

The liberal position does not seem promising. An examination of some arguments for the other extreme, the conservative position, will help determine whether it offers a preferable alternative policy, or whether some moderate position should be adopted.

One conservative argument is offered by John Noonan, whose general approach in addressing the issue of when personhood begins is to eliminate points other than conception on the basis that they are arbitrary.[31] He considers the criterion of viability, the point at which the fetus is able to live outside of the mother. Because of technological advances, the point of viability can be very unclear. The answers to questions such as whether a fetus in an artificial womb is viable (or whether it is a fetus at all) would then determine its moral standing; but basing standing on socially determined definitions is arbitrary. Further, this criterion is not morally relevant according to Noonan. Not being viable entails being dependent on another for one's well-being, including perhaps one's continued existence, but there is no reason for denying personhood on the basis of being dependent. Indeed, it is the vulnerable and dependent who ought to be afforded the strongest protections. Consideration of extremely dependent adult human beings will allegedly confirm this thesis.

A second possible criterion is that of experience. It is sometimes suggested that a being cannot have full moral standing until it has the capacity to feel and to suffer, and that this capacity is not had until well after conception. Noonan responds that this is not the case, and that this criterion cannot mark any genuine distinctions among the fetal stages, since even a zygote is alive and responsive to its environment.[32] He also considers other, less plausible criteria, such as parental sentimentality and social visibility, and he concludes that conception is the only point at which personhood can, consistently, be said to begin. In an effort to strengthen this claim, he then gestures at a positive reason for thinking that conception is the critical point, which is that conception is when the entity receives its genetic code. Through this offering, Noonan apparently takes his otherwise purely negative argument (his reasoning against opposing views) to be reinforced.

A first observation here is that Noonan has identified a major difficulty in the abortion debate, namely, the difficulty of picking out a precise point at which the fetus becomes a person. Because pregnancy necessarily involves a very gradual process of fetal development, the identification of any such point will certainly seem arbitrary. However, as has been noted several times in earlier chapters, the (acknowledged) difficulty of drawing lines does not imply that no lines ought to be drawn. What needs to be shown is that the early fetus (the zygote) can have morally relevant interests, and this has not been done. Citing the fact (if it is a fact) that a zygote is responsive to its environment fails to establish that it has any moral standing at all, let alone full moral standing; plants and single-celled organisms, for instance, are responsive in this way, but these things are certainly not persons (beings with "full" moral standing) and they likely lack moral standing altogether. By citing conception as the point at which the genetic code is received, Noonan at best identifies the point at which something becomes a human being. His confusion in thinking that this is equivalent to becoming a person in the morally relevant sense is evidenced by the language he employs. For instance, he talks about "humanity" and "becoming human," and claims that "a being with a human genetic code is man."[33] Because no relevant connection between being human and being a person is provided, Noonan's conservative argument is unpersuasive.

The difficulty of demonstrating that a very early fetus has interests has led some conservatives to attempt a different route to their desired conclusion. The claim is that, while it can be conceded that the early fetus has no interests, the fetus's moral standing derives from its potential to have interests. If left alone (i.e., if not killed), it will likely develop into a being that has all the interests of the prototypical adult human person, and thus will itself be a person.[34] To strengthen this argument, appeal is made to statistical probabilities; the probability of a fetus developing into a person is judged to be greater than 80 percent. The probabilities for individual spermatozoa and oocytes, meanwhile, are overwhelmingly small. It thus makes sense to speak of the fetus, but not gametes, as having potentiality. This deflects the criticism that if a simple zygote has potential interests and thus moral standing, then individual sex cells have potential interests and thus moral standing. If plausible, that criticism would warrant a policy of banning the use of contraception, in the name of the right to life of individual gametes, and this seems absurd. Employing probabilities, however, the "potentiality principle" is appropriately applied to the fetus in the same way that it applies to all persons. As Devine writes, "Even a normal, awake adult can be thought of as a person for essentially the same reason as an embryo: both are capable of using speech and so on, although the embryo's capacity requires the more time and care before it is realized."[35]

To this argument, it may be responded that Devine has conflated the notions of potentiality and capacity, and that there is a relevant difference between them. Potentiality, on a standard definition, is such that an entity has the potential for quality X if it has never had X, but, given a certain course of events, will come to have X. Thus, the proposition that the fetus possesses the potential to have interests, and is thus a potential person, is accurate. But in the above quotation, potentiality is replaced with the notion of capacity, and this is problematic. L. W. Sumner's characterization of a capacity is appropriate here:

> Possession of a capacity at a given time does not entail that the capacity is being manifested or displayed at that time. A person does not lose the capacity to use language, for instance, in virtue of remaining silent or being asleep. The capacity remains so long as the appropriate performance could be elicited by the appropriate stimuli.[36]

The early fetus does not appear to have the capacity to suffer or to feel anything, and certainly it does not have the capacity to use speech as implied by Devine. Potentialities may have ramifications for a forward-looking moral theory and so may be relevant to the question of abortion within the goal-based theory of rights. On the interest-based theory, however, unless the entity has interests, it cannot have rights. Because it can only be said of the early fetus that it possesses the potential to have interests and does not in fact have interests, then on the interest-based theory it cannot have rights, and in fact it cannot have any moral standing at all. Therefore, the early fetus lacks the right to life alleged by conservatives.

Of course, the conservative may object to the designation of the fetus as a "potential person." Stephen Schwarz, for instance, argues that the fetus is an actual (rather than potential) person, despite the observation that it doesn't function as a person.[37] It is in this respect, he claims, that fetuses and unconscious (but otherwise normal) adult human beings are similar. Neither displays the characteristic functioning of a person, but each will do so in the normal course of events. Each, therefore, has the capacity to function as a person, and while the types of capacity may differ,[38] that difference is not morally relevant. There is therefore no basis for ascribing personhood to one (the unconscious adult) and not the other (the early fetus).

Despite the new name tag, that which is possessed by the early fetus is still merely potentiality and not capacity. This move by Schwarz amounts to little more than verbal reshuffling, and in the end cannot ground the conservative conclusion. The heart of the problem is Schwarz's insistence that a normal adult human and the zygote from which it developed are the same person. Such a claim is supported only by a very peculiar view of personal identity. In the context of the abortion debate, a more defensible theory of personal identity might be a reductionist view of the sort described by Derek Parfit. According to the reductionist view, if, say, Gerald Ford is transformed, very slowly, into a 30-year-old Greta Garbo, it does not make sense to say that the person resulting from this process is, in any sense, Gerald Ford. Both physically and psychologically (complete with memories and dispositions), that person is Greta Garbo. This conclusion can only be denied by appealing to some "further fact" of identity (such as a Cartesian Ego), a move that ultimately fails.[39] The gradual transformation of a newly fertilized egg into a nine-month-old fetus (or newborn infant) is analogous to the Gerald Ford–Greta Garbo transformation, according to Parfit; thus, it cannot be said that a single-celled zygote and the late-term fetus into which it develops are the same person.[40]

It seems that neither the conservative nor the liberal position on abortion is well-founded. This finding suggests that a moderate policy, in which abortion is permissible up to a certain time during pregnancy, might be superior to either extreme. Before exploring that possibility, however, it is worth highlighting some of the more constructive findings from the foregoing discussions.

First, as Tooley points out, there are no substantive differences between the moral standing of a late-term fetus and the moral standing of an infant. While the intuitive temptation is to count this observation as a strike against the liberal, Tooley instead employs the unconventional strategy of using it to support the justification of infanticide. Until a preferable criterion for moral standing is identified, Tooley's suggestion must remain a candidate, and in any case the similarity between fetus and infant is itself likely to be relevant. Second, as Thomson points out, the unique relationship between fetus and mother, in which the former is parasitic upon the body of the latter for several months, must be taken into account. Thomson is right in her observation that philosophical discussions of abortion run the risk of focusing too narrowly on the status of the fetus, and we would do well to avoid falling into the same sort of reasoning. Third, as Noonan points out, the specification of a precise point at which personhood (or moral standing generally) is acquired is likely an impossibility. Noonan therefore recommends avoiding the attempt to do so altogether. It will be seen that there are moral reasons for thinking that this is not the best strategy, but his broader message, that a "magic point" during the course of pregnancy may simply not exist, is well-taken. The fourth (and related) consideration is that, as Parfit points out, a reductionist view of personal identity may be the most appropriate model for application to the span of fetal development (from conception until birth).

Bearing these in mind, consideration of a moderate abortion policy should now be undertaken. As mentioned in this chapter's introduction, such a policy will not be easy to maintain. Given the apparent inadequacies of the alternatives, however, an attempt should be made. If too many

problems persist, it may have to be conceded that the abortion controversy is an issue for which the language of rights is genuinely unhelpful.

The question of moral standing is as good a place to start as any. Three
broad criteria might be considered: rationality, sentience, and life itself.[41]
While rationality is generally considered a sufficient condition for moral
standing,[42] there are problems with the assertion that it is a necessary
condition. Most basically, there are interests that are in no way connected
with rationality. It is reasonable that a being that can experience pain has
an interest in avoiding pain, and clearly, possession of rationality is not
necessary to experience pain. Of course, it is impossible for such a being
to communicate to us rational creatures, via language or use of concepts
at least, that it is experiencing pain. The best a cat can do, for example, is
to cry out when its tail is stepped on; it cannot ask the perpetrator to be
more careful in the future. But the negative reaction to a painful stimulus
should suffice as a demonstration that at least some nonrational beings
have interests and thus, on the interest-based theory, moral standing;
Cartesian explanations, according to which pain reactions are purely me-
chanical rather than demonstrative of states of awareness, should be rejected.[43] This does not entail that a strong right to life is possessed by
many nonrational beings, but it does mean that further discussion (regarding, e.g., the prevailing conditions and the interests at stake) is warranted.

Here, then, is some theoretical (rather than merely intuitive) force
against the view, offered by Tooley, that late-term fetuses and infants
alike possess no moral standing. They can feel pain and thus have some
interests and some moral standing. Again, this does not, in itself, mean
that the liberal position has been defeated. It may still be the case that
whatever moral standing is had by the fetus is overridden in the context
of abortion, perhaps (but not necessarily) for reasons similar to those offered by Thomson. It does imply that the route to the liberal position
taken by Tooley and Warren is unfounded.

A life-based criterion for moral standing looks initially to have more
plausibility. It may be argued that any entity that is alive has a good of its
own, in that it can be benefited or harmed; there is a way in which things
can be said to go better or worse for that entity. The idea is that all living
things are "teleological centers of life." They are "unified systems of goal-
oriented activities directed toward their preservation and well-being."[44]
Because the natural functioning of an organism can be helped or harmed,
the organism itself can be helped or harmed; it therefore has interests,
and for this reason is said to have moral standing.

This criterion would ascribe moral standing not only to humans and
animals but to plants as well. It would also mean that all fetuses have
moral standing, which is the conclusion at which conservatives want to

arrive. But a criterion that assigns moral standing so widely may be problematic, especially if the beings are alleged to have full moral standing.
The idea of a plant having a right to life is strongly counterintuitive.[45]
Imagining a world in which duties toward plants are as morally compelling as duties toward human beings is difficult to say the least. Yet,
this radical egalitarianism of moral standing may have to be adopted if
the conservative position is to be supported by appeal to a life-based criterion. It may not suffice for a fetus to have merely some moral standing
if it is to have a right to life, held against its mother.

There are sound reasons, however, for rejecting the life-based criterion.
It alleges that insofar as plants can be benefited or harmed, they have interests, but this assumes an underlying conception of interests that is
somewhat dubious. Specifically, it assumes an objective conception of interests, according to which the entity possessing the "needs" does not
have to be capable of being aware of its needs, in any sense. In other
words, an interest can be a need that does not, and indeed cannot, matter
to the entity in question. Even a rudimentary consciousness, on this reasoning, is not necessary for having interests. But then it is difficult to see
why these sorts of interests are morally relevant. The mere fact that an
entity is self-regulating, and that a "disturbance" causes a self-adjust-
ment of some sort, appears to be grounding the claim that self-regulating
systems have interests the infringement of which would be prima facie
morally wrong. As the critical premise, the fact of self-regulation appears
insufficient to establish the desired conclusion.[46] The requirement that
the need must matter to the being explains the exclusion of things like
machines (whose value, it is assumed, can only be derivative) from having interests. The recommendation, then, is for the adoption of a subjective conception of interests, according to which interests must have a
conative being as their subject.[47] In this conception, what Goodpaster,
Taylor, and others have called interests, possessed by plants, are really
something else or are appropriately labeled morally irrelevant interests.

It may be objected that this line of reasoning begs the question as well.
The (mere) fact of consciousness appears to be grounding the claim that
self-regulating systems with some sense of awareness have interests the
infringement of which would be prima facie morally wrong. All living
things clearly strive for their own survival, and in so doing they make
use of whatever faculties they have at their disposal. Consciousness, according to this line, should be viewed merely as one such faculty (though
a significant one). Again, though, for this approach to be persuasive, a
sense of intentionality must be ascribed to beings that have no consciousness (e.g., plants must be thought of as "striving" for their survival), and this seems an illicit move. Even so, allowing such beings to
have some (but certainly not full) moral standing can be tolerated. Be-

cause the addition of consciousness can plausibly be said to add greatly to the depth, breadth, and intensity of interests, this allowance will not ultimately amount to much. Since only moral agents can have any duties toward plants, and since moral agents are themselves "persons," the weighing of interests in circumstances of conflict will almost invariably result in the overriding of the plant's interests. Thus, if things like plants have any moral standing at all, they have what may be called "trivial" moral standing. Because it is trivial, discussion hereafter will treat plants (and all such entities, which are "merely" alive) as having no moral standing.

The implication is that moral standing is acquired some time between the beginning of life and the acquisition of rationality. More specifically, if certain nonrational beings have interests (because they can experience pain and other feelings), and if life itself is insufficient to establish (any significant) moral standing, sentience seems to be the appropriate criterion. In simplest terms, sentience is to be understood as the ability to enjoy and to suffer.[48] It is the ability to be benefited or harmed in any way that matters to the being in question.[49] By "matters," it is not necessary for the being to be continuously or consciously aware of the interest; it does mean that the infringement of the interest causes a negative reaction indicating that, in some sense, the being cares about that infringement.[50]

As the criterion for moral standing, sentience has the advantage of admitting of degrees. Its application to the gradual process of fetal development is thus relatively unproblematic. There is no magical point at which sentience is acquired, and in this way Noonan's concern can be accommodated. Rather, it is attained gradually. In addition to separating beings with some moral standing from beings with none, sentience can also serve as a comparison criterion, as the standard for determining which beings, from among those having at least some moral standing, have more than others. Sentience avoids the intuitive problems of over-inclusiveness (associated with the life-based criterion) and underinclusiveness (associated with the rationality-based criterion), and its plausibility is supported by theoretical considerations of subjective interests, discussed above. The next step is to apply the criterion of sentience to abortion.

It has been suggested that the very early fetus is not sentient. It is essentially a clump of cells (and even a single-celled zygote at the very beginning) with no capacity to experience anything. As early as six weeks after conception, the development of the physical attributes necessary for sentience has begun.[51] By the fourteenth week (roughly the end of the first trimester), most of the neural components necessary for sentience can be detected. Thus, it makes sense to say that sentience is acquired over the course of that eight-week stage and is had at the end of that stage, at which time the fetus can be said to have some moral standing. Over the course of the next several months, the development of the various relevant aspects (forebrain, cerebral cortex, brainstem, and the neural connections among them) continues, until approximately the middle of the seventh month, at which time the components of the nervous system are indistinguishable from those of the infant.

These observations have the following implications for the permissibility of abortion. During the first trimester, abortion, considered in itself, is permissible for any reason. Although it is an act of killing a living being, it is not the killing of a being with any moral standing; rather, it is the prevention of the formation of a being with moral standing. In this way, first-trimester abortion is morally comparable to killing a plant and is thus comparable to contraception. Intuitive resistance to this conclusion is unfounded. It may be objected that since the stage of sentience acquisition occurs during the first trimester, some moral standing should be attributed earlier. However, since any first-trimester moral standing would be very minimal, it can be classified as "trivial" moral standing. The competing interests of the mother, therefore, need be very minor in order for her right to choose to prevail.

After the cessation of the growth of the neural components necessary for sentience (roughly in the seventh month), the fetus can be said to be fully sentient.[52] The late-term (that is, third-trimester) fetus is thus a "person" in the morally relevant sense. This means that late-term abortions are (generally) impermissible and should be prohibited. The interest grounding the alleged right to an abortion, personal autonomy, is outweighed by the interest of the fetus (a person in the third trimester) in continued existence. Describing its right to life negatively, as the right not to be killed, is inappropriate, as Tribe points out.[53] It is a positive right, a claim, held against its mother (or indeed against anyone in a position to furnish assistance) that she provide the support needed for its continued existence. Thus, a correlative duty to provide such support, possessed by the mother, is alleged to exist. This right of the fetus is justified on the interest-based theory, since it passes the tests posed by Raz. The interest in continued existence is valuable, and (in general) is sufficiently strong to warrant holding the mother under a duty; the competing prima facie right of the mother to choose, based on an interest of personal autonomy, is outweighed.

The late-term fetus's right to life is not absolute, however. One overriding condition obtains when the pregnancy poses a threat to the life of the mother. In such circumstances, the right to an abortion is justified in two ways. The first justification is based on a principle of self-defense, according to which an innocent person may protect herself against the threat of another. When the aggression is of such severity as to endanger the life of the potential victim, she may respond in kind, taking the life of the aggressor if necessary. A threat to one's life may not even be necessary to justify such a reaction; a strong case can be made that the use of deadly force in self-defense is permissible when the only alternative is to endure a certain substantial degree of harm (but not death). Further, the aggressor need not be morally culpable, or even "aggressing" in any strong sense. In Thomson's discussion, distinctions are made among a "villainous aggressor" (one who attacks a victim and is responsible for his actions); an "innocent aggressor" (one who attacks, but because of a mental abnormality is not, and cannot be, responsible for his actions); and an "innocent threat" (one who, by virtue of his relationship to the potential victim, poses a threat to her life but does not "act" at all and is not responsible for the situation).[54] Thomson argues that in all three cases, the potential victim has a right to life that justifies taking the life of the aggressor (or threat). This conclusion follows from the interest-based theory; a personal autonomy interest grounds the Hohfeldian privilege to kill in self-defense.[55] The innocent aggressor and innocent threat (but not the villainous aggressor) also possess such a privilege; but since their privilege is not stronger than the one possessed by the potential victim, the victim does no wrong in defending herself.[56]

The analogy to abortion should be clear. The fetus is an innocent threat to the life of the mother, and its mother is justified in taking its life in order to defend herself. The justification is the existence of a right (in the form of a privilege) to self-defense, grounded by an interest of personal autonomy (or, perhaps, a core interest in well-being generally).

There is a second way in which the mother's right to a late-term abortion is justified when her life is in danger. It has been assumed to this point that the third-trimester fetus is a person. In the background, however, are echoes of Tooley's view that rationality must have at least some relevance for personhood. While rationality is not a necessary condition for moral standing, it can be said that the possession of rationality enhances one's interests, in that it allows for a fuller understanding of them. No very deep understanding is necessary. An adult suffering an asthma attack has some understanding that there is a problem with the workings of his body, even if he is ignorant of the workings of the lungs. Further, he can understand some of the potential consequences of his predicament, and this understanding enhances his interest in overcoming his problem. The addition of rationality to an otherwise fully sentient being may not have dramatic ramifications for the degree of moral standing, but there are some. Thus, rather than describing late-term fetuses and infants as persons, it is more accurate to describe them as "near persons," in order to indicate the difference between possessing and lacking rationality.

This difference should not be overemphasized; in general, an infant suffering an asthma attack ought to receive the very same assistance as an adult in similar circumstances. The difference between "persons" and "near persons" will be of practical import only when there is an "other things equal" conflict between the parties, that is, when both face the same unpleasant fate that only one will suffer. Difficult pregnancies and births, in which it seems clear that either the mother will live (or suffer severe physical debilitation) or the fetus will live, are examples of such conflicts. In these situations, it is at least the case that the mother has no duty to allow the fetus to survive rather than herself; she therefore possesses a privilege to choose her own life. (She certainly may choose her fetus at her own expense; the relevant point is that she has no duty to do so.)

This second justification has other implications that don't necessarily follow from the first. In particular, the doctor appears to be compelled to save the mother, at the expense of the fetus, when there is no way of ascertaining the mother's preference (e.g., when she is unconscious). This is the principle that comes into play in "burning building" examples, in which a rescuer has the time and ability to save only one of two potential victims; one will be saved and the other will die. When one potential victim is a "person" and the other is a "near person," it is argued that the rescuer has a duty to save the person.[57] The doctor faces an analogous situation.[58]

Another implication is that the practice of partial-birth abortion should not be prohibited, at least when the mother's life is at stake.[59] Those opposed to the practice emphasize that most of the fetus has been born,[60] and that it is therefore as much infanticide as it is abortion. In this they are correct, but the occurrence of birth is not itself morally significant. The moral standing of the fetus is not altered as a result of birth. Indeed, not until the onset of rationality (at least several months after birth) does the infant become (or begin to become) a "full person." The case of partial-birth abortion presents an "other things equal" conflict between a "near person" and a "full person," and thus, first, the mother may choose her life over that of her fetus, and second, the doctor has a duty to choose the mother's life if her preference cannot be ascertained. The same moral prescription would obtain if the conflict were between a mother and her three-month-old infant; the situations are morally equivalent. In this way, Tooley's insight can be accommodated.

To this point, the interest-based theory of rights has generated policies for the first and third trimesters of pregnancy. During the first trimester, the woman's "right to choose" overrides all conflicting considerations; therefore, the policy ought to allow a woman to obtain an abortion for any reason during this period. During the third trimester, the fetus's "right to life" overrides many (but not all) conflicting considerations; therefore, a policy prohibiting abortion, except when cases of the sort described above obtain, is called for. The remaining task is the determination of what policy is appropriate during the middle trimester of pregnancy.

During this period, the fetus is said to have some (but not full) moral standing, but this does not entail the immorality of middle-trimester abortions. A comparison of the competing interests is still required. The interests of the woman wishing to have an abortion (personal autonomy in particular) are significant; the interests of the fetus warrant closer examination. It has been said that during the first trimester, the fetus's interests (if any) are trivial. During the fourth month, it is reasonable that they continue to be of lesser weight than those of its mother, and so the permissive policy should hold. While the fetus is sentient, and its interests (in terms of number, quality, and intensity) are growing, they are still outweighed. Recall that the fetus's alleged right to life is a claim to positive assistance, and thus requires more on the part of its objects (the bearers of the correlative duty) than would a "mere" (negative) right not to be killed.

The fifth month poses more difficulties. While "unjust killing" (wording representative of the language employed by conservatives) should certainly be avoided, denial of needed assistance is somewhat less compelling. During the sixth month, however, the fetus is approaching full sentience. Because its interests are such that it is quite close to achieving personhood or "near-personhood," there is good reason for thinking it ought to be afforded its mother's assistance.

The foregoing considerations suggest that the most defensible policy recommended by the interest-based theory of rights would allow for unrestricted abortion through the fifth month of pregnancy, and deny it thereafter, except in cases where the life or health of the mother is at stake. Pending further research on prenatal development,[61] this is a fairly reasonable point at which the moral weight of the fetus's interests can be thought to surpass that of its mother.

8.3 Rights of Abortion: The Goal-Based Theory

Throughout the chapters in Part 2, the particular conception of rights has not played a significant role in the various analyses. For reasons discussed in Chapter 2, the benefit conception has been used in conjunction with the interest-based theory of rights, and the choice conception has been used alongside the goal-based theory. Nothing substantial has turned on these assignments, which have been used primarily as explanatory aids.

This does not hold for the present case, however. As noted in the previous section, the debate over abortion rights is largely a debate over what sorts of beings can have rights. Appeals to rights possessed by the fetus are out of place in the choice conception, since a fetus is clearly incapable of the managerial abilities required of a rightholder on that conception. Any appeal to fetal rights must therefore employ the benefit conception (whether or not this is done consciously). Because we are doing philosophy "from the inside out" (i.e., beginning with current practical problems rather than with theory), we should abandon in the present section the practice of using the choice conception with the goal-based theory.[62]

With this in mind, the task of determining which goal should be pursued must be addressed. Two initial candidates for goals (each of which should be familiar by now) might be agreeable to proponents of both the liberal and conservative positions. One candidate is well-being. Conservatives are likely to accept well-being as the goal, since their concern pertains to the status of the fetus, and their aim is to protect it by disallowing abortion. Liberals will be somewhat tolerant of this goal, since they point to a variety of worries regarding the mother's well-being as justification for her right to obtain an abortion. However, liberals also endorse a woman's right to choose even when well-being is not an issue of primary concern; her freedom to choose is appealed to, and so the goal of freedom will likely be preferable to liberals. While a fetus's freedom is not typically thought of as the primary concern of the conservative, there is some room within the notion of freedom to accommodate the conservative nonetheless.

When these considerations are tallied, the goal of freedom recommends itself as the superior alternative, so long as it is conceived broadly, in order to account for the well-being of the fetus (and thus pacify the conservative). On this construal, freedom includes the value of well-being; if one's well-being is adversely affected, then (other things being equal) one's freedom is correspondingly adversely affected (though freedom may be affected in ways not pertaining to well-being).[63] In this way, the goal of freedom should be acceptable to proponents of both the liberal and conservative positions. The abortion debate may then be described in terms of freedom: the freedom of the mother to obtain an abortion conflicts with the freedom of the fetus, which (on the proposed formulation) would be infringed if it were aborted.

The scope of moral standing implied by this goal appears, at first blush, to be identical to that implied by the principles of the interest-based theory of rights. Specifically, sentience seems the appropriate criterion in the goal-based theory. Unless a being is sentient, it cannot experience freedom; nonsentient beings cannot, even in a rudimentary sense, experience anything. Meanwhile, a sentient being can have its freedom violated if such freedom is construed negatively, as the absence of constraints; thus, the (negative) freedom of a sentient but not rational being is respected simply by leaving it alone.[64] For these reasons, sentience appears initially to be a necessary and sufficient condition for moral standing. The accuracy (or inaccuracy) of this initial supposition should become evident as the discussion continues.

Before proceeding, it is worthwhile to review the nature of the harm of killing generally.[65] A forward-looking moral theory may initially appear to have difficulty accommodating such harm, for once death occurs, there no longer exists a subject whose good (in this case, freedom) can be assessed. It is often the case that a person's death has negative consequences for others, such as friends and family members, but the negative aspect of death for the victim himself may not be so clear.[66] The resolution here is that the harm to the victim consists in the total and permanent deprivation of all goods, including freedom, with which we are primarily concerned. The intentional act of killing is thus very serious. Because the freedom lost in death is clearly more substantial than the freedom lost in being subjected to a rule prohibiting killing, rules prohibiting killing would have positive effects on the overall amount of freedom.[67] In the goal-based theory of rights, this result implies the existence of a (moral) right not to be killed, correlative with a duty not to kill.[68]

This understanding of the harm of death accords with the initial hypothesis regarding the scope of moral standing. Nonsentient entities cannot have moral standing; because they cannot possess freedom, they are not capable of losing freedom. The foregoing also agrees with our commonsense intuitions that, other things being equal, the death of a fully rational being is more regrettable than the death of a "merely" sentient (i.e., nonrational) being.[69] The former loses much more, since freedom is greatly enhanced by the possession of rationality. The awareness of one's long-term options, and the ability to adjust one's long-term planning accordingly, are not had by nonrational creatures, whose freedom is much more primitive.

While the harm of death can thus be accounted for on the goal-based theory, the nature of the harm of not being created poses more serious difficulties. Attempts to describe harm invariably entail references to the victim. In the case of not being created, however, there is no victim and there never was one. Indeed, any sentence with "the victim of the harm of not being created" as its subject verges on being nonsensical, since there is nothing to which that subject refers.[70] While some may think the case of death is similar in this respect, the difference is that death, again, entails loss; there was a person, and the total and permanent deprivation of his freedom constitutes the loss.

At this point, it seems that the liberal position is destined to be prescribed by the goal-based theory. Aborting an early fetus is refraining
from creating a being with moral standing; it is thus comparable to contraception and is wholly permissible. While aborting a late-term fetus is
killing, it is a nonrational being whose freedom is lost; such freedom is
comparable to that had by an animal and is therefore likely to be outweighed by the freedom gained by the mother. Abortion at any time during pregnancy seems permissible. Moreover, infanticide may also be unproblematic. Because there are no substantive differences between a
late-term fetus and an infant, the infant's freedom is also of a primitive
sort and will be overridden by the mother's gain. Only when the onset of
rationality begins will this prescription change. (Assuming the above
claims regarding comparisons of freedom, infanticide may still be impermissible when alternatives such as adoption are available in society.)

However, there exists an apparently significant objection to this rather
straightforward line of reasoning. While the notion of potentiality was
found in the interest-based theory to be unhelpful to the cause of the
fetus, it may have much more significance in the goal-based model. If so,
then even the very early fetus may warrant moral protection. The reason
for thinking that potentiality is relevant is that freedom is normally in the
future of the fetus, and in a forward-looking theory the future must matter. Within such a theory, there appears to be no morally relevant difference between refraining from creating more freedom in the world on the
one hand (which aptly describes early abortions) and failing to allow the
development of the freedom of an already-sentient being (or even a "near
person") on the other hand (which describes late-term abortions).[71] It is
tempting to say that the good of an early fetus must count in the
cost/benefit analysis. However, because an early fetus has no moral
standing, it is unclear just whose good this is. Referring to future persons
is somewhat misleading, since in any particular case a new person may
or may not come into existence, depending on a number of factors. Sumner therefore utilizes the term "dependent persons" to designate "all
those who will exist (at some time) only if some particular course of action is chosen by the mother pondering an abortion."[72] Employing this
term, the content of the objection can be captured in the following way:
accounting for the good of independent but not dependent persons in the
cost/benefit analysis is arbitrary and thus may well lead to inaccurate
conclusions. Moreover, once the good of dependent persons is added to
the mix, it is argued that abortion will be seen as wrong and that the conservative position will have to be adopted.

One way of responding to this objection might be to depart from the
traditional standard of maximization and appeal instead to a theory of
the right according to which the greatest average good should be

achieved.[73] (The difference between maximization and greatest average is significant only when the good of dependent persons enters into the calculations.) In the maximizing approach, obtaining an abortion is impermissible when carrying the pregnancy to term will produce a net overall gain in freedom. Other things being equal, the conservative prescription will hold in the maximizing strategy even when the net increase is less than the existing average level of freedom. However, this is not the case on the averaging approach, according to which the potential for a mere overall increase in freedom is not, in itself, sufficient to prohibit the abortion; the increase must not reduce the existing average.

Support for the averaging approach is not wholly unfounded. It seems perfectly consistent with the general consequentialist doctrine, "The greatest good for the greatest number."[74] If maximization were the goal, then why not just "the greatest good"? The problem is that this approach establishes, at most, that it may be the case that abortion is impermissible. This is because it may (or may not) be the case that the increase in freedom associated with the creation of a new being bolsters the existing average and thus entails a duty to create it. Further, the approach itself might be problematic in its implications. It could be that (perhaps extreme) population contraction may be called for, as when the existence of fewer persons will lead to more freedom per individual.[75] In the current reasoning, women would have duties not to procreate in such circumstances, and the prescribed social policy would be intolerant of procreation. There may even be a call for the elimination of a number of persons in order to reach the desired optimum number; further, the question of which specific persons should be eliminated may be a function of the averages that would result from various possible assortments of subsets of particular persons.

The primary difficulty with the averaging approach, however, is its violation of the impartiality condition that is a necessary aspect of an acceptable consequentialist theory. When the same amount of freedom can be produced either by creating a new person or by performing some other act that does not entail a new person, the averaging approach necessarily prescribes the latter. According to Sumner, the good of dependent persons thus counts for less, and this is unacceptable.[76]

Other responses to the potentiality problem attempt to reduce the degree to which the good of dependent persons should play a role in the analysis, but these responses face exactly the same problem. It has been suggested that the good of dependent persons should be discounted, such that the final outcome of the cost/benefit analysis in the case of abortion will be unaffected by the introduction of their good into the calculations.[77] Others have weighted positive and negative effects differently in an effort to achieve the same result.[78] Impartiality is violated in either case.

There may be some redeeming aspects of the averaging approach that mitigate the force of some of the problems associated with it. The bottom line, though, is that it fails to sustain the liberal position on abortion. Once the good of dependent persons is taken into account, abortion during any stage of pregnancy may well be impermissible.

Still, there seems to be something very odd indeed about the maximizing approach. The language during the preceding discussion has focused more on the notion of duties than on rights. This is understandable insofar as the language of rights is not easily incorporated into the present situation. However, the aim of the project at hand is to address practical problems within the context of rights, and so the various rights implications must be considered. If, as it now seems on the direct cost/benefit analysis, there exists a duty not to obtain an abortion even during the very early stages of pregnancy, then there appears to be a right not to be the victim of an abortion.[79] Specifying the subject of this right is hard enough; we have decided to proceed with Sumner's "dependent person" designation, though there are potential metaphysical difficulties associated with this notion that have been overlooked. Assuming these can be addressed, however, specifying the content of the right poses a whole new set of problems. The assignment of any particular right to a dependent person seems problematic, since there is nothing that can concurrently have that right. Redescribed, the problem is that a right with meaningful content cannot be ascribed to a dependent person. In the abortion context, the unease with which a dependent person is accorded a right "to become," or a right "to develop into a person," is evident.

An attempt to avert this difficulty might be made by appealing to the following sort of example. A wrongdoer plants a bomb in a populated building and programs it to detonate in three hours. It does so, causing death and injury. It seems natural enough to say that the wrongdoer has violated his duty not to harm others, and that the victims' rights not to be harmed have been violated. But this should be the case regardless of whether the wrongdoer programs the detonation to be in three hours, three weeks, three years, or even three hundred years. In the case that the detonation is successfully programmed for three hundred years in the future,[80] the sets of persons existing in the two time periods are (presumably) exclusive; the wrongdoer is long gone by the time his plot is realized, and none of the victims was around at the time the bomb was set. Even so, according to this line of reasoning, there is no reason to abandon the initial characterization of the situation, according to which the wrongdoer has violated the rights of the victims. But then those victims, who at the time of the wrongful act (setting the bomb) were dependent persons, can have rights despite the fact that they are dependent.

This case is somewhat disanalogous with abortion, however, since the victims in the bomb example are, at the time their rights are violated, independent persons. It can be said of these independent persons that they hold rights against members of past generations not to take actions that endanger their well-being (or freedom generally; the specific good is presently unimportant). Or, it can be said of the dependent persons at the time of the wrongful act that they hold rights against the wrongdoer (and others) conditionally, the condition being that they in fact do become independent persons, since if this condition is not met they will not suffer the death and injury from the bomb blast. The problem obtains when an attempt is made to ascribe to dependent persons rights that are not conditional in this way.[81]

The foregoing suggests the following conclusions regarding the abortion of early fetuses. On a direct cost/benefit analysis with freedom as the relevant goal, there exists a duty not to obtain abortions. This is because a woman considering an abortion faces two options, one of which (carrying the fetus to term) will produce more overall freedom than the other. However, for the above reasons it cannot be said that there is a right held by early fetuses not to be aborted. It seems, therefore, that for the first time in this book we have an instance in which the language of rights fails. There is no right of the fetus, but neither is there a right of the mother; her duty not to obtain an abortion entails her lack of a Hohfeldian privilege to do so. In the direct cost/benefit analysis, there are no rights anywhere; yet there is a morally preferable policy.

Despite their previous vehement appeals to fetal rights in the abortion debate, conservatives are likely to be quite prepared to abandon those claims in exchange for the endorsement (by this theory) of their proposed social policy. However, because the implications only of the direct cost/benefit analysis have been suggested, declaring the conservative position to be recommended by the goal-based theory would be premature. A full analysis requires investigating whether there are indirect reasons for thinking that constraints, in the form of rights to obtain abortions, might be called for.

In this vein, it may be that these considerations in favor of the conservative position prove too much. Even early abortions appear impermissible on the direct analysis because of the increase in freedom associated with the creation of a new person. But this justification implies not only a duty to refrain from obtaining abortions but also a general duty to procreate. Recall that according to the potentiality principle relied on by conservatives, the distinction between refraining from creating a new person on the one hand and ending the life of an existing person on the other is (irrespective of side effects) irrelevant. This means that contraception is wrong, and moreover, that the failure to procreate is wrong. In a maximizing approach, the more freedom the better. Because in each case the addition of a new person (normally) creates more freedom than is consequently lost by others, on each occasion of choice (of whether to create a new person) the appropriate action is to procreate.

This conclusion of the direct analysis cannot be avoided. The gain in freedom generated by the creation of a new person will normally outweigh the loss. There may be exceptions, such as when a fetus is diagnosed with a disease that would cause its life to be filled with horrible suffering.[82] In general, though, the duty to procreate is intact. It may be thought that, as population increases and reaches critical levels, the duty to procreate is canceled, but this is unlikely to be the case; gains in freedom continue to be had with the addition of new children. While additional losses of freedom will be felt by others as problems associated with overpopulation escalate, it must be remembered that because of diminishing returns, the loss felt with the addition of each particular child will in all likelihood be rather moderate, and will not be so great as to outweigh the gain.

Thus, the direct analysis entails not only a duty to refrain from obtaining abortions, but also a duty to procreate. If another conclusion is to be reached, it must follow from indirect considerations. Recall that indirect considerations take into account what is likely to occur in the long run, regardless of the prescriptions associated with each particular instance of choice. Because in the long run a duty to procreate is likely to be self-defeating in the manner described above, there are good reasons for thinking that certain constraints are appropriate.

In order to determine exactly which constraints should be recognized, the difference between killing and failing to create should again be appealed to. It has already been suggested that a social policy prohibiting killing is called for on the goal-based analysis. Permitting such a practice would make life intolerable, and the side effects on freedom would be at least as serious as the central effects (i.e., the effects on the victims themselves). The case of procreation is less clear. A social policy may call for the creation of new persons to be required, prohibited, or permissible. Were a policy to uniformly require procreation, then in the long run problems associated with overpopulation would eventually obtain, and for reasons given above this would be self-defeating. Neither the conservative nor the liberal intends the pursuit of freedom to entail that scenario. Under certain conditions, moderate population growth may be called for, and a policy mandating that couples produce a certain minimum number of children might then be appropriate (although rights would play no role in the justification of such a policy).[83] Abortion may be impermissible in these circumstances. Current conditions, however, do not warrant such a measure; this is the case not only in the United States (which is the focus of this project) but globally.

At the other extreme, a policy uniformly prohibiting procreation would also be self-defeating, and for fairly straightforward reasons; the extinction of the human species cannot be thought to promote more freedom in the world than its indefinite continuation. Again, though, under certain conditions a policy limiting (but not altogether prohibiting) population growth may be in order. Such a policy is currently in effect in China, and other parts of the world threatened with overpopulation might be well-served by adopting a restrictive policy. Abortion in these circumstances may be not only permissible but mandatory. In the United States, however, there is at present no cause for this limitation.

The direct implication of these considerations is that procreation should be neither required nor prohibited, but should be permissible. Couples (or individual women) may decide to create a new being, and they may also refrain from doing so. The broader implication is that within the goal-based theory there are sound reasons for recognizing a distinction between killing a being with moral standing and refraining from creating such a being. Once this distinction is recognized and applied to the context of abortion, the following results are obtained. First, abortions during the first trimester of pregnancy are perfectly permissible. Decisions during this period do not pertain to killing a being with moral standing. Recall that prior to sentience, a being cannot experience anything and so cannot experience freedom; hence, no central consequences for its freedom follow from its demise. Despite the fact that in each particular case (or at least in most cases) carrying the fetus to term would create more freedom, there are good reasons for constraining the pursuit of the goal by not ascribing to the mother a duty to do so. This lack of a duty implies a Hohfeldian privilege on her part; in other words, the mother has a right to obtain an abortion.

Second, abortions of sentient fetuses (i.e., second- and third-trimester fetuses, according to the very general time line established in the previous section) are a matter of killing rather than refraining from creating. The question to be addressed is whether that killing is justifiable, and in the current theory the answer must be a function of freedoms. During the fourth and fifth months of pregnancy, the freedom of the fetus is very rudimentary. This is because the degree of freedom a being can have tends to be correlative with the degree to which it is sentient (other things being equal). Because the sentience of the fourth- or fifth-month fetus is quite basic, the freedom it possesses (and thus the freedom it can lose through being killed) is limited. The freedom gained by the mother is likely to be greater, and so abortion should be permissible during this period.

Things appear to be somewhat different, however, in the case of the late-term fetus, whose moral standing is similar to that of an infant. Side effects aside, the loss of freedom associated with late-term abortion is comparable to the loss of freedom associated with infanticide. If a new mother concludes that she had been mistaken several months earlier in thinking that having the child would be in her best interest, it may be the case that the freedom she would gain by killing her infant (in order to avoid raising it) would outweigh its lost freedom; though its sentience is fairly well developed, it is not yet rational. However, we should be moved by the consideration that there is a third alternative which is superior in terms of freedom, namely the possibility of adoption. Introducing this alternative allows for the freedom of both the mother and the child to remain intact.

The question is whether the case of late-term pregnancy presents any morally relevant differences. One clear difference is that prohibiting abortion does have certain consequences for the mother's freedom. Denying her the opportunity to obtain an abortion entails the use of her body for a period of time. Even so, that freedom loss appears to be outweighed by the potential loss of freedom on the part of the (by now fairly sentient) fetus. Since an infant is not significantly different, it may be asked whether a new mother's freedom may be infringed (to an extent comparable to that endured in a normal pregnancy) for two or three months so that the child will survive. The answer points to a duty on the part of the mother not to kill it in such circumstances. (The existence of certain complications that pose additional threats to the mother's freedom will cancel the duty.) Similarly, in the context of late-term pregnancy, requiring of the mother a few months of her time appears to generate less lost freedom than allowing the fetus to be killed. In this context, the general duty not to kill is not overridden (as it is during fourth- or fifth-month pregnancies) by the fact that greater freedom is to be obtained by allowing the killing.

With this reasoning, then, the conclusion is that early abortions (those occurring through approximately the fifth month) are permissible. The mother possesses a right in the form of a Hohfeldian privilege to choose abortion, since indirect considerations of the cost/benefit analysis indicated a lack of a duty to procreate. Meanwhile, abortions during the final trimester are impermissible. The fetus has been found to have a right (so long as the benefit conception of rights is retained) in the form of a Hohfeldian claim not to be killed. Assigning a policy to the sixth month is not easy, since the nonrational aspects of sentience develop quickly during this time. For an added measure of security, it perhaps makes sense to recognize the rights of the fetus during this time.

One might object to this reasoning. Earlier, it was claimed that indirect considerations ground the recognition of a distinction between refraining from creating on one hand and killing on the other hand. If sentience is the threshold for this distinction, then the implication would seem to be that abortion prior to sentience is permissible and abortion after the onset of sentience is impermissible. The objection points out that only the first of these implications is recognized in the conclusions stated in the preceding paragraph.

The objection is misguided, however, in assuming that postthreshold abortion must be impermissible. Rather, the implication is that abortion must be considered much more carefully after the first trimester since it is a case of killing (and not merely failing to create), but this does not in itself entail a prohibitive policy. Killing is occasionally permissible in other contexts, even the killing of persons (in the morally relevant sense). Once it is recognized that abortion after the first trimester is a case of killing, the question of whether it is permissible killing must be addressed, and this was the aim of the above discussion. The conclusion, again, is that such killing is permitted during the fourth and fifth months but not afterward.

A different objection would challenge the finding that late-term abortions are not instances of permissible killing. Late-term fetuses are not rational, and have no more capacity for freedom than many animals. The claim that the abortion of such fetuses is impermissible because of the degree of freedom they possess implies the existence of a variety of duties toward animals, and also a variety of animal rights correlative with those duties. But this is undoubtedly incorrect; we certainly have no positive duties to animals, and even many negative duties are easily overridden.

The response to this general reductio is to accept the alleged absurdity. It is indeed the case that certain animals have at least as much capacity for freedom as late-term fetuses. Rather than rejecting the prescription regarding abortion, however, it can be accepted that on the goal-based theory of rights, several animals do have rights (perhaps even positive rights) held against human beings. Certain particular negative rights (such as rights not to be hunted, eaten, or used for experimental purposes) would have to be examined individually. If the outcomes were to call for these rights to be recognized, then certain social practices would have to be adjusted. Commonsense intuitions are not so dramatically opposed to these findings as to render them unacceptable. Further, this response will likely seem more appealing when it is realized that the scope of positive duties owed to animals would be rather limited for indirect reasons. Were there too many positive duties owed to too many animals, life for humans would become intolerable, and the overall amount of freedom would ultimately be negatively affected.

The implications of the above conclusions regarding the permissibility of abortion on the goal-based theory are therefore not absurd. Those conclusions, which call for abortion to be permissible through the fifth month of pregnancy and impermissible thereafter (except in those cases where the mother's freedom is unduly threatened, such as when her well-being is at stake), should be accepted as the ones that follow from the goal-based theory of rights.

Notes

1. In this chapter, "fetus" will refer to a being that is the product of conception for the entire duration of pregnancy, from conception to birth. More technical definitions distinguish among the fetus, embryo, and zygote, but for present purposes, "zygote" will refer to a type of fetus, a very early fetus. The term "embryo" will not be used at all.

2. Or, alternatively, dual criteria may be utilized. This was the approach taken by the Supreme Court in the landmark Roe v. Wade decision, 410 U.S. 113 (1973). The Court granted a woman a constitutional right to choose during the first trimester of pregnancy (as a derivative of the right to privacy), and granted the fetus constitutional protection during the third trimester (on the basis of viability). Correspondingly, states may not restrict abortion during the first trimester, and (with few exceptions) must not allow it during the third. Restriction during the middle trimester was ruled permissible, but only on the basis of a paternalistic principle: "preservation and protection of maternal health," a legitimate state interest, grounded the permissibility of state-imposed restrictions during this period. Paternalism was found in the previous chapter to be a dubious principle for government intervention, and the moral relevance of viability can be assessed independently of the Court's ruling. Thus, no further reference to this case is necessary in this chapter.

3. The degree to which these points are critical may vary slightly within each camp; the extreme conservative denies even the permissibility of contraception, while the extreme liberal appears to allow even for the permissibility of infanticide (as will be seen).

4. Christine Pierce and Donald VanDeVeer, Introduction to People, Penguins and Plastic Trees (Belmont, CA: Wadsworth, 1995), 7.

5. A standard argument of this sort is offered by Lucinda Cisler, "Unfinished Business: Birth Control and Women's Liberation," in Sisterhood Is Powerful, ed. Robin Morgan (New York: Random House, 1970), 272–76.

6. Tooley, "Abortion and Infanticide," in The Rights and Wrongs of Abortion, ed. Marshall Cohen, Thomas Nagel and Thomas Scanlon (Princeton: Princeton University Press, 1974).

7. "In Defense of Abortion and Infanticide," in The Abortion Controversy, ed. Louis P. Pojman and Francis J. Beckwith (Boston: Jones and Bartlett, 1994), 184.

8. Those partial to the benefit conception of rights will reject from the outset the claim that rights should be dependent on desires.

9. Again, all three go together on the interest-based theory.

10. Regarding the morally relevant distinctions between having a claim and making a claim, see Feinberg, "The Nature and Value of Rights," in The Philosophy of Human Rights, ed. Morton E. Winston (Belmont, CA: Wadsworth, 1989), 68–71.

11. Kant, Critique of Pure Reason (New York: St. Martin's Press, 1965), 19–23, 129–31.

12. Tooley, "Abortion and Infanticide," 62. Tooley and others who hold rationality to be necessary for moral standing owe a good deal to Kant. See Lectures on Ethics (New York: Harper and Row, 1963), 239.

13. Tooley, "Abortion and Infanticide," 79. Since in Kant's view humans possess an a priori conceptual apparatus, concepts without language seems a logical possibility. Such is not the case if the Wittgensteinian line is taken, since thought itself is said to be constituted by the social system of conventional signs.

14. Tooley allows for the existence of "simple desires," but denies that they can be relevant in determining whether an entity can have rights. See "In Defense of Abortion and Infanticide," 193.

15. A slightly different objection is that these simple desires have corresponding simple concepts that, morally, are as relevant as those of the more sophisticated Kantian variety. When Tom Regan, for instance, talks about the moral relevance of being a "subject-of-a-life," he appears to be referring to these other sorts of concepts. See The Case For Animal Rights (Berkeley: University of California Press, 1983), 243–45.

16. On this point see Sumner, Abortion and Moral Theory (Princeton: Princeton University Press, 1981), 60–61.

17. Warren, "On the Moral and Legal Status of Abortion" in Morality in Practice (4th ed.), ed. James P. Sterba (Belmont, CA: Wadsworth, 1994).

18. Ibid., 153–54.

19. See Steven Rose, The Conscious Brain (London: Penguin Books, 1976), Chapter 7. Warren concedes that pain is probably felt by late-term fetuses.

20. In her postscript to this article, she admits that the act of killing an infant is not murder, but (in a move that confers merely derivative value on infants) she claims that such killing may be morally prohibited for reasons pertaining to societal values.

21. The assumption for now is that problems associated with reflective equilibrium can be overcome. In other words, it is assumed that the permissibility of infanticide is not in such dramatic conflict with our considered judgments as to render it unacceptable.

22. Thomson, "A Defense of Abortion" in The Rights and Wrongs of Abortion.

23. To this point, the assumption has been that the right to life is to be conceived negatively, as the right not to be killed. Among the circumstances in which it may be overridden are instances of killing in self-defense. See Thomson's "Self-Defense," Philosophy and Public Affairs 20 (1991). Analogously, then, it will at least be the case that a woman whose life is threatened by the fetus has the right to kill

it, even when the fetus is innocent. (Thomson, "Rights and Deaths," in The Rights and Wrongs of Abortion, 117.)

24. "A Defense of Abortion," 4–7.

25. Laurence H. Tribe, Abortion: The Clash of Absolutes (New York: W.W. Norton and Company, 1990), 130.

26. This portrayal of pregnancy is from Bernard Nathanson, Aborting America (New York: Doubleday, 1979), 220.

27. "A Defense of Abortion," 17.

28. Thus, consent is not necessary. For a somewhat different argument for this claim, see Francis J. Beckwith, "Arguments From Bodily Rights: A Critical Analysis," in The Abortion Controversy, 167–68.

29. The ongoing assumption will be that the doctor may act on behalf of the mother. The permissibility (or lack thereof) of the doctor performing the procedure mirrors the mother's privilege (or lack thereof).

30. "Rights and Deaths," 118.

31. John T. Noonan, Jr., "Abortion Is Morally Wrong," in The Abortion Controversy.

32. Thus, unlike his response to the viability criterion, Noonan's response here does not appear to reject the criterion altogether, but to suggest that it actually bolsters his position.

33. Noonan, 183.

34. This is, roughly, the argument adopted by Philip Devine, "The Scope of the Prohibition against Killing" in The Abortion Controversy.

35. Ibid., 226.

36. Sumner, Abortion and Moral Theory, 237–38.

37. Schwarz, "Personhood Begins at Conception," in The Abortion Controversy.

38. Ibid., 241–42. Schwarz distinguishes among "latent-1," "latent-2," and "immediately present" capacities.

39. Derek Parfit, Reasons and Persons (Oxford: Clarendon Press, 1984), Chapter 11 (especially 236–43).

40. Of course, the genetic code, appealed to by Noonan, could serve as the "further fact" of identity, but since the two beings are both physically and psychologically distinct, this criterion for identity cannot serve the purpose desired by Noonan.

41. These are the generally accepted candidates for criteria within the scope of individualistic moral theories, i.e., theories that assign moral standing only to individual entities. See, e.g., Kathi Jenni, "Dilemmas in Social Philosophy: Abortion and Animal Rights," Social Theory and Practice 20 (1994), 60–64; Pierce and VanDeVeer, People, Penguins and Plastic Trees, 9–10; Martin Schonfeld, "Who or What Has Moral Standing?" American Philosophical Quarterly 29 (1992), 353–54. Other theories, typically appealed to within a context of environmental ethics, assign moral standing to groups of entities, such as species or entire ecosystems. See, e.g., Aldo Leopold, "The Land Ethic," in Environmental Ethics, ed. Louis P. Pojman (Boston: Jones and Bartlett, 1994); Holmes Rolston III, "Duties to Endangered Species," in Environmental Ethics, ed. Robert Elliot (Oxford: Oxford University Press, 1995), 66–69; Laura Westra, "Ecology and Animals: Is There a Joint Ethic of

Respect?" Environmental Ethics 11 (1989). These are problematic for a variety of reasons, and so the scope will be confined to individualistic theories.

42. The sole exception might be God, conceived as perfectly rational but incapable of being harmed.

43. See Rollin, The Unheeded Cry (Oxford: Oxford University Press, 1989), 123. Whether the apparently negative reactions of plants to certain stimuli indicate the presence of interests will be addressed momentarily.

44. Paul W. Taylor, "The Ethics of Respect For Nature," in People, Penguins and Plastic Trees, 133–34.

45. Those holding the (extreme) biocentric view maintain that such intuitions are a product of bias, and that consistent moral reasoning will yield the existence of strong duties owed to all living beings. See Kenneth Goodpaster, "On Being Morally Considerable," Journal of Philosophy 75 (1978), 312; Taylor, "Biocentric Egalitarianism," in Environmental Ethics, ed. Pojman, 76.

46. On this point see Rollin, "Sentience Is the Criterion for Moral Standing," in Environmental Ethics, ed. Pojman, 31.

47. This is the view of Joel Feinberg, "The Rights of Animals and Unborn Generations," in Philosophy and Environmental Crisis, ed. William T. Blackstone (Athens, GA: University of Georgia Press, 1971), 49–51.

48. Sumner, Abortion and Moral Theory, 142.

49. Rollin, "Sentience Is the Criterion for Moral Standing," 31.

50. In order to distinguish conative beings from plants that may appear to react negatively, certain evidence (e.g., biochemical, neurophysiological) may have to be examined. An implication is that some (higher) animals have the same moral standing as late-term fetuses and infants. Though somewhat counterintuitive, the idea that we have certain substantial moral duties to those animals (which we are likely failing to discharge) ought not to be dismissed; in previous centuries, intuitions regarding the moral status of human slaves were similarly oriented. Many animals, however, will possess a level of moral standing below that of the human infant, owing to their lesser interests (measured in terms of quality, quantity, and intensity).

51. The timing (in terms of the age of the fetus, from conception) is rough here. I am relying only on Rose, The Conscious Brain, Chapter 7, which is certainly not the only source for the specifics of prenatal development. However, the specifics are not relevant; if the timing of the various developments described in this section turns out to be somewhat different, then adjustments can be made. What is relevant is the connection between moral standing and those developments.

52. This claim will be qualified momentarily.

53. Abortion: The Conflict of Absolutes, 130.

54. Thomson, "Self-Defense."

55. In this case, the privilege is a mere privilege; it is not accompanied by a periphery of claims of noninterference held against the innocent threat (or aggressor), who possesses the exact same privilege. Of course, each possesses claims of noninterference against others; in general, third parties may not (without consent) involve themselves in conflicts between innocent parties.

56. For reasons associated with the second justification for life-threatening exceptions to the prohibition on late-term abortion (discussed below), third-party

intervention on behalf of the fetus is impermissible. The mother, however, is en-tirely within her rights to contract with a doctor in her attempt to defend herself.

57. Carruthers appeals to something like this in explaining why a normal adult human, rather than an animal, should be saved. See The Animals Issue (Cam-bridge: Cambridge University Press, 1992), 68.

58. This is not true if the fetus is assumed to be a "full person."

59. Cases in which partial-birth abortion is necessary, e.g., to save the woman's uterus so that she may have more children, but her life is not in danger, pose more difficulties. In such cases, an interest of a "full person," though significant, is pitted against a more significant interest of a "near person." Assessing the rel-evant moral weights in such cases is very difficult indeed. Answers to such situ-ations need not be attempted here, since the aim of the current project is merely to arrive at a general abortion policy.

60. During the 1997 Senate debate prior to the vote in which President Clin-ton's veto of a ban on partial-birth abortion was sustained, Senator Rick Santo-rum (R-Penn) relied chiefly on this fact in arguing against the practice.

61. Again, this is an important qualification, since the development of sen-tience may follow a somewhat different time line from the general one referred to in this section.

62. Despite his stated preference for the choice conception, Sumner concedes that it is inappropriate in the context of abortion. See The Moral Foundation of Rights (Oxford: Oxford University Press, 1987), 206.

63. There may or may not be problems associated with freely limiting one's own freedom. Any such difficulties would not pertain to the context of abortion, however.

64. Admittedly, the freedom of a minimally sentient being is very limited in-deed.

65. For now, the killing only of "persons" (in the morally relevant sense) will be addressed.

66. Common sense dictates that death, in itself, must in some way be negative for the victim. Sumner distinguishes these "central effects" (consequences for the victim himself) from "side effects" (consequences for others) (Abortion and Moral Theory, 201.) See also Jonathan Glover, Causing Death and Saving Lives (London: Penguin Books, 1977), 113–15.

67. Such rules would likely be defeasible in order to accommodate cases of self-defense, as well as certain other situations.

68. If only the negative effects on those associated with the victim grounded the prohibition, then they—and not the victim himself—would possess the right that he not be killed.

69. The "other things equal" qualification serves to hold the side effects con-stant. It is conceivable that substantial negative side effects resulting from the death of a particular animal, say, would make killing that animal less permissible than killing a certain human (the side effects of which would be negligible) on a forward-looking theory.

70. Whether such a sentence is indeed nonsense (or whether it is simply a false sentence) is, predictably enough, a function of the underlying theory of language. No position need be taken for our purposes. For representative outlines of two

principal theories, see Bertrand Russell, "On Denoting," Mind 14 (1905); and Peter Strawson, "On Referring," in Essays in Conceptual Analysis, ed. Anthony Flew (London: MacMillan, 1956).

71. This consideration is raised by David E. Soles, "Sentience and Moral Standing," Dialogue 24 (1985).

72. Abortion and Moral Theory, 209. Those "who will exist (at some time) regardless of the course of action chosen" are "independent persons."

73. This is the approach adopted by Richard Brandt, "Some Merits of One Form of Rule-Utilitarianism," University of Colorado Studies Series in Philosophy (1967).

74. The origin of this oft-cited phrase can be traced to Frances Hutcheson (who himself was probably not a consequentialist). See "An Enquiry Concerning Good and Evil," in The British Moralists: 1650–1800 (Volume One), ed. D. D. Raphael (Indianapolis: Hackett, 1991), 284.

75. See Sumner, "Classical Utilitarianism and the Population Optimum" in Obligations to Future Generations, ed. R.I. Sikora and Brian Barry (Philadelphia: Temple University Press, 1978), 104–6.

76. Ibid., 101–3.

77. Mary Williams, "Discounting Versus Maximum Sustainable Yield," in Obligations to Future Generations.

78. Jan Narveson, "Future People and Us," in Obligations to Future Generations.

79. The right may or may not be strictly correlative with the duty in the Hohfeldian sense.

80. Perhaps the wrongdoer, a compulsive perpetrator of sinister deeds, possesses a desire to be remembered for his exploits even in the distant future.

81. This explains why there is no contradiction in claiming that the early fetus has no right to life, but that it does have a right that its mother not use drugs or alcohol or take other actions that may endanger its future well-being. There is no contradiction because this latter right is conditional in the manner described above.

82. On this point see Glover, Causing Deaths and Saving Lives, 147–49.

83. A variety of qualifications and exceptions would have to accompany this policy in order for it to be morally justified.

9

Concluding Remarks

The experiment is now complete. Although no particular hypothesis was being tested, we can now review the findings and consider what conclusions they may suggest.

Regarding the issue of redistributive taxation, three potential policies were considered. According to the interest-based theory of rights, the libertarian position was found not to be justified. Libertarians are correct that some external goods are necessary in order to formulate and carry out a life plan. However, while a personal autonomy interest does ground rights to some property, it cannot ground absolute property rights in the face of competing claims to assistance that are also based on personal autonomy. The socialist egalitarian policy, in which an equal distribution of wealth across society is recommended, was also not justified in this theory, since property rights would be much too conditional in such a scheme. Rather, because the interest-based theory recognizes moderate rights to control over one's property that would be overridable only when there are competing claims by those with insufficient personal autonomy, a liberal welfare policy was prescribed by the theory.

The same conclusion was reached from an analysis that utilizes the goal-based theory. Because there are diminishing marginal returns of freedom as wealth increases at a constant rate, a direct cost/benefit analysis yielded the conclusion that wealth should be equalized across society. However, because of indirect adverse effects likely to be associated with such an extreme policy (such as increased disincentive and discontent), there are reasons for thinking that constraining pursuit of the goal by upholding property rights of moderate strength would ultimately be a more successful strategy.

The interest-based analysis of affirmative action was a more complex process because of the various interests that were in play. A general right to compensation for past and present injustices and for the current inequality of opportunity, possessed by all blacks, was found to be justified. However, the case for a derivative and more specific right to preferential treatment in the context of employment is problematic on two counts. First, the interests grounding such a right would not, in fact, be effectively attended to if the right were recognized by social policy; in this way affirmative action is self-defeating. Second, the corresponding duties associated with a right to preferential treatment are not reasonable in that they violate the legitimate rights of the would-be duty-bearers to equal consideration. These findings negate both the required affirmative action and permissible affirmative action positions, and imply mandatory race-neutral hiring policies.

Empirical evidence was used in the goal-based analysis to suggest that the same conclusion follows from that model. Economic advances for blacks slowed considerably in the wake of the "goals and timetables" strategy mandated by the Department of Labor, and while the reasons for this phenomenon are somewhat unclear, such evidence indicates that even if the goal of a "colorblind" society seems to call for a policy of affirmative action (which is itself unclear), constraining direct pursuit of the goal by disallowing racial preferences is in order.

It was acknowledged at the beginning of the discussion on pornography that certain restrictions on the production and distribution of such materials are appropriate. Thus, the question was whether the industry should be prohibited altogether or whether practices within the bounds of the acceptable restrictions should be permitted. Considerations of paternalism and legal moralism in the context of the interest-based theory were found to be insufficient justifications for prohibition. Feminist protests, which focused largely on the harms to women generated by the very existence of the industry, were also considered. In the end, however, the causal connections alleged by feminists were too weak to ground the banning of pornographic practices. The personal autonomy interest grounding the freedom to engage in such practices is sufficiently strong to resist challenges that cannot demonstrate a fairly direct connection with the infringement of a competing interest. The goal-based analysis, meanwhile, allowed for either freedom or equality as the goal to be pursued; on both counts it was argued that a policy of restriction rather than outright prohibition would be a better strategy.

Assessing the moral permissibility of abortion on the interest-based theory consisted largely in evaluating the moral status of the fetus, which turned out to be a two-part task. First, there exists the question of when the fetus acquires any moral standing at all, that is, when the fetus can have any interests and thus have rights on the interest-based theory. After examining several candidate criteria for moral standing, sentience was determined to be the most plausible. Second, even with this conclusion in hand, there remained the question of when the fetus was of sufficient moral standing (i.e., when its interests were of sufficient strength) to override the interests of the mother grounding her right to obtain an abortion. Because there are no specific points at which these thresholds are achieved, and because the answers to these questions must be in terms of developmental rather than temporal achievement, arriving at definitive practical guidelines is difficult. In the end, it was suggested that a policy allowing abortion through the fifth month of pregnancy but (generally) disallowing it thereafter was most reasonable; this claim, however, was qualified by recognizing the possibility that a somewhat different time line may correlate more accurately with the developmental stages of the fetus that determine its level of moral standing.

Thus, in all four cases, the implications of the two theories of rights are the same. The temptation is to conclude that the language of rights can therefore be salvaged, and more strongly—insofar as it constitutes an effective way of capturing complex moral content—that the language of rights ought to be employed in debates over social issues. Since the application of rights theories to such issues yields meaningful conclusions that appear to converge, it would seem that we can use the language of rights without having to investigate the normative underpinnings each time we utilize it. That sort of theoretical investigation would be required only occasionally; periodic confirmation of the status of rights claims is desirable.

However, this conclusion regarding the usefulness of "rights talk" relies heavily on the claim that all coherent rights theories do indeed entail the same normative implications, a claim that may be referred to as the "convergence thesis." When relying on the results of this book for its support, the convergence thesis seems a substantial inferential leap. In making a case for such a generalization, several points should be remembered. First, it is indeed the case that only a sampling of theories and issues has been considered, and the possibility that other theories and issues might yield less favorable results is very real. Prudence calls for further analysis in this respect. However, the finding of convergence in all four cases examined herein is cause for at least some optimism. Therefore, in addition to further experimentation of the sort conducted in Part 2, there are grounds for an examination of whether there is something inherent in the nature of rights theories that promotes unity in the theories' normative implications. A starting point for such an examination might be the basic values that, as it happened, played significant roles in this project. The values of personal autonomy (or freedom more generally) and equality, for example, were crucial for both theories in a number of the analyses. If some value(s) along these lines can be found, then the convergence thesis can be arrived at deductively rather than inductively, and, correspondingly, it will be more likely to be accepted. It then follows that the conclusion regarding the functional value of the language of rights will be more acceptable as well.

There will certainly arise an objection to the results of this project which is typically invoked in philosophical discussions of applied ethical issues. The claim will be that the theories were at times simply misapplied to the issues, such that conclusions other than the specific ones arrived at are in order. For instance, a counterargument might be offered for the conclusion that the goal of gender equality is achieved more effectively when, contrary to the claim in section 7.3, prohibition of the pornography industry (rather than mere restrictions of various sorts) is enacted. The more cynical reader will go so far as to suggest that the individual arguments in Part 2 were guided (consciously or unconsciously) toward the individual conclusions that would ultimately point toward the convergence thesis.

It is unclear what is supposed to follow from this charge. It cannot be doubted that the possibility of misapplication always exists. Review of the arguments of the sort advanced in Part 2 is thus entirely appropriate. However, it may be that in lodging this protest, the skeptic is suggesting that applied ethics ventures are simply not worthwhile. Such a conclusion, though, is not supported.

The skeptic's objection may be metaphysical; namely, it may deny the existence of objectively valid moral principles. This book would thus be deemed insignificant insofar as it relies on the existence of such principles and appeals to them in an effort to reach resolutions. We acknowledged in the opening chapter that a certain commitment to realism would pervade this project. That assumption facilitates the idea that the content of law (including social policy) ought to be informed by moral considerations. The alternative is to admit of some version of relativism. This possibility may not, as it turns out, wholly conflict with the motivation behind this book, since a backdrop of cultural relativism still allows for prevailing norms to guide legislative consideration.[1] If the approach of "philosophy from the inside out" is emphasized, and the claim is made that the implications of prevailing rights theories (regardless of any objective validity) on prevailing social issues are examined in this work, then the objection can be met on the skeptic's own terms.

The response to the metaphysical skeptic thus takes the following form. First, he may simply be wrong in his supposition, in which case further work would be necessary to generate reasons in favor of the realist position. Second, it can be allowed that he is correct. But, since individual societies can be criticized on grounds of logical inconsistency, including the inconsistency with which moral principles (albeit relative) may be applied, an analysis of the sort undertaken in this book is indeed worthwhile. Either alternative defeats the claim that applied ethics ventures are inherently useless, although adoption of the former response—that the metaphysical skeptic may simply be wrong in his supposition—seems necessary if the convergence thesis is eventually to be deductively established.

By contrast, the epistemological skeptic is indifferent to the status of moral principles. His claim is conditional: If there are objective moral principles, they cannot be known with certainty. The value of investigations aimed at discovering them is therefore limited. But such a drastic conclusion seems uncalled for. The alternative is to allow this inability to acquire certain moral knowledge to dictate a complete withdrawal from practical inquiry, and this hardly seems a productive strategy. That certain ethical knowledge is an unattainable ideal in no way implies that pursuit of the ideal ought not to take place. Such pursuit will indeed be deemed fruitless when measured against a standard of actual attainment, but there is no reason why that standard should carry the day.

Thus, it should be resolved that the sort of philosophical investigation undertaken in this book is indeed worthwhile. In addition, the omnipresent possibility that a rights theory has been misapplied to a particular issue should not give rise to ample suspicion of the final results. Here again, the alternative is to refrain altogether from making arguments for certain conclusions. Instead, substantive arguments with reasonable conclusions, well supported by finely detailed premises, should be attempted. Indeed, this is what has been attempted herein, and it is hoped that the breadth and depth of the arguments put forth suggest that they were not formulated superficially or with the underlying intention of arriving at converging conclusions. The observation that the results follow no particular political agenda should provide evidence for this latter claim.

Moving on to another sort of objection, it may be pointed out that the leading ethical theories, such as those of Mill and Kant, have essentially been ignored in this project. These leading theories have not attained popularity and widespread acceptance by accident; rather, the reasonable conclusion is that they are well founded and offer substantive moral methodologies. Had these approaches been employed, disparate conclusions in particular cases would certainly have emerged; yet, they have apparently been shunned in this book in favor of frameworks offered by two late twentieth century philosophers. Such a move is highly questionable, especially since a "retreat" to these frameworks is necessary in order to reach convergent conclusions. Further, it may be alleged that this is even more problematic than first appearances would indicate, since even these frameworks in their original forms were not utilized. Rather, they were altered in various ways that, it can be argued, affected their normative implications in specific instances. In this way, too, the convergence thesis may appear to be a self-fulfilling prophecy.

Several remarks are in order here. First, it does seem clear that rights claims, when embedded in straightforward (Millian) utilitarian and Kantian moral frameworks, would indeed yield divergent results in specific cases. However, the claim is that these approaches are lacking in that they are largely inapplicable to the moral difficulties of the sort considered in Part 2. Mill's "happiness," it was said, is too general a notion on which to base rights claims, and Kant's absolutism generates difficulties at least as serious. Second, their general moral approaches are followed nonetheless; the methodologies employed by Joseph Raz and L. W. Sumner are clearly in the spirit of Kant and Mill, respectively, and so the charge that these "traditional" approaches have been altogether abandoned is unfair.

Third, the precise forms of the models described by Raz and Sumner were modified not in order to alter the conclusions they might generate but because they, too, were not wholly applicable. For instance, Sumner called for the formulation of a single, global goal to be pursued, while Raz relied on the notion of humanism as an external standard for assessing the value of individuals' chosen aims—a move that is problematic for application of his rights framework to a pluralistic society. Again, any departures were motivated by the ambition to make ethics practicable and capable of living up to its reputation as an action-guiding discipline. The objection that ethical theory is in some sense "sacred" and immune to alteration is unfounded. The warning directed toward practitioners of applied ethics, iterated several times in the pages of this book, bears repeating. When standard moral theory does not mesh with real-life moral problems, it is the theory that must be malleable if there is to be any reconciliation, and there is no reason for thinking that making the requisite modifications is in some way impermissible.

The remaining few words are reserved for some far-reaching speculation. The potential plausibility of the convergence thesis is already highly speculative; it has been claimed that substantial additional work must be undertaken if it is ever to be adequately demonstrated. As described above, the convergence thesis pertains only to rights theories; it is the idea that assorted theories of rights-justification, when applied to a single practical issue, will all recommend the same moral prescription. However, if—as was conceded in the opening chapter—rights are not the basic elements of morality, but are derived from more foundational moral principles, the convergence thesis may imply a certain unity among moral theories generally and not just among rights theories. It goes without saying that this is the far-reaching aspect of the speculation.

For now, however, the focus is on rights specifically. While they have in recent times been deployed carelessly, there is no cause for their dismissal from the realm of moral discourse. On the contrary, the language of rights can be very effective in capturing rather complex moral content. In a deliberative democracy especially, there is certainly a place for the notion of moral rights in debates over public policy and social issues generally.

Notes

1. It is assumed that subjectivism is a problematic brand of relativism.

Bibliography

Arneson, Richard J. "Property Rights in Persons." In Economic Rights, (eds.) Ellen Frankel Paul, Fred D. Miller, Jr., and Jeffrey Paul. Cambridge: Cambridge University Press, 1992.

Avineri, Shlomo and Avner de-Shalit (eds.). Communitarianism and Individualism. Oxford: Oxford University Press, 1992.

Baynes, Kenneth. The Normative Grounds of Social Criticism. Albany: State University of New York Press, 1992.

Beauchamp, Tom L. "The Justification of Reverse Discrimination." In Robert D. Heslep (ed.), Social Justice and Preferential Treatment. Athens, GA: University of Georgia Press, 1977.

Becker, Lawrence. Property Rights. London: Routledge and Kegan Paul, 1977.

Beckwith, Francis J. "Arguments From Bodily Rights: A Critical Analysis." In Louis P. Pojman and Francis J. Beckwith (eds.), The Abortion Controversy. Boston: Jones and Bartlett, 1994.

Bentham, Jeremy. "Introduction to the Principles of Morals and Legislation." In Louis P. Pojman (ed.), Ethical Theory. Belmont, CA: Wadsworth, 1989.

_____. The Works of Jeremy Bentham. Ed. John Bowring. Edinburgh: William Tate, 1843.

Berlin, Isaiah. "Two Concepts of Liberty." In Michael Sandel (ed.), Liberalism and Its Critics. New York: New York University Press, 1984.

Blackstone, William T. (ed.). Philosophy and Environmental Crisis. Athens, GA: University of Georgia Press, 1971.

_____. "Reverse Discrimination and Compensatory Justice." In Robert D. Heslep (ed.), Social Justice and Preferential Treatment. Athens, GA: University of Georgia Press, 1977.

Boxill, Bernard. Blacks & Social Justice. Lanham, MD: Rowman and Littlefield, 1992.

Brandt, Richard. "Some Merits of One Form of Rule-Utilitarianism." University of Colorado Studies, Series in Philosophy. Boulder, CO: University of Colorado, 1967.

Braybrooke, David. Meeting Needs. Princeton: Princeton University Press, 1987.

Brint, Michael and William Weaver (eds.). Pragmatism in Law and Society. Boulder, CO: Westview Press, 1991.

British Home Office. Report of the Committee on Obscenity and Film Censorship. London: Her Majesty's Stationery Office, 1979.

Cameron, Deborah and Elizabeth Frazer. "On the Question of Pornography and Sexual Violence: Moving Beyond Cause and Effect." In Catherine Itzin (ed.),

Pornography: Women, Violence and Civil Liberties. Oxford: Oxford University Press, 1993.

Carruthers, Peter. The Animals Issue. Cambridge: Cambridge University Press, 1992.

Chester, Gail and Julienne Dickey (eds.). Feminism and Censorship: The Current Debate. London: Prism Press, 1988.

Christman, John. The Myth of Private Property. Oxford: Oxford University Press, 1994.

Cisler, Lucinda. "Unfinished Business: Birth Control and Women's Liberation." In Robin Morgan (ed.), Sisterhood Is Powerful. New York: Random House, 1970.

Claiborne, William. "Judge Blocks Measure on Affirmative Action," Washington Post (Nov. 27, 1996).

Cohen, Marshall, Thomas Nagel, and Thomas Scanlon. Equality and Preferential Treatment. Princeton: Princeton University Press, 1977.

_____. The Rights and Wrongs of Abortion. Princeton: Princeton University Press, 1974.

Copp, David. "The Right to an Adequate Standard of Living: Justice, Autonomy and the Basic Needs." In Ellen Frankel Paul, Fred D. Miller, Jr., and Jeffrey Paul (eds.), Economic Rights. Cambridge: Cambridge University Press, 1992.

D'souza, Dinseh. Illiberal Education. New York: The Free Press, 1991.

Devine, Phillip. "The Scope of the Prohibition Against Killing." In Louis P. Pojman (ed.), The Abortion Controversy. Boston: Jones and Bartlett, 1994.

Devlin, Patrick. The Enforcement of Morals. London: Oxford University Press, 1965.

Dhavan, Rajeev and Christie Davies (eds.). Censorship and Obscenity. Lanham, MD: Rowman and Littlefield, 1978.

Donnerstein, Edward, Daniel Linz, and Steven Penrod. The Question of Pornography: Research Findings and Policy Implications. New York: The Free Press, 1987.

Duggan, Lisa. "False Promises: Feminist Anti-Pornography Legislation in the U.S." In Gail Chester and Julienne Dickey (eds.), Feminism and Censorship: The Current Debate. London: Prism Press, 1988.

Duggan, Lisa, Nan Hunter, and Carole Vance. "Feminist Anti-Pornography Legislation." In James P. Sterba (ed.), Morality in Practice (4th ed.), Belmont, CA: Wadsworth, 1994.

Dworkin, Andrea. "Against the Male Flood: Censorship, Pornography and Equality." In Catherine Itzin (ed.), Pornography: Women, Violence and Civil Liberties. Oxford: Oxford University Press, 1993.

_____. "Power." In Susan Dwyer (ed.), The Problem of Pornography. Belmont, CA: Wadsworth, 1995.

Dworkin, Gerald. "Paternalism." In Joel Feinberg and Hyman Gross (eds.), Philosophy of Law (5th ed.). Belmont, CA: Wadsworth, 1995.

Dworkin, Ronald. "Do We Have a Right to Pornography?" In Susan Dwyer (ed.), The Problem of Pornography. Belmont, CA: Wadsworth, 1995.

_____. "Liberty and Pornography." In Susan Dwyer (ed.), The Problem of Pornography. Belmont, CA: Wadsworth, 1995.

_____. Life's Dominion. New York: Alfred A. Knopf, 1993.

_____. A Matter of Principle. Cambridge, MA: Harvard University Press, 1985.

_____. "Pragmatism, Right Answers, and True Banality." In Michael Brint and William Weaver (eds.), Pragmatism in Law and Society. Boulder, CO: Westview Press, 1991.

_____. Taking Rights Seriously. Cambridge, MA: Harvard University Press, 1977.

_____. "Women and Pornography." In New York Review of Books, October, 1993.

Dwyer, Susan (ed.). The Problem of Pornography. Belmont, CA: Wadsworth, 1995.

Easton, Susan. The Problem of Pornography: Regulation and the Right to Free Speech. London: Routledge, 1994.

Einsiedel, Edna F. "The Experimental Research Evidence: Effects of Pornography on the 'Average Individual.'" In Catherine Itzin (ed.), Pornography: Women, Violence and Civil Liberties. Oxford: Oxford University Press, 1993.

Elliot, Robert (ed.). Environmental Ethics. Oxford: Oxford University Press, 1995.

Etzioni, Amitai. The Limits of Privacy. New York: Basic Books, 1999.

_____. The New Golden Rule: Community and Morality in a Democratic Society. New York: Basic Books, 1996.

Ezorsky, Gertrude. Racism and Justice: The Case For Affirmative Action. Ithaca: Cornell University Press, 1992.

Feinberg, Joel. Harm to Others. Oxford: Oxford University Press, 1987.

_____. "The Nature and Value of Rights." In Morton E. Winston (ed.), The Philosophy of Human Rights. Belmont, CA: Wadsworth, 1989.

_____. "The Rights of Animals and Unborn Generations." In William T. Blackstone (ed.), Philosophy and Environmental Crisis. Athens, GA: University of Georgia Press, 1971.

Feinberg, Joel and Hyman Gross (eds.). Philosophy of Law (5th ed.). Belmont, CA: Wadsworth, 1995.

_____. Philosophy of Law (2nd ed.). Encino, CA: Dickinson, 1975.

Finnis, John. Fundamentals of Ethics. Oxford: Clarendon Press, 1983.

_____. Natural Law and Natural Rights. Oxford: Clarendon Press, 1980.

Fishkin, James S. Justice, Equal Opportunity and the Family. New Haven: Yale University Press, 1983.

Flew, Anthony (ed.). Essays in Conceptual Analysis. London: Macmillan, 1956.

Freeman, Richard B. "Changes in the Labor Market for Black Americans, 1948–72." Brookings Papers on Economic Activity 1 (1973).

Frey, R. G. (ed.). Utility and Rights. Minneapolis: University of Minnesota Press, 1984.

Friedman, Milton. Capitalism and Freedom. Chicago: University of Chicago Press, 1982.

Fullinwinder, Robert K. "Preferential Hiring and Compensation." Social Theory and Practice 3 (1975).

Gauthier, David. Morals By Agreement. Oxford: Oxford University Press, 1986.

Gewirth, Alan. The Community of Rights. Chicago: University of Chicago Press, 1996.

_____. Reason and Morality. Chicago: University of Chicago Press, 1978.

Gillian, Patricia. "Therapeutic Uses of Obscenity." In Rajeev Dhavan and Christie Davies (eds.), Censorship and Obscenity. Lanham, MD: Rowman and Littlefield, 1978.

Gilligan, Carol. In a Different Voice. Cambridge, MA: Harvard University Press, 1983.

Glazer, Nathan. Affirmative Discrimination: Ethnic Inequality and Public Policy. Cambridge, MA: Harvard University Press, 1975.

Glendon, Mary Ann. Rights Talk: The Impoverishment of Political Discourse. New York: The Free Press, 1991.

Glover, Jonathan. Causing Death and Saving Lives. London: Penguin Books, 1977.

Goldman, Alan H. "Affirmative Action." In Marshall Cohen, Thomas Nagel, and Thomas Scanlon (eds.), Equality and Preferential Treatment. Princeton: Princeton University Press, 1974.

_____. "Limits to the Justification of Reverse Discrimination." Social Theory and Practice 3 (1975).

_____. "Reparations to Individuals or Groups?" In Barry R. Gross (ed.), Reverse Discrimination. Buffalo: Prometheus Books, 1977.

_____. "Reverse Discrimination and the Future: A Reply to Irving Thalberg." The Philosophical Forum 6 (1974–75).

Goldman, Alvin I. and Jaegwon Kim (eds.) Values and Morals. Boston: D. Riedel, 1978.

Goldmann, Robert B. and A. Jeyaratnum (eds.). From Independence to Statehood. London: Frances Pinter, 1984.

Goodin, Robert. Reasons for Welfare. Princeton: Princeton University Press, 1988.

Goodpaster, Kenneth. "On Being Morally Considerable." Journal of Philosophy 75 (1978).

Gross, Barry R. "Is Turn About Fair Play?" In Barry R. Gross (ed.), Reverse Discrimination. Buffalo: Prometheus Books, 1977.

Gross, Barry R. (ed.). Reverse Discrimination. Buffalo: Prometheus Books, 1977.

Hacker, P. M. S. and Joseph Raz (eds.). Law, Morality and Society. Oxford: Clarendon Press, 1971.

Hare, R. M. "Justice and Equality." In James P. Sterba (ed.), Justice: Alternative Political Perspectives. Belmont, CA: Wadsworth, 1992.

_____. Moral Thinking: Its Levels, Method and Point. Oxford: Oxford University Press, 1981.

_____. "Rights, Utility and Universalization: A Reply to J.L. Mackie." In R. G. Frey (ed.), Utility and Rights. Minneapolis: University of Minnesota Press, 1984.

Harman, Gilbert. "Moral Relativism as a Foundation for Natural Rights." Journal of Libertarian Studies 4 (1980).

Hart, H. L. A. "Are There Any Natural Rights?" In David Lyons (ed.), Rights. Belmont, CA: Wadsworth, 1979.

_____. Law, Liberty and Morality. Stanford: Stanford University Press, 1963.

Hartnack, Justus. Human Rights. Lewiston, NY: Edwin Mellen, 1986.

Hawkins, Gordon and Franklin E. Zimring. Pornography in a Free Society. Cambridge: Cambridge University Press, 1991.

Hayek, Friedrich A. The Constitution of Liberty. Chicago: University of Chicago Press, 1960.

_____. "Liberty, Equality and Merit." In James P. Sterba (ed.), Justice: Alternative Political Perspectives. Belmont, CA: Wadsworth, 1992.

Heslep, Robert D. (ed.). Social Justice and Preferential Treatment. Athens, GA: University of Georgia Press, 1977.

Hobbes, Thomas. Leviathan. (Ed. C. B. MacPherson.) London: Penguin Books, 1968.

Hohfeld, Wesley. Fundamental Legal Conceptions. (Ed. Walter Wheeler Cook) New Haven: Yale University Press, 1919.

Hook, Sidney. "The Bias in Anti-Bias Regulations." In Barry R. Gross (ed.), Reverse Discrimination. Buffalo: Prometheus Books, 1977.

_____. "Discrimination, Color Blindness and the Quota System." In Barry R. Gross (ed.), Reverse Discrimination. Buffalo: Prometheus Books, 1977.

Hook, Sidney (ed.). Law and Philosophy. New York: New York University Press, 1964.

Hospers, John. Libertarianism. Los Angeles: Nash, 1971.

_____. "The Libertarian Manifesto." In James P. Sterba (ed.), Justice: Alternative Political Perspectives. Belmont, CA: Wadsworth, 1992.

Hume, David. A Treatise of Human Nature. (Ed. L. A. Selby-Bigge) Oxford: Oxford University Press, 1978.

Humphreys, Sheila M. (ed.). Women and Minorities in Science. Boulder, CO: Westview Press, 1982.

Hutcheson, Francis. "An Enquiry Concerning Good and Evil." In D. D. Raphael (ed.), The British Moralists: 1650–1800 (Vol. 1). Indianapolis: Hackett, 1991.

Hynes, H. Patricia. "Pornography and Pollution: An Environmental Analogy." In Catherine Itzin (ed.), Pornography: Women, Violence and Civil Liberties. Oxford: Oxford University Press, 1993.

Itzin, Catherine. "A Legal Definition of Pornography." In Catherine Itzin (ed.), Pornography: Women, Violence and Civil Liberties. Oxford: Oxford University Press, 1993.

_____. "Pornography and Civil Liberties." In Catherine Itzin (ed.), Pornography: Women, Violence and Civil Liberties. Oxford: Oxford University Press, 1993.

_____. "Sex and Censorship: The Political Implications." In Gail Chester and Julienne Dickey (eds.), Feminism and Censorship: The Current Debate. London: Prism Press, 1988.

_____ (ed.). Pornography: Women, Violence and Civil Liberties. Oxford: Oxford University Press, 1993.

Jenni, Kathi. "Dilemmas in Social Philosophy: Abortion and Animal Rights." Social Theory and Practice 20 (1994).

Jones, Hardy E. "On the Justifiability of Reverse Discrimination." In Barry R. Gross (ed.), Reverse Discrimination. Buffalo: Prometheus Books, 1977.

Kagan, Shelly. Normative Ethics. Boulder, CO: Westview Press, 1998.

Kant, Immanuel. Critique of Pure Reason. (Trans. Norman Kemp Smith.) New York: St. Martin's Press, 1965.

_____. Grounding for the Metaphysics of Morals. (Trans. James W. Ellington.) Indianapolis: Hackett, 1981.

_____. Lectures on Ethics. (Trans. Lewis Infield.) New York: Harper and Row, 1963.

Kappeler, Susanne. "No Matter How Unreasonable." Art History 2 (1988).

Katzner, Louis. "Is the Favoring of Women and Blacks in Employment and Edu-
cational Opportunities Justified?" In Joel Feinberg and Hyman Gross, Philoso-
phy of Law (2nd ed.) Encino, CA: Dickinson, 1975.
Kimmel, Michael S. (ed.). Men Confront Pornography. New York: Meridian Books,
1990.
Kutchinsky, Berl. "Legalized Pornography in Denmark." In Michael S. Kimmel
(ed.), Men Confront Pornography. New York: Meridian Books, 1990.
Kymlicka, Will. Contemporary Political Philosophy. Oxford: Oxford University
Press, 1990.
_____. Liberalism, Community and Culture. Oxford: Clarendon Press, 1989.
Langevin, R., D. Paitich, and A. Russon, "Are Rapists Sexually Anomalous, Ag-
gressive, or Both?" In R. Langevin (ed.), Erotic Preference, Gender Identity and
Aggression in Men: New Research Studies. Hillsdale, NJ: Lawrence Erlbaum,
1985.
Langevin, R (ed.). Erotic Preference, Gender Identity and Aggression in Men: New Re-
search Studies. Hillsdale, NJ: Lawrence Erlbaum, 1985.
Langton, Rae. "Speech Acts and Unspeakable Acts." In Susan Dwyer (ed.), The
Problem of Pornography. Belmont, CA: Wadsworth, 1995.
_____. "Whose Right? Ronald Dworkin, Women and Pornographers." In Susan
Dwyer (ed.), The Problem of Pornography. Belmont, CA: Wadsworth, 1995.
Leopold, Aldo. "The Land Ethic." In Louis P. Pojman (ed.), Environmental Ethics.
Boston: Jones and Bartlett, 1994.
Levenbrook, Barbara Baum. "On Preferential Admission." Journal of Value Inquiry
14 (1980).
Lindblom, C. E. Politics and Markets. New York: Basic Books, 1977.
Linsley, William A. "The Case Against Censorship of Pornography." In Dolf Zill-
man and Jennings Bryant (eds.), Pornography: Research Advances and Policy Con-
siderations. Hillsdale, NJ: Lawrence Erlbaum, 1989.
Locke, John. Two Treatises of Government. (Ed. Peter Laslett.) Cambridge: Cam-
bridge University Press, 1963.
Lomasky, Loren E. Persons, Rights and the Moral Community. Oxford: Oxford Uni-
versity Press, 1987.
Longino, Helen E. "Pornography, Oppression and Freedom: A Closer Look." In
Susan Dwyer (ed.), The Problem of Pornography. Belmont, CA: Wadsworth, 1995.
Lyons, David. "Human Rights and the General Welfare." Philosophy and Public Af-
fairs 6 (1977).
_____. "Mill's Theory of Justice" in Alvin I. Goldman and Jaegwon Kim (eds.),
Values and Morals. Boston: D. Riedel, 1978.
_____. "Rights, Claimants and Beneficiaries." In David Lyons (ed.), Rights. Bel-
mont, CA: Wadsworth, 1979.
_____. Rights, Welfare and Mill's Moral Theory. Oxford: Oxford University Press,
1994.
_____. "Utility and Rights." In Jeremy Waldron (ed.), Theories of Rights. Oxford:
Oxford University Press, 1984.
Lyons, David (ed.). Rights. Belmont, CA: Wadsworth, 1979.MacCormick, Neil.
"Rights in Legislation." In P. M. S. Hacker and Joseph Raz (eds.), Law, Morality
and Society. Oxford: Clarendon Press, 1971.

Machan, Tibor. Individuals and Their Rights. LaSalle, IL: Open Court, 1989.

MacIntyre, Alasdair. After Virtue. Notre Dame: University of Notre Dame Press, 1984.

_____. Whose Justice? Which Rationality? Notre Dame: University of Notre Dame Press, 1988.

Mackie, J. L. "Can There Be a Right-Based Moral Theory?" In Jeremy Waldron (ed.), Theories of Rights. Oxford: Oxford University Press, 1984.

_____. The Cement of the Universe: A Study of Causation. Oxford: Oxford University Press, 1974.

_____. Ethics: Inventing Right and Wrong. London: Penguin Books, 1977.

_____. "Rights, Utility and Universalization." In R. G. Frey (ed.), Utility and Rights. Minneapolis: University of Minnesota Press, 1984.

MacKinnon, Catharine A. Feminism Unmodified. Cambridge, MA: Harvard University Press, 1987.

_____. Only Words. Cambridge, MA: Harvard University Press, 1993.

MacPherson, C. B. "Berlin's Division of Liberty." In C. B. MacPherson (ed.), Democratic Theory: Essays in Retrieval. Oxford: Clarendon Press, 1973.

_____. The Political Theory of Possessive Individualism. Oxford: Oxford University Press, 1962.

MacPherson, C. B. (ed.). Democratic Theory: Essays in Retrieval. Oxford: Clarendon Press, 1973.

Malamuth, N. M. and James V. P. Check. "Sexual Arousal to Rape Depictions: Individual Differences." Journal of Abnormal Psychology 92 (1983).

Marshall, W. L. "Pornography and Sex Offenders." In Dolf Zillman and Jennings Bryant (eds.), Pornography: Research Advances and Policy Considerations. Hillsdale, NJ: Lawrence Erlbaum, 1989.

Martin, Rex. Rawls and Rights. Lawrence, KS: University Press of Kansas, 1985.

Marx, Karl and Friedrich Engels, The Communist Manifesto. New York: Bantam Books, 1992.

McCloskey, H. J. "Respect for Human Moral Rights versus Maximizing Good." In R. G. Frey (ed.), Utility and Rights. Minneapolis: University of Minnesota Press, 1984.

Messick, David M. "Philosophy and the Resolution of Equality Conflicts." Social Justice Research 10 (1997).

Michelman, Frank. "Conceptions of Democracy in American Constitutional Argument: The Case of Pornography Regulation." Tennessee Law Review 56 (1989).

Mill, John Stuart. On Liberty. (Ed. John Gray.) Oxford: Oxford University Press, 1991.

_____. Principles of Political Economy. London: Penguin Books, 1970.

_____. Utilitarianism. (Ed. George Sher.) Indianapolis: Hackett, 1979.

Moore, G. E. Principia Ethica. London: Cambridge University Press, 1966.

Morgan, Robin (ed.). Sisterhood Is Powerful. New York: Random House, 1970.

Murray, Charles. "Affirmative Racism." In James P. Sterba (ed.), Morality in Practice (4th ed.) Belmont, CA: Wadsworth, 1994.

Nagel, Thomas. "A Defense of Affirmative Action." Report from the Center for Philosophy and Public Policy 1 (1981).

_____. "Equal Treatment and Compensatory Discrimination." In Marshall Cohen, Thomas Nagel, and Thomas Scanlon (eds.), Equality and Preferential Treatment. Princeton: Princeton University Press, 1977.

_____. Equality and Partiality. Oxford: Oxford University Press, 1991.

_____. The View From Nowhere. Oxford: Oxford University Press, 1986.

Narveson, Jan. "Contractarian Rights." In R. G. Frey (ed.), Utility and Rights. Minneapolis: University of Minnesota Press, 1984.

_____. "Future People and Us." In R. I. Sikora and Brian Barry (eds.), Obligations to Future Generations. Philadelphia: Temple University Press, 1978.

Nathanson, Bernard. Aborting America. New York: Doubleday, 1979.

Newton, Lisa H. "Reverse Discrimination as Unjustified." In Barry R. Gross (ed.), Reverse Discrimination. Buffalo: Prometheus Books, 1977.

Nickel, James W. "Should Reparations Be to Individuals or Groups?" In Barry R. Gross (ed.), Reverse Discrimination. Buffalo: Prometheus Books, 1977.

Nielson, Kai. "Radical Egalitarianism." In James P. Sterba (ed.), Justice: Alternative Political Perspectives. Belmont, CA: Wadsworth, 1992.

Noonan, Jr., John T. "Abortion Is Morally Wrong." In Louis P. Pojman and Francis J. Beckwith (eds.), The Abortion Controversy. Boston: Jones and Bartlett, 1994.

Nozick, Robert. Anarchy, State and Utopia. New York: Basic Books, 1974.

_____. Philosophical Explanations. Cambridge, MA: Harvard University Press, 1981.

Okin, Susan Moller. Justice, Gender and Family. New York: Basic Books, 1989.

Parfit, Derek. "Is Common-sense Morality Self-Defeating?" In Samuel Scheffler (ed.), Consequentialism and Its Critics. Oxford: Oxford University Press, 1988.

_____. Reasons and Persons. Oxford: Clarendon Press, 1984.

Parker, Kathleen. Executive Edge. Emmaus, PA: National Center for Career Strategies, 1990.

Parmar, Pratibha. "Rage and Desire: Confronting Pornography." In Gail Chester and Julienne Dickey (eds.), Feminism and Censorship: The Current Debate. London: Prism Press, 1988.

Paul, Ellen Frankel, Fred D. Miller, Jr., and Jeffrey Paul (eds.). Economic Rights. Cambridge: Cambridge University Press, 1992.

Perlo, Victor. Economics of Racism U.S.A. New York: International Publishers, 1975.

Pierce, Christine and Donald VanDeVeer (eds.). People, Penguins and Plastic Trees. Belmont, CA: Wadsworth, 1995.

Pojman, Louis P. Ethics: Discovering Right and Wrong. Belmont, CA: Wadsworth, 1990.

_____. "The Moral Status of Affirmative Action." In James P. Sterba (ed.), Morality in Practice (5th ed.). Belmont, CA: Wadsworth, 1997.

_____. (ed.) Environmental Ethics. Boston: Jones and Bartlett, 1994.

_____. (ed.). Ethical Theory. Belmont, CA: Wadsworth, 1989.

Pojman, Louis P. and Francis J. Beckwith (eds.). The Abortion Controversy. Boston: Jones and Bartlett, 1994.

Putnam, Hilary. Realism With a Human Face. Cambridge, MA: Harvard University Press, 1990.

Rada, R. T. Clinical Aspects of the Rapist. New York: Grune and Stratton, 1978.

Raphael, D. D. (ed.). The British Moralists: 1650–1800 (Volume One). Indianapolis: Hackett, 1991.

Rawls, John. "Justice as Fairness: Political Not Metaphysical." Philosophy and Public Affairs 14 (1985).

_____. "Legal Obligation and the Duty of Fair Play." In Sidney Hook (ed.), Law and Philosophy. New York: New York University Press, 1964.

_____. A Theory of Justice. Cambridge, MA: Harvard University Press, 1971.

Raz, Joseph. The Morality of Freedom. Oxford: Oxford University Press, 1986.

_____. "Promises and Obligations." In P. M. S. Hacker and Joseph Raz (eds.), Law, Morality and Society. Oxford: Clarendon Press, 1971.

_____. "Right-Based Moralities." In R. G. Frey (ed.), Utility and Rights. Minneapolis: University of Minnesota Press, 1984.

Regan, Tom. The Case for Animal Rights. Berkeley: University of California Press, 1983.

Rollin, Bernard E. Animal Rights and Human Morality. Buffalo: Prometheus Books, 1992.

_____. "Sentience Is the Criterion for Moral Standing." In Louis P. Pojman (ed.), Environmental Ethics. Boston: Jones and Barlett, 1994.

_____. The Unheeded Cry: Animal Consciousness, Animal Pain and Sentience. Oxford: Oxford University Press, 1989.

Rolston, Holmes, III. "Duties to Endangered Species." In Robert Elliot (ed.), Environmental Ethics. Oxford: Oxford University Press, 1995.

Romano, Carlin. "Between the Motion and the Act." The Nation, November 15, 1993.

Rorty, Richard. "The Banality of Pragmatism and the Poetry of Justice." In Michael Brint and William Weaver (eds.), Pragmatism in Law and Society. Boulder, CO: Westview Press, 1991.

_____. "Human Rights, Rationality and Sentimentality." In Stephen Shute and Susan Hurley (eds.), On Human Rights. New York: Basic Books, 1993.

Rose, Steven. The Conscious Brain. London: Penguin Books, 1976.

Ross, W. D. The Right and The Good. Oxford: Clarendon Press, 1930.

Rothbard, Murray. For a New Liberty. New York: Macmillan, 1973.

Rowan, John R. "Philosophy on Messick and Social Conflict: Resolving the Resolution Process." Social Justice Research 10 (1997).

Russell, Bertrand. "On Denoting," Mind 14 (1905).

Russell, Diana E. H. "Pornography and Rape: A Causal Model." In Catherine Itzin (ed.), Pornography: Women, Violence and Civil Liberties. Oxford: Oxford University Press, 1993.

Ryan, Alan. Property and Political Theory. Oxford: Blackwell, 1984.

Sandel, Michael (ed.). Liberalism and Its Critics. New York: New York University Press, 1984.

_____. Liberalism and the Limits of Justice. Oxford: Blackwell, 1984.

_____. "Morality and the Liberal Ideal." In James P. Sterba (ed.), Justice: Alternative Political Perspectives. Belmont, CA: Wadsworth, 1992.

Sartorius, Rolf. "Persons and Property." In R. G. Frey (ed.), Utility and Rights. Minneapolis: University of Minnesota Press, 1984.

Scanlon, T. M. "Contractualism and Utilitarianism." In Amartya Sen and Bernard Williams (eds.), Utilitarianism and Beyond. Cambridge: Cambridge University Press, 1982.

_____. "Rights, Goals and Fairness." In Samuel Scheffler (ed.), Consequentialism and Its Critics. Oxford: Oxford University Press, 1988.

_____. "A Theory of Free Expression." Philosophy and Public Affairs 1 (1972).

Scheffler, Samuel (ed.). Consequentialism and Its Critics. Oxford: Oxford University Press, 1988.

Schonfeld, Martin. "Who or What Has Moral Standing?" American Philosophical Quarterly 29 (1992).

Schwarz, Stephen. "Personhood Begins at Conception." In Louis P. Pojman and Francis J. Beckwith (eds.), The Abortion Controversy. Boston: Jones and Bartlett, 1994.

Sells, Lucy W. "Leverage for Equal Opportunity Through Mastery of Mathematics." In Sheila M. Humphreys (ed.), Women and Minorities in Science. Boulder, CO: Westview Press, 1982.

Sen, Amartya and Bernard Williams (eds.). Utilitarianism and Beyond. Cambridge: Cambridge University Press, 1982.

Sher, George. "Justifying Reverse Discrimination in Employment." In Marshall Cohen, Thomas Nagel and Thomas Scanlon (eds.), Equality and Preferential Treatment. Princeton: Princeton University Press, 1977.

Shue, Henry. Basic Rights. Princeton: Princeton University Press, 1980.

_____. "Security and Subsistence." In Morton E. Winston (ed.), The Philosophy of Human Rights. Belmont, CA: Wadsworth, 1989.

Shute, Stephen and Susan Hurley (eds.). On Human Rights. New York: Basic Books, 1993.

Sikora, R. I. and Brian Barry (eds.). Obligations to Future Generations. Philadephia: Temple University Press, 1978.

Simmons, A. John. The Lockean Theory of Rights. Princeton: Princeton University Press, 1992.

_____. Moral Principles and Political Obligations. Princeton: Princeton University Press, 1979.

Simon, Robert. "Preferential Hiring: A Reply to Judith Jarvis Thomson." In Marshall Cohen, Thomas Nagel and Thomas Scanlon (eds.), Equality and Preferential Treatment. Princeton: Princeton University Press, 1977.

Slote, Michael. Common-sense Morality and Consequentialism. London: Routledge and Kegan Paul, 1985.

Smart, Carol (ed.). Feminism and the Power of Law. London: Routledge, 1989.

Smart, J. J. C. and Bernard Williams. Utilitarianism: For and Against. Cambridge: Cambridge University Press, 1963.

Soles, David E. "Sentience and Moral Standing." Dialogue 24 (1985).

Sowell, Thomas. " 'Affirmative Action' Reconsidered." In Gross (ed.), Reverse Discrimination.

_____. Civil Rights: Rhetoric or Reality? New York: William Morrow, 1984.

_____. The Economics of Politics and Race. New York: William Morrow, 1983.

_____. Ethnic America. New York: Basic Books, 1981.

_____. Markets and Minorities. New York: Basic Books, 1981.

_____. Preferential Policies: An International Perspective. New York: William Morrow, 1990.

Sreenivasan, Gopal. The Limits of Lockean Rights in Property. Princeton: Princeton University Press, 1994.

Steinem, Gloria. "Erotica and Pornography: A Clear and Present Difference." In Susan Dwyer (ed.), The Problem of Pornography. Belmont, CA: Wadsworth, 1995.

Sterba, James P. "From Liberty to Welfare." In James P. Sterba (ed.), Justice: Alternative Political Perspectives. Belmont, CA: Wadsworth, 1992.

_____(ed.). Justice: Alternative Political Perspectives. Belmont, CA: Wadsworth, 1992.

_____(ed.). Morality in Practice (4th ed.). Belmont, CA: Wadsworth, 1994.

_____(ed.). Morality in Practice (5th ed.) Belmont, CA: Wadsworth, 1997.

Strawson, Peter. "On Referring." In Anthony Flew (ed.), Essays in Conceptual Analysis. London:MacMillan, 1956.

Sumner, L.W. Abortion and Moral Theory. Princeton: Princeton University Press, 1981.

_____. "Classical Utilitarianism and the Population Optimum." In R. I. Sikora and Brian Barry (eds.), Obligations to Future Generations. Philadelphia: Temple University Press, 1978.

_____. The Moral Foundation of Rights. Oxford: Oxford University Press, 1987.

_____. Welfare, Happiness and Ethics. Oxford: Oxford University Press, 1996.

Sunstein, Cass. Democracy and the Problem of Free Speech. New York: Macmillan, 1993.

Sweet, Corinne. "Pornography and Addiction." In Catherine Itzin (ed.), Pornography: Women, Violence and Civil Liberties. Oxford: Oxford University Press, 1993.

Taylor, Charles. "Atomism." In Shlomo Avineri and Avner de-Shalit (eds.), Communitarianism and Individualism. Oxford: Oxford University Press, 1992.

Taylor, Paul W. "Biocentric Egalitarianism." In Louis P. Pojman (ed.), Environmental Ethics. Boston: Jones and Bartlett, 1994.

_____. "The Ethics of Respect for Nature." In Christine Pierce and Donald VanDeVeer (eds.), People, Penguins and Plastic Trees. Belmont, CA: Wadsworth, 1995.

Thomson, Judith Jarvis. "A Defense of Abortion." In Marshall Cohen, Thomas Nagel and Thomas Scanlon (eds.), The Rights and Wrongs of Abortion. Princeton: Princeton University Press, 1977.

_____. "Preferential Hiring." In Marshall Cohen, Thomas Nagel and Thomas Scanlon (eds.), Equality and Preferential Treatment. Princeton: Princeton University Press, 1977.

_____. The Realm of Rights. Cambridge, MA: Harvard Unviersity Press, 1990.

_____. "Rights and Deaths." In Marshall Cohen, Thomas Nagel and Thomas Scanlon (eds.), The Rights and Wrongs of Abortion. Reprinted from Philosophy and Public Affairs 2 (1973).

_____. "Self-Defense." Philosophy and Public Affairs 20 (1991).

Tooley, Michael. "Abortion and Infanticide." In Marshall Cohen, Thomas Nagel and Thomas Scanlon (eds.), The Rights and Wrongs of Abortion. Reprinted from Philosophy and Public Affairs 2 (1972).

_____. "In Defense of Abortion and Infanticide." In Louis P. Pojman and Francis J. Beckwith (eds.), The Abortion Controversy. Boston: Jones and Bartlett, 1994.

Tribe, Laurence H. Abortion: The Clash of Absolutes. New York: W.W. Norton and Company. 1990.

Tully, James. A Discourse on Property. Cambridge: Cambridge University Press, 1980.

United States Commission on Civil Rights. The Economic Progress of Black Men in America. Washington: U.S. Commission on Civil Rights, 1986.

United States Commission on Obscenity and Pornography. Report of the Commission on Obscenity and Pornography. New York: Bantam Books, 1979.

Waldron, Jeremy. "Enough and as Good Left for Others." Philosophical Quarterly 29 (1979).

_____. The Right to Private Property. Oxford: Clarendon Press, 1988.

_____. "Two Worries About Mixing One's Labor." Philosophical Quarterly 33 (1983).

Waldron, Jeremy (ed.). Theories of Rights. Oxford: Oxford University Press, 1984.

Warren, Mary Anne. "On the Moral and Legal Status of Abortion." In James P. Sterba (ed.), Morality in Practice (4th ed.). Belmont, CA: Wadsworth, 1994.

Weaver, James. "The Social Science and Psychological Research Evidence: Perceptual and Behavioral Consequences of Exposure to Pornography." In Catherine Itzin (ed.), Pornography: Women, Violence and Civil Liberties. Oxford: Oxford University Press, 1993.

Weiner, Myron. "The Pursuit of Ethnic Inequalities through Preferential Policies." In Robert B. Goldmann and A. Jeyaratnum (eds.), From Independence to Statehood. London: Frances Pinter, 1984.

Weinreb, Lloyd L. Oedipus at Fenway Park: What Rights Are and Why There Are Any. Cambridge, MA: Harvard University Press, 1994.

Welch, Finnis. "Affirmative Action and Its Enforcement." American Economic Review (May, 1981).

Westra, Laura. "Ecology and Animals: Is There a Joint Ethic of Respect?" Environmental Ethics 11 (1989).

Williams, Mary B. "Discounting versus Maximum Sustainable Yield." In R. I. Sikora and Brian Barry (eds.), Obligations to Future Generations. Philadelphia: Temple University Press, 1978.

Wilson, William J. The Truly Disadvantaged. Chicago: University of Chicago Press, 1987.

Winston, Morton E. (ed.). The Philosophy of Human Rights. Belmont CA: Wadsworth, 1989.

Zillman, Dolf and Jennings Bryant (eds.). Pornography: Research Advances and Policy Considerations. Hillsdale, NJ: Lawrence Erlbaum, 1989.

Index